The Wealth of England

The Medieval Wool Trade and its Political Importance
1100–1600

by

Susan Rose

OXBOW | books
Oxford & Philadelphia

First published in 2018.
Reprinted in paperback in 2020 in the United Kingdom by
OXBOW BOOKS
The Old Music Hall, 106–108 Cowley Road, Oxford OX4 1JE

and in the United States by
OXBOW BOOKS
1950 Lawrence Road, Havertown, PA 19083

Paperback edition: ISBN 978-1-78925-382-5
Digital Edition: ISBN 978-1-78570-737-7 (epub)

A CIP record for this book is available from the British Library

Library of Congress Control Number: 2017962123

For a complete list of Oxbow titles, please contact:

UNITED KINGDOM
Oxbow Books
Telephone (01865) 241249
Email: oxbow@oxbowbooks.com
www.oxbowbooks.com

UNITED STATES OF AMERICA
Oxbow Books
Telephone (610) 853-9131, Fax (610) 853-9146
Email: queries@casemateacademic.com
www.casemateacademic.com/oxbow

Oxbow Books is part of the Casemate Group

Front cover: July; sheep shearing near the Chateau du Clain in Poitiers F7V in Les très riches heures du Duc de Berry. *(Royal Library of Belgium Creative Commons CC BY-SA 3.0)*
Back cover: Sheep going off to summer pastures from the Da Costa Hours *(Morgan Library New York)*

To Anne, Mimi and Sue, friends for life

The Renaissance view of the life of a shepherd; engraving by Agostino Verrazano, 1490–1540 (Warburg Institute)

Contents

List of Figures

List of Maps and Tables

Preface

The concept for this book follows on from that for my earlier book on the wine trade in the same period. My aim has been to place the wool trade firmly in the context of English medieval society looking at it more widely than a concentration solely on its mechanics and economic impact. It is largely based on the work of earlier scholars to whom I owe an enormous debt of gratitude. The seminal work of T. H. Lloyd has made it possible to obtain a detailed idea of the nuts and bolts of the wool trade and its complex finances. Eileen Power's Ford lectures delivered in 1939, later published as *The Wool Trade in English Medieval Society,* must be some of the most influential of all those in this prestigious series. The figures and tables in *England's Export Trade, 1275–1547,* the work of Eleanor Carus-Wilson and Olive Coleman, are equally an invaluable resource for anyone wishing to look at trade in these years. I have also profited greatly from more recent work by many eminent scholars in the field of economic and social history. Professor Peter Spufford helped me greatly by discussing with me the problems caused by the debasement of currencies both in England and the Netherlands in the late fifteenth and sixteenth centuries. I would also like to thank Dr Paul Dryburgh and Dr Alan Kissane who very kindly let me see some of their work on the market for wool in Lincolnshire in the early fourteenth century before publication. I am of course responsible for all errors of fact or interpretation in this work.

One of the greatest boons to the historian writing nowadays has been the amount of material available online, including not only invaluable reference works but also digital versions of out-of-print books and important primary sources. As a writer now retired from any academic post I have been very fortunate that the Open University has allowed me to maintain my access to their extensive digital collections both of reference works and journals. I could not have attempted this work without this. My thanks are due to the University and the Faculty of Arts. I have also benefitted from the work of the cheerful and efficient staff at the British Library, the Institute of Historical Research and the National Archives at Kew. The maps have been drawn by Peter Wilkinson. Last, but by no means least, I have been supported throughout the work on this book by my husband, who has put up with sheep and wool dominating conversations for some time and has helped greatly on expeditions to photograph sites for the pictures.

Susan Rose, Highgate, 2017

Map 1. The major wool producing areas and markets in England c.1250–c.1550

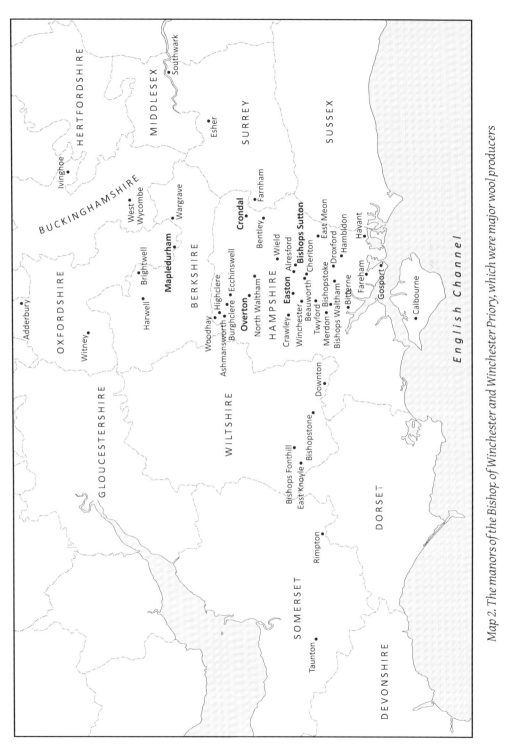

Map 2. The manors of the Bishop of Winchester and Winchester Priory, which were major wool producers

Introduction

In the first of her Ford lectures delivered in January 1939, Eileen Power asserted that for England in the Middle Ages, 'her commerce and her politics alike were built upon wool'.[1] She pointed out that wool financed war with England's neighbours and allowed 'honest burgesses' to climb 'into the ranks of the nobility, only outstripped in their progress there by the dishonest ones who arrived first. It is the aim of this book to examine and assess the influence of the wool trade on the economy, the politics and the society of medieval England. Did the money raised from taxing the export of wool enable English kings to pursue policies otherwise quite out of reach of the rulers of only the major part of a small island off the coast of north west Europe? Did English society develop in a particular way because of the importance of this trade?

The period covered will be that from around the middle of the thirteenth century to around the middle of the sixteenth century. Although it is certain that wool was traded from England across the North Sea to the Low Countries at much earlier periods than this detailed evidence of the trade is hard to come by before the mid thirteenth century. In 1558 England lost control of Calais to the French. The Company of the staple which had had controlled most of the export trade in wool from the late fourteenth century found itself thrown out of its base in the town and never regained its former dominance. The wool trade was already in decline at this time with most attention focused on the closely related export trade in woollen cloth. In the late 1550s there were great changes in the political and economic context in which merchants had to operate whatever the nature of their business. This study is therefore for the most part brought to an end at this time. The extension of export trade into other commodities and far beyond the boundaries of Western Europe and the related adoption of new forms of business organisation are left for others to discuss.

In this book full use is made of primary sources in print and where these are not available also a selection of primary source material in the National Archives. The invaluable work of earlier scholars is used via a wide range of secondary sources including books, journal articles and unpublished theses. Visual sources have also been consulted and the book includes many illustrations from contemporary documents. There are also photographs of buildings which still exist and which were built at least in part with money made in the wool trade or the closely linked trade in woollen cloth. The bibliography includes all the sources which were used extensively in the writing of this book. The author owes a large debt of gratitude to those whose researches have

---

1 E. Power (1941), *The Wool Trade in English Medieval History,* Oxford: Oxford University Press, 17.

made so much relevant material easily available although she alone is responsible for errors and also for her interpretations of the evidence.

The book itself is divided into four parts. The first section, Production, looks first of all at what was written by contemporaries about the best way to care for sheep. There is a small group of treatises, written from the late thirteenth to the sixteenth centuries, which are full of advice about how to look after large flocks and deal with the diseases to which sheep are prone. It must be said that there is also advice on how to be on one's guard against possible fraud by the shepherd. In a second chapter the practice rather than the theory of medieval sheep farming is examined. Our information largely comes from the accounts kept by those in charge of the large flocks of monastic houses or other estates in church hands. The rate of survival of estate accounts from ecclesiastic landlords is much better than that for secular landholdings even those of the greatest noble families. Information can be extracted from these sources about the way flocks were divided with wethers (adult castrated male sheep) kept separately from the ewes while some estates also had separate flocks of lambs after they had been weaned. Matters like the shearing and washing of the sheep are covered along with the provision of winter feed and shelter. The evidence used comes from sources like the copious records of the Bishopric of Winchester, and other material from Norwich Cathedral Priory and Croyland Abbey in the fens. Visual sources are also used in an attempt to discover whether distinct breeds of sheep existed at this time. The evidence for this is in fact very scanty; there were probably no more than small regional variations between flocks. There was nothing like the modern situation with a website devoted to sheep farming including a lengthy alphabetical list going from Badger Face Welsh Mountain sheep to Zwarbles with the characteristics of each carefully described.[2] Even if information about possible different breeds of sheep is lacking, merchants and producers were well aware that wool came in different qualities. Generally speaking the best wools came from the Welsh Marches and the Cotswolds and the least valued from the most northern counties, Northumberland, Durham and Cumberland and also Cornwall where the wool was said to be far too hairy.

The second section, Trade, looks at how wool was bought and sold from different perspectives and in different periods. It begins by focusing at first on the way monastic houses disposed of their wool in the later thirteenth century when the most important buyers were those from the wealthy and important Italian merchant houses. It is clear that more or less from the earliest days of this trade credit played a very important role. This is particularly the case with the Cistercian houses in the north of England, which are often believed to have financed the building of their magnificent abbeys and churches from the profits of the wool trade. New research has also cast light on the way the market worked in Lincolnshire where a much more varied group of producers traded with local middlemen as well as the agents of the Italian trading

---

2 http://www.nationalsheep.org.uk/know-your-sheep/sheep-facts/ [consulted on 26/1/17].

houses. The second chapter in this section deals with the way that the crown began to intervene directly in the wool market in the mid fourteenth century. Edward III has been described as acting like a 'wool monger extraordinary'.[3] His motivation was financial; he was in dire need of money in order to conduct the campaigns of the first phase of the Hundred Years War. The wealth generated by the trade was too tempting a source of ready money to be ignored by the royal government. The various schemes the King employed to divert some of the profits of the wool trade into his own hands are examined with an assessment of how these schemes, varying from increased export duties to direct intervention in the market for wool and the establishment of the Staple system, affected the trade itself.

A further chapter then looks at the basic statistics of the wool trade as far as they can be ascertained. The prices of wool of different qualities at different dates are discussed along with estimates of the total amount of wool on the market. This leads on to a discussion of the importance of the trade in woollen cloth which is of course linked to that in raw wool. In this and other chapters in this part of the book emphasis is laid on the nature of the sources for the information provided with an assessment of their reliability.

The final chapter in this section looks in some detail at the business lives of some fifteenth and sixteenth century wool merchants for whom there are good surviving sources. These are principally the letter collections associated with the Stonor, Cely and Johnson families. Those of the Stonor and Cely families have been published while those of the Johnson family are available in an unpublished thesis. These collections reveal in considerable detail the way the wool trade was conducted and how it changed between the later fifteenth century and the 1540s. The ubiquitous use of credit and bills of exchange in the export trade is noticeable as well as the way the current political situation impacted on English merchants and their customers in the Low Countries. There are also surviving account books kept by graziers and broggers living on the edge of the Cotswolds and the Midlands which provide an insight into the way wool was produced and bought up by local men rather than either aliens or London merchants in the early sixteenth century.

The third part of the book, Politics, deals with the importance of the wool trade to the Crown and how this changed over our period. The primary value of the wool trade to England's rulers lay in the revenue it generated. The way this invaluable source of ready money allowed the crown to follow policies which might otherwise have been beyond its reach is discussed. Some emphasis is also laid on the importance of the revenue raised from the wool trade as security for loans to the crown whether from foreign bankers or wealthy denizens. The final chapter looks at the complex relationship between the Company of the staple and the Crown which developed in the course of the fifteenth century. This was particularly evident after the passage

---

3 T. H. Lloyd (1977), *The English Wool Trade in the Middle Ages*, Cambridge: Cambridge University Press, 144.

of the *Act of Retainer* of 1461 which made the Company entirely responsible for the financing of the defence of Calais. This chapter takes the story of the staple up to 1558 when Calais was taken by the French.

The final part of the book, Decline, begins by looking at the hostility to pastoral farming in general and the wool and cloth trades in particular which was expressed in pamphlets and in the Commons in the first decades of the sixteenth century. Thomas More's well-known image in his *Utopia* of the sheep eating the men was echoed in other contemporary writings which held that the extension of pasture lands at the expense of tillage was the root cause of poverty, homelessness, the abandonment of villages and the destruction of communities. A second chapter then discusses some of the remedies proposed for what was called the 'disorderly market' of wool most of which involved stricter control of the way both wool and cloth were sold. The most popular tactic was the exclusion of middlemen or broggers blamed for the rise in prices in the 1540s and 50s. The concluding chapter tries to determine whether the wool trade can rightfully be claimed to be the source of the wealth of England. What evidence survives to this day of the wealth of wool merchants and clothiers? Did some parts of society benefit more than others? What other advantages did the wool trade bring in its wake? My answers to these questions make plain the great importance of the success of the wool trade in medieval England in forming the particular nature of English society and governance. Eileen Power's 'honest brokers' were the forebears of owners of great estates. The wool trade ensured that agriculture even in remote areas always had links with commerce and was not concerned solely with subsistence. The representation of both wool producers and wool merchants in parliament ensured that the interests of the trade could not be ignored. It was appropriate in the Middle Ages and it is appropriate today for a wool sack to be a prominent feature of the Upper House of Parliament. It constitutes a powerful reminder that England's power and influence has to a considerable extent depended on its success as a nation of traders.

Part 1

Production

Chapter 1

The Good Shepherd and His Flock; the Approach to Sheep-Farming 1100–1600

Sheep were probably first domesticated in England around about 4000–3500 BC during the Neolithic period and by Roman times were commonly found on most farms providing wool for home-spun clothing, milk for making cheese and meat. There may have been as many as 7.5 million sheep peacefully grazing English pastures by the time the great inquest of property and ownership was compiled in what became Domesday Book, perhaps outnumbering the people by more than two to one.[1] As the trade in wool became more widespread and more profitable, the management of sheep became a matter of some importance for many landowners and their tenants. It was not essential to life in the same way as grain farming, but it held out prospects of an increase in riches even as early as the beginning of the twelfth century.

Contemporary writing

There are, however, very few treatises or any other kind of writing from this period which give any but the barest details of the way to care for sheep. This was the kind of knowledge which was part of the common stock of country folk; recording it in writing would have seemed impractical and a waste of time to most people. It was neither exotic nor rare but utterly commonplace; writers, mostly clerics at least before *c.*1350, were not often concerned with such mundane matters, while few shepherds if any would have been able to read or have access to texts like this. Those who were literate left such things to their servants. In England, however, there is a very small group of treatises, most of which date from the end of the thirteenth century, which deal with agricultural matters. Landowners were becoming much more interested at this time in having some idea of the profitability of their holdings and where and how income was generated; for this reason, they needed guidance on how to keep and understand accounts. Advice on keeping accounts and recording the yields, whether in money or in produce of both arable and livestock farming, led to some discussion of the best methods of producing the best returns.

Another motive for a more systematic approach to land management was the increasing influence of statute law on land holding, especially laws introduced during

---

1 D. Hurst (2005), *Sheep in the Cotswolds; the Medieval Wool Trade*, Stroud: Tempus, 31.

the reign of Edward I. Manorial extents which listed and valued all the assets of a manor also became much more frequent particularly after the *Extenta Manerii* was issued by the Crown, a document asking detailed questions about a manor and its produce intended to provide the basis for the valuation of land holdings.[2] These treatises were intended not so much for the lords of large estates but for the lawyers and bailiffs employed on this kind of property, men who did not have a university education but the kind of practical training found in the Inns of Court. It is doubtful if they were ever read by agricultural workers themselves.

The earliest of the group, from the last decades of the thirteenth century, is known as the *Seneschaucy*. Its main aim was to set out clearly the duties of each official or servant on a manor, including the shepherd. This was taken as a model and much of its content incorporated in a work known as *La Dite de Hosebondrie* or *Husbandry*, originally written in Norman French, which dates from sometime after 1276. This work had quite a wide circulation. There are more than 34 MS copies in existence while it was also printed and translated into English as early as the late fifteenth century. The introduction states that it was written by one Walter of Henley. He had clearly had experience as a bailiff on a large demesne[3] estate and later became a member of the Dominican order. His book describes the way in which a large estate, where the demesne lands are managed by a bailiff on behalf of the landowner, should be run.

His book was, in fact, for all 'who have lands and tenements and may not know how to keep all the points of husbandry, as the tillage of land and the keeping of cattle'.[4] Much of his material also appears in a work called *Les Reules Saynt Robert* to which the name of Robert Grosseteste, the scholar and bishop of Lincoln, was attached.

The *Seneschaucy*, the model for Walter's work, has a special section on the work expected of a shepherd. His prime duty was to guard the sheep from attacks by dogs, and to prevent them straying into dangerous bogs and moors. He and his watchdog must spend the night 'in the fold with the sheep'. Sheep were clearly enclosed in a fold made of hurdles every night with, on large estates separate folds for the wethers, (castrated male sheep) the breeding ewes and the hoggs or hoggets (female sheep which had not yet lambed). One shepherd could be expected to look after either 400

---

2 The *Extenta Manerii* produced *c.*1276 in the reign of Edward I is sometimes called a statute (4 Edw. I) which it was not. Extents in general are discussed in R. Lennard (1929), 'What is a Manorial Extent?' *Ec HR* 44, 256–63.

3 The demesne was the part of a large medieval land grant whether owned by a nobleman or the Church which was cultivated by the owner directly; that is to say the produce was either for the support of the landowner's own household or was sold for his direct benefit. Other parts of the estate would be held either by unfree tenants or villeins who provided a variety of services to the owner, or tenants who held their land on leases with money rents. Tenanted land was normally held in small parcels amounting to a virgate or yardland (about one quarter of a hide between 30–40 acres [*c.*12–16 ha]).

4 Words from the opening paragraph in the translation by E. Lamond (1890), *Walter of Henley's Husbandry*, London, Longman, Green & Co, 3.

wethers, 300 ewes, or 200 hoggs. He must be of acknowledged good character, even, the *Seneschaucy* states, if he was friendly with the miller (notoriously the most prone to fraud of all manorial servants.) He must not leave the flock 'to go to fairs, markets or wrestling matches or to spend the evenings with friends or go to the tavern'. He must reliably and faithfully account for flock numbers and any losses by death or disease.[5]

Walter of Henley's work does not go into any more details regarding the work of the shepherd apart from recommending that the he must treat the sheep well.

> 'Looke that your sheapherd be not testye (angrie) for thorow anger some of the shepe may be harassed wherof they may die Looke wheather your sheape goe feading with the shepheard going amongst them for if the sheepe goe shunning (avoiding) him it is no signe that he is gentle unto them'.[6]

Other aspects of the care of sheep are not mentioned. One of the main benefits of having a sheep flock on a manor, however, was the fertilising effect of sheep folded on arable land before it was sown. He says,

> Also the folded land (lande that is doung with the folde) the nearer that it is to the sowing tyme the better it is. And from the first ladie day [15th August] cause your folde to be pitched abroad (according to the number of your sheep) be it more or lessse, for in that tyme they carie out no (the sheep make much) doung.[7]

Apart from this he lays most emphasis on the use of ewes' milk for making butter and cheese. In his view 20 sheep fed on the rich pasture of a salt marsh should produce in the summer as much milk for butter and cheese as two cows while for those pastured on fallow land or less rich meadows 30 sheep will produce as much as three cows. Wool production is treated as something of a sideline, coming largely from sheep which are sold for meat or who are culled from the flock.[8]

A much more detailed discussion of the best way to care for sheep can be found in *Le Bon Berger* by Jean de Brie.[9] De Brie apparently rose from being a goose herd in the French countryside to being in the service of Arnoul de Grant Pont, treasurer of the Sainte Chapelle in Paris, and later in that of Jehan de Hetomesnil, one of the royal councillors and a Master of Requests, as well as a canon of the Sainte Chapelle.

5 D. Oschinsky (1971), *Walter of Henley and Other Treatises on Estate Management and Accounting*, Oxford: Oxford University Press, translation of the *Seneschaucy*, 273, 287. This work also includes the *Les Reules Saynt Robert*.

6 *Ibid.*, 337.

7 *Ibid.*, 329.

8 D. Oschinsky (1971), *Walter of Henley*. The translation is that made in the sixteenth century by William Lambarde and printed originally in 1577, 329, c.74; 335, c.88; 337, c.96 *et seq.*

9 C. W. Carroll and L. Hawley Wilson (2012), *The Medieval Shepherd: Jean de Brie's Le Bon Berger* (1379), Tempe Arizona: Arizona Center for Medieval and Renaissance Studies.

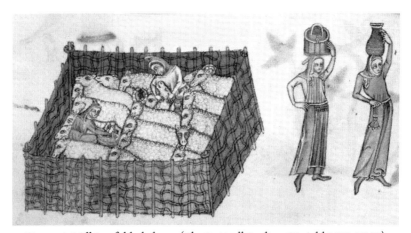

Figure 1. Milking folded sheep (The Luttrell Psalter: BL Add MSS 42130)

A prologue to the surviving printed versions (there are four dating from *c*.1486–1542) states that Jean de Brie wrote the book in 1379 for presentation to Charles V of France. No MS version of the text has been found leading some to doubt that this is a genuine fourteenth century text. Some of it seems to reflect the religiosity of the period of the Reformation; the image of Christ as the Good Shepherd was a favourite at the time and appears in this text. The book also includes classical references which may be due to later editing of the printed text. On the other hand the book also speaks of the need for a shepherd to be 'of good morals' and to avoid taverns and all dishonest places, phrases which echo those of the two earlier English treatises which may have been known to the author.

It also has in the main body of the work an eminently practical approach to the business of being a successful shepherd. It does, of course, relate to sheep-rearing practices in northern France; we cannot be certain how comparable these were to practices in England. Nevertheless much of the content would seem to have a wide application. The author lists the equipment a shepherd should have: a case of ointment to deal with the scabs of mange is essential, along with a knife to cut out the mites. He should carry a scrip with food for himself and his dog and also a leash for the dog and, of course, a crook with a hook for catching sheep by the leg when necessary. His clothing is also described, including a large felt hat which would be very good for keeping off the rain and which should include a large folded-back 'pocket' in the front. This was intended for the storage of any wool clippings he needed to show his master. Mittens, either knitted from wool or made out of cloth, were recommended for use in the winter. They could be hung from the shepherd's belt when he needed to use his hands. Finally a shepherd might take a musical instrument with his flock into the fields, perhaps some form of flute or bagpipes.[10] This may sound like some sort of pastoral conceit but illustrations of shepherds in the fields dating from at least

10 *Ibid.*, 95, 103, 105.

the thirteenth century show shepherds playing wind instruments of various kinds.

In this book, a month by month calendar also sets out a schedule for a shepherd's work. The writer takes for granted that the sheep were taken into a fold at night. In this instance a more permanent building, like the sheepcotes widely used in our period, was implied, not just an enclosure surrounded by hurdles, since opening doors and windows for good ventilation was often mentioned. The shepherd was also instructed about removing the dung; this must never be done in May but, on the other hand, it was very good to do this in December.[11] The care of ewes in lambing time was set out in some detail. 'Lambs dropped in the field were likely to be eaten by ravens,

Figure 2. *Woodcut of two shepherds; from* Le compost et calendrier des bergères, *1499 (Warburg Institute)*

kites and crows' if the shepherd was not rapidly on the scene. The shepherd 'should not sleep too soundly at night' so that he could deal with newborns. The writer's own experience was plain as he described how the ewe cleaned and stimulated the newborn and how suckling should begin. He also had a lot to say about the plants on which the sheep should graze at different times of the year. For example gorse was a danger in March since it was 'poorly digested' and 'very harmful to ewes in their throat's gullet'. A shepherd needed to make sheep which had eaten gorse drink immediately to avoid further problems. Poppies, that is those 'with a round leaf and red hairy stem' made sheep ill in June. In September the flocks should feed on wheat stubble in the morning and oat stubble later in the day but 'barren and rocky lands' should be avoided because this was where something called *mugue sauvage* grew. This plant which had yellow flowers and a clover-like leaf infected sheep with a possibly

---

11 *Ibid.*, 145.

Figure 3. Image of shepherds and their sheep from a fifteenth century edition of Vergil's Bucolica *(BL King's 24)*

deadly disease called *yrengier*. This is said to be caused by eating the seed case of the plant 'on which spiders, vermin and poisonous things feed themselves'.[12]

The shepherd had to guard against other dangers including the flock getting too hot or too damp. This was a particular problem after the sheep had been shorn in June. The shepherd was advised to keep a close eye on his bell wether.[13] If this animal stopped, became completely quiet, stamped his feet and shook his tail, this was a good sign that the whole flock was suffering from the heat. The sheep should be led into a shady valley where they might benefit greatly from grazing on camomile.[14] There is finally a whole section on sheep diseases and possible remedies with some concentration on mange or sheep-scab. This was best treated with an ointment made of 'old lard, quicksilver, rock alum, copperas and verdigris'

---

12 C. W. Carroll and L. H. Wilson (2012), *Medieval Shepherd*, 117, 131, 139. The editors identify *mugue sauvage* as lily of the valley which is very poisonous but is nothing like the plant described nor would it be growing in September; they link *yrengier* with the French word for spider *araignier* but the detailed description of this in the book sounds like a parasite infection. The method of treating the disease is to be found on p. 163 and a cure for sheep who have been eating poppies on p. 161.

13 The bell wether was a castrated male sheep wearing a bell which led the flock from place to place; the shepherds of the Mesta in Spain employed a similar system.

14 C. W. Carroll and L. H. Wilson (2012), *Medieval Shepherd*, 132–3.

mixed with 'a bit of flour made from the seeds of a medlar tree and plain ashes' steeped in old lard.[15]

The problems of newborn lambs were also included along with methods of castrating the young male sheep. The final section advises that a shepherd's dog should be trained only to grab sheep by the ear and that it would learn to follow his master by having his jaw and front feet rubbed with bacon rind. The book concluded with Jean de Brie's hope that 'all discerning young shepherds may receive his advice with good will'.[16]

Much later, in the sixteenth century, Thomas Tusser composed and published in a series of versions his *Five Hundredth Points of Good Husbandrie united to as many of Good Housewiferie*. Tusser was not a great success as a farmer himself in East Anglia but his work in verse was widely read and distributed throughout England. His work does not include a great deal about sheep farming and most of the advice is commonsensical; ewes with lambs are in danger from dogs and foxes. They should be protected from marshy land and need good food. He declares:

> Watch therefore in Lent to thy sheep go and loke
> For dogs will have vittles by hooke or by crooke
> And by brembles and bushes in pasture too full
> Poore sheepe be in danger and loseth their wull

He also spends some time on the best way to deal with milking the ewes and the value of the dung from folded sheep like earlier writers. He has relatively little to say specifically about wool as a crop although he does advise that in June:

> Washe sheepe (for the better) where water doth run
> And let him go cleanly and drie in the sun

Sheep should also be shorn carefully;

> Reward not they sheepe (when you take off his cote)
> With twitches and patches as brod as a groat.

Otherwise flies will attack the wounds. His most interesting passage is perhaps where he hints at some form of selective breeding. He points out that ewes which regularly produce twin lambs are a valuable asset.

> Ewes yearly by twinning rich maistres do make
> The lambs of such twinners for breeders go take.

---

15 *Ibid.*, 111, 139, 155.

16 *Ibid.*, 145–6, 165, 167.

The reason for this is reflected in his aphorism that:

> Young lamb well sold
> Fat lamb worth gold[17]

Some more evidence for the widespread understanding of the advantages (and in this particular case the hoped-for disadvantages) of selective breeding emerges from the evidence put before the courts in a quarrel over land between Peter Temple and Sir Anthony Cooke, both graziers with substantial flocks in 1562–1564. Temple claimed that Cooke's employees had made gaps in the hedges around the disputed pastures so that rams could serve the ewes at the wrong time of the year. The consequence would be that the lambs would be born too early and would die. More seriously he also claimed that Cooke's men had put in up to 80 Welsh rams 'of a very coarse kind of wool' leaving him no choice but to buy 8 ells of canvas 'to cover the hinder parts of the ewes'.[18] There is no record of whether this had the desired effect but the accusation reveals some understanding and a general acceptance of the importance of inherited characteristics in breeding.

Apart from writings aimed at improving the way sheep were cared for, other sources also cast some light on the shepherd's life. Prominent among these are the texts of miracle plays which often included one in the cycle based on the story in the New Testament of how the shepherds keeping their flocks on the hills above Bethlehem heard of the birth of Jesus. In the Chester Shepherds' play the first shepherd talks of walking 'wylde' on the hills, building a shelter under bushes, always concerned to save his 'seemely wedders' from storms, in fact wandering all the way from the Conway estuary to the Clyde. The shepherd is often weary but all the time his thoughts are on how he may keep his flock healthy and treat their illnesses such as 'scabbe', 'rotte' and 'cough'. He has many herbal remedies and also 'tarre in a pott'. He is often lonely but can call to other shepherds by blowing his horn. One of them has with him his 'good dogge Dottyknolle/that is nothing cheeffe of his chidynge'.[19] The first shepherd in the Second Towneley play complains bitterly of the cold of winter on the sheep-walks; his hands are chapped and his legs are weak. The second shepherd echoes his complaint; he must go, 'now in dry/now in wete/now in snaw, now in slete/when my shone freys to my fete'. This text dating from the early sixteenth century also lays some emphasis on the way sheep runs have displaced arable fields and sees the shepherd's life as a solitary one.[20]

---

17 All quotations are from Thomas Tusser (1878), *Five Hundred Pointes of Good Husbandrie*, ed. W. Payne and J. Herrage. London: Trubner. Consulted on line at https://openlibrary.org/books/OL23299840M/Five_hundred_pointes_of_good_husbandrie.

18 N. Alcock (1981), *Warwickshire Grazier and London Skinner 1532–1555*, Oxford: Oxford University Press, 244.

19 *The Chester Mystery Plays; the Adoration of the Shepherds* (n.d) lines 1–5, 13–15, 33, 178.

20 *The Towneley Plays; the Second Shepherds' Play*; Surtees Society (1835), 98–99.

Another possible insight into the life of a medieval shepherd comes from a somewhat different text written sometime between 1261 and 1268. This is a formulary, or collection of model letters and other documents which might be needed by the conscientious administrator of a large estate. It also provides an explanation of why the *Seneschaucy* puts so much emphasis on the need for a shepherd to be upright and trustworthy.[21] It was put together by Robert Carpenter, the former bailiff of the manor of Shorwell in the Isle of Wight. One of the documents in the collection, ostensibly a model account for a reeve, includes a section explaining how a shepherd may very easily defraud his employer and also how an unscrupulous reeve can maliciously injure a shepherd. There has been some discussion as to the purpose of the section; was Robert helpfully pointing out possible frauds to bailiffs and reeves? Or was he remembering how he had cheated his own employer? It certainly seems reasonable to suppose that, as the dodges to cheat a landlord are recorded in a very matter of fact way, such behaviour was not uncommon.

The examples it gives include the following ways of cheating the landlord: A shepherd could exaggerate the number of barren ewes in his flock or the number that had aborted their lambs; even if only a few lambs were 'hidden' in this way, just a small increase in the number of living lambs in the flock would add up to 'extra lambs' which could be sold to the profit of the shepherd. In the same way, if the number of lambs that had died was under-reported to the landlord or his bailiff, the 'extra' lambskins could be enough to line a coat for the shepherd. Other examples relate to hiding the evidence if the shepherd had stolen sheep from the flock by 'borrowing' beasts from a colleague to make up the numbers when the flock was counted. Dishonest shepherds might also keep back some of the milk to be used for cheese-making for the landlord to the shepherd's own advantage. A reeve on the other hand could injure a shepherd's reputation by manipulating fleece weights and the number of spoiled fleeces suggesting this was due to the shepherd's lack of care of his flock rather than his own negligence in some respect.[22]

There is no way of knowing to what extent all the advice given to landowners and sheep farmers was followed. The few glimpses of the reality of a shepherd's life have force. It is, however, very rare to find any comment by a producer on the way his flocks were managed. Some scribbled notes dated 1486 appear at the end of a sheep account for Michaelmas 1482–1483 kept by Roger Townshend of East Raynham in Norfolk. He notes that the dunging of his pastures has been approved and that old hurdles must be collected for re-use or sale. He emphasises the absolute necessity of the shepherd being present when the count of the flocks takes place. Finally he noted that the shepherds should, 'be warre of gresyng fowle mornynges, Reynes and Stranys weder

---

21 E. Lamond, ed. (1890), *Walter of Henley's Husbandry*, 95.

22 M. Carlin (2011), 'Cheating the boss: Robert Carpenter's embezzlement instructions (1261x1268) and employee fraud in medieval England,' in B. Dodds and C. D. Liddy eds, *Commercial Activity: Markets and Entrepreneurs in the Middle Ages*, Woodbridge: Boydell, 183–97.

dogges and all thynges'.[23] Townshend himself had personal experience of the losses caused by bad weather since he had lost many lambs in the hard winter of 1480–1481.[24]

Another similar note is that made by Peter Temple in the 1540s; in one account he is assessing if he has made a profit from renting nearly 470 acres (190 ha) of pasture for cattle and sheep. He had 600 ewes and 340 lambs on the fields but reminds himself, 'memorandum now I have provyd this pound wyll not kepe xc sheep.'[25]

This contrasts with the systematic reasoned accounts kept by Robert Loder at the beginning of the seventeenth century. He sets out the arguments at some length as to what profit he might expect from his flock of 500 sheep taking into account all the expenses (not including 'all the casualties...in buying rotten shep etc') and the current price of wool.[26] The *Rules of St Robert* written between 1240 and 1242 included material about the expected rate of stocking accepted at this period.

> 'Each acre of fallow should support two sheep at the least' was the basic rule of thumb for sheep while his twenty sixth rule stated that 'the wool of a thousand sheep in good pasture ought to yield at least fifty marks yearly, the wool of 2,000 sheep 100 marks and so on counting by thousands. The wool of a thousand sheep in medium pasture ought to yield at the least forty marks, and in coarse and feeble pasture thirty marks.'[27]

There is no way of knowing if these rules held good in practice. If we wish to discover more about the methods and approaches used in practice by landowners, their tenants and their shepherds and the type of sheep in their care in this period, we need to turn to other sources of information.

Types of sheep

It is difficult to be certain about the appearance or type of sheep which were valued and cared for by medieval farmers. Eileen Power in her Ford lectures (still the most widely available discussion of the wool trade in medieval England), felt able to state firmly that there were two breeds of medieval sheep. These were those producing short-stapled wool used to make heavy broadcloth and somewhat larger sheep with long-stapled wool used to make lighter woollens, worsteds and serges.[28] This view has been widely challenged. Many more recent scholars would be very reluctant to accept

---

23 'Beware of grazing on foul mornings, rains and strange weather dogs and all things'.

24 C. E. Moreton and C. Richmond (2000), 'Beware of grazing on foul mornings; a gentleman's husbandry notes'. *Norfolk Archaeology* 43, 500–3.

25 N. Alcock (1981), *Warwickshire Grazier*, 98–9.

26 G. E. Fussell (1936), *Robert Loder's Farm Accounts 1610–1620*, London: Royal Historical Society Camden 3rd series 53, 41.

27 E. Lamond (1890), *Walter of Henley*, 399.

28 E. Power (1941), *The Wool Trade in English Medieval History*, Oxford: Oxford University Press, 21.

that clearly differentiated breeds existed in this period, although there were certainly local variations in sheep types. More or less all wool produced in England up to around the middle of the sixteenth century was short-stapled while the increased production of long-stapled wool and the different breeds we are accustomed to today are, in their view, the product of innovations in the seventeenth and eighteenth centuries. It seems, for example, that the Cotswold

Figure 4. Modern sheep of the Cotswold breed

sheep of today, which has a relatively long-staple curly fleece, was developed in the course of the late sixteenth and early seventeenth centuries. In our period many sheep had a body shape, both in this region and elsewhere, not unlike that of the sheep endemic to the island of Soay in the Hebrides, with a compact body and slender limbs and neck, standing around 64 cm at the withers. Their wool was white and would be considered nowadays as short-stapled or, in a few cases, like that of those in the Cotswolds, possibly of medium length.[29] Camden's remark in his *Britannia*, first published in 1586, that the sheep in the Cotswolds had long necks and square bodies does not really support the idea that the modern Cotswold breed with its shaggy fleece and large size had developed by the late sixteenth century.[30]

Visual and material sources

Representations of sheep in medieval MSS show little in the way of breed characteristics. The animals are usually white-faced, the ewes being without horns. In the calendar sections of Books of Hours (which were illuminated in France or Flanders rather than England for the most part) sheep sometimes feature in a winter scene for the month of February where, in a landscape buried in a heavy snowfall, the peasants huddle round the fire in their home and the sheep are a woolly mass in a sheep-house or roofed sheepcote nearby. The building shown seems to link well with the folds described in *Le Bon Berger*. A sheep-shearing scene may also occur for one of the summer months, July in the case of the *Très Riches Heures du Duc de Berry*, where the male shearer wears

29 P. L. Armitage (1983), 'The early history of English longwool sheep', *The Ark, the Monthly Journal of the Rare Breeds Survival Trust* 10, 90–7.

30 W. Camden, *Britannia*, facsimile edition (1970), Hildesheim: Georg Olms, 257.

Figure 5. Image for February from Les très riches heures du Duc de Berry, *showing a sheepcote (Royal Library of Belgium, Creative Commons CC BY-SA 3.0)*

a hat much like that also described in *Le Bon Berger*.[31] In shearing scenes the sheep are usually lying across the lap of the shearer often with their legs hobbled with twine; the shears being used are very similar to the hand shears still occasionally used to-day. The *Luttrell Psalter* includes a different scene; this is of folded ewes being milked. None of the animals depicted, however, show much in the way of clearly differentiated breed characteristics.

Northleach Church contains several images of sheep which are part of the decoration of memorial brasses originally on tombs commemorating notable wool merchants from the fifteenth century. That of John Fortey (1458) shows a long-legged sheep with a curled fleece; it has been suggested that this may have been an attempt to portray a long-woolled sheep or an early member of the distinctive Cotswold breed of modern times with their very shaggy fleeces. The brass on the tomb of William Midwinter from 1500 shows a similar animal. John Taylour's brass from 1490 shows a sheep standing on a woolsack bearing the Taylour merchant mark. This animal is very like to those in the MSS illuminations with less attention paid to the representation of the fleece. The later brass (1525) in memory of Thomas Bushe unusually shows horned animals both male and female. It is clearly unwise to place too much weight on these images. We have no knowledge of

31 See the illustration on the front cover.

Figure 6. Sheep emerging from their fold and going off to the summer pastures from the Da Costa Hours *(The Morgan Library and Museum MS M.399. fol. 5v)*

their makers in many instances nor where they worked or of their knowledge of the sheep of the day. It is perhaps safest to say that there is no clear evidence provided by these images that there were more than minor local difference between sheep types and their appearance in different parts of England.[32]

The most detailed discussion of the nature of medieval English sheep and their wool is that undertaken by M. L. Ryder in a series of articles. Although there is ample evidence that the owners of large flocks often moved them from place to place on their estates there is little sign of any form of systematic selective breeding, whether to improve wool quality or for any other desirable characteristic. Some sheep with black or greyish wool are sometimes mentioned in accounts but it is clear that the vast majority were white. It is plain, however, that the wool produced varied in quality, something that was well known to the merchants whose price lists survive. Ryder also looked at skeletal remains of sheep and conducted a very detailed analysis of the wool used in a wide range of surviving medieval and later textiles. This enabled him to conclude that the sheep of medieval England were very similar in size to the sheep still found on the Hebridean island of Soay and on Shetland. The most prominent difference is the rarity of coloured fleeces among the medieval sheep while those from the islands nowadays have dark-coloured hairy fleeces. Sheep of either sex might be horned although this was uncommon. Using the method usual in the modern wool trade to categorise the medieval wool samples which he examined, Ryder found that most wool was 'hairy medium/generalised medium'. This meant that the wool varied from hairy wool difficult to card and only suitable for very rough cloths coming from sheep in northern upland areas to wool of reasonable quality which could be used for the thick woollen cloth that was much liked in medieval times. There was some fine wool, as much as 21% of the total in thirteenth and fourteenth century samples from Southampton. None of the wool samples examined had a long staple. Generally the staple was between 25 mm and 40 mm long. Some sheep of breeds originating in the seventeenth or eighteenth centuries have a staple length of over 300 mm.[33]

Does this mean that the very high reputation of English wool among European merchants was unjustified? The poet John Lydgate wrote in the early fifteenth century:

> Off Brutis Albion his wolle is cheef richesse
> In prys surmountimg euery otir thyng
> Sauf greyn and corn; marchauntis al expresse
> Wolle is cheeff tresour in this land growing
> To riche and poore this best fynt clothing:
> Alle naciouns afferme up to the fulle,
> In al the world ther is no bettir wolle.[34]

---

32 All these tombs can be seen in D. Hurst (2005), *Sheep in the Cotswolds*, 21–2.

33 M. L. Ryder (1966), 'The history of sheep breeds in England,' *Agricultural History Review* 12, 1–12 and 65–82; (1984), 'Medieval sheep and wool types,' *Agricultural History Review* 32, 14–28.

34 J. Lydgate, *The Debate of the Horse, Goose and Sheep,* quoted in D. Hurst, *Sheep in the Cotswolds*, 121.

Figure 7. Modern sheep of the Soay breed

Was this either not true or based on the abysmal quality of wool from other sources? The answer seems to be that the relatively small quantity of fine wool was of exceptional quality while much of the rest was acceptable for making the kind of woollen cloth or broadcloth then in most demand. English flocks as a whole certainly produced a greater quantity of wool suitable for making good quality woollen cloth than the majority of those in the remainder of Western Europe, at least until the early fifteenth century.

It is also the case that the varying quality of English wools from different producers and different regions of the country was well recognised and understood by the market from the earliest times. There are various price lists from the twelfth century and later in existence which make this plain. Ryder's samples included some from Perth and Aberdeen in Scotland which would have been very similar to the wools from Northumberland and the Borders. These were acknowledged by the English Crown in the late fourteenth century to be of such low quality that they were exempted from the Staple legislation. This required virtually all wool for export to go through the Staple at Calais. His 'fine wool' samples came mainly from Baynard's Castle in London (the centre of the English end of the export trade) and Southampton, the main port used by merchants from Genoa and Florence who largely bought from producers in the Cotswolds and the Welsh Marches. These wools would have justified the high reputation of the best English wool.

One of the most detailed price lists is that compiled by Francesco Balducci Pegoletti, a member of the well-known Italian banking and trading partnership of the Bardi. It dates from around 1318 and lists no fewer than 194 monasteries from which the Bardi were accustomed to buy raw wool. The best price was paid for wool from a

Benedictine nunnery in Stanfield in Lincolnshire, and from Cistercian abbeys in Thame, Oxfordshire, Dore in Herefordshire and Tintern in Monmouthshire. If Pegoletti's suppliers are grouped by region, the highest prices were paid in Lincolnshire, in Grantham and the parts of Lindsey and the lowest in Yorkshire. The prices set by the crown for the royal purveyance or compulsory purchase ordered in 1337 were highest for wools from Hereford and Shropshire (the highly coveted March wools) and lowest for the northern counties from Westmorland to Northumberland. In 1454 when minimum export prices were put forward by the Commons in Parliament the wools from the Cotswolds and Lindsey were priced at the highest rate while it was suggested that wool from a mixture of counties in the southeast and north of England was of the lowest quality.

A compendium of prices and practices for merchants called *The Noumbre of Weyghtes* put together some time in the reign of Edward IV (broadly 1460–1483) sets out the prices usual at the Calais Staple for English wools. 'March' wool from Leominster is by far the most expensive followed at some distance by fine Cotswold wool. Once more the cheapest comes from Yorkshire and the southeast.[35] In the same book an example of how the profit may be calculated on a wool sale is given and this takes as the standard wool traded at Calais 'Cots' or the middle quality of wool from that region. The Cely brothers, whose trading activities at the end of the fifteenth century are known in detail because of the survival of much of their business correspondence, did not buy the most expensive wools. The bulk of their trade was in good to middle 'Cots' with a smaller quantity of the cheaper wools of Kesteven and Lindsey.[36]

Apart from their place of origin wool was also graded in other ways, some of which reflected on the shepherd. One reason why wool produced by many Cistercian abbeys was well regarded was, it has been suggested, because care was taken in sorting and packing the wool before sale. This was quite a lengthy process which relied largely on the skill and integrity of those undertaking the work. In the trade the wool from young sheep perhaps from the first shearing was for example less desirable than that from older animals. Although sheep were washed before shearing the care with which this was done varied. Some producers were also less than scrupulous in carefully separating what was called 'clift wool' from the remainder of the fleece. This was soiled and matted wool from the belly and back legs of a sheep. 'Morlings' was the wool from the fleeces of dead sheep, probably showing the effects of scab or some other infection. 'Locks' were even less regarded remnants of straggly wool left over from the shearing process. All these, sometimes classed as 'refuse', might find a market of some sort but the shepherd of a well-managed flock might hope to reduce the losses from too many

35 Tables at the end of T. H. Lloyd (1973), *The Movement of Wool Prices in Medieval England*, Cambridge: Cambridge University Press for the EcHR, 70–71, record the information from these lists.

36 A. Hanham (1985), *The Celys and their World: an English Merchant Family of the Fifteenth Century*, Cambridge: Cambridge University Press, 112.

damaged or low quality fleeces.[37] Sheepskins or fells which might come from sheep dead of disease, as well as those culled as past breeding or sold for their meat, also found a ready market. In the sixteenth century some fells were bought to be tanned into leather particularly by glovers. They sold on the wool plucked from the skins to wool merchants. Otherwise the fells were sold in much the same way as fleece wool.

The washing of sheep usually took place in running water, a stream or river. At least three places in England are called after the practice, Sheepwash in North Devon on the River Torridge, a place on the Cod Beck on the North York moors and a village on the Wansbeck near Morpeth. By the early nineteenth century what might be called 'sheep-baths' were sometimes built by damming a stream or by linking to a spring. In the Cotswolds these were stone lined basins with an access for the sheep. That near Cleeve Hill is a typical example.[38] Winchcombe Abbey brought all its flocks to Sherborne for washing and shearing. The abbot and his entourage moved to Sherborne for a month while the sheep were washed in the Sherborne brook. Their local tenants owed services connected with washing the sheep, shearing and preparing and packing the wool for sale and were rewarded with a feast at the end of the work.[39]

The accounts for 1269–1270 kept by the central *bercaria* or wool-house of the Cistercian abbey at Beaulieu include a sum for the washing and shearing of their flocks on their properties at Faringdon, near the mother house in the New Forest and elsewhere. The workers received rations of bread and were also refreshed with 173 gallons of good ale and a further 57 gallons of mixed ale.[40] There is no mention of the 'warden pies' full of spices and 'raisins of the sun' provided for the sheep shearing feast in Shakespeare's *The Winter's Tale* when all 24 shearers sported nosegays and entertained the company with songs.[41] Even without these additions, however, washing and shearing was clearly a convivial moment in the farming year.

There are also well-attested archaeological remains of the sheepcotes or sheep-houses like those depicted in the calendar sections of some Books of Hours. In the Cotswolds sheepcotes were sometimes as much as 64 m long and 7 m wide. The aim was to house a whole flock of as many as 300–400 sheep. The accumulated dung from a sheep-house was a valuable form of fertiliser. These cotes were also used for lambing while hay and other winter fodder were stored in the loft under the roof. Some were built near remote upland pastures and others near the centre of the manor.[42]

Beaulieu Abbey had sheepcotes on its granges at Faringdon, at Suberton and in the New Forest. These had thatched roofs while that at Faringdon was at least in

---

37 E. Power and M. M. Postan (1933), *Studies in English Trade in the Fifteenth Century*, London: Routledge, 51.

38 D. Hurst (2005), *Sheep in the Cotswolds*, 181–7.

39 *Ibid.*, 123.

40 S. F. Hockey (1975) *Accounts of Beaulieu Abbey*, London: Camden 4th series for the Royal Historical Society, 165–6.

41 Shakespeare, *The Winter's Tale*, Act IV, scene II.

42 D. Hurst (2005), *Sheep in the Cotswolds*, 101–4.

partly built of stone. The abbey also made hay for winter feed on its own pastures and grew oats for the same purpose. These supplies were not always enough and more had to be bought in by the abbey.[43] At least by the end of the fifteenth century many tenant holdings had a range of agricultural buildings of which the most common of those used for housing animals were sheepcotes. Information from court rolls kept on manors in the Cotswolds in the years 1497–1525 show that repairs were often required on sheepcotes particularly at Broadway.[44] After the heyday of sheep-farming had passed in the seventeenth century, some sheepcotes were apparently well enough constructed to be converted into houses for local people.

The widespread practice of housing sheep in the winter months also led to the common provision of extra fodder for the flocks especially the breeding ewes most of which would have been in lamb in the winter months. The roof space made an excellent place to store hay. Large quantities might be needed. At Minchinhampton in 1378–1379 eight 'wainloads' fed 200 wethers and 21 'wainloads' 171 hoggs.[45] Walter of Henley advocated housing sheep between Martinmas (12 November) and Easter. He implied that they should be provided with hay, but warned that if wethers were housed separately, care should be taken that any hay should be mixed with well-threshed wheat or oat straw. Otherwise 'they come to the manger starving and push back the weak and choke themselves without chewing the small hay.' Mixing the hay with straw prevented this. He also advised that peapods and vines were good winter feed for sheep.[46] In the early seventeenth century Robert Loder calculated that he would have to spend around £20 on hay and straw for 240 sheep overwintered on his property at Awfield. This would be for fully mature sheep; he calculated that for 100 tegs (sheep of less than 2 years old) he would need ten loads of hay.[47]

Another very obvious characteristic of medieval sheep husbandry, as soon as evidence becomes available in some quantity, is that wethers (the castrated male sheep), breeding ewes, and hoggets or hoggs (young female sheep between 1 and 2 years old) were often kept in distinct flocks. This was the case with the Norwich Cathedral priory flocks in the fifteenth century. The ewe flocks were breeding units with the lambs kept with their mothers until they were separated and added to the wether or hogg flocks.[48] The fleeces of wethers were heavier and more valuable than

43 *Accounts of Beaulieu Abbey*, 165–6.

44 C. Dyer (2012), *A Country Merchant; Trading and Farming at the End of the Middle Ages*, Oxford, Oxford University Press, 190 and table 6.6.

45 C. Dyer (1995), 'Sheepcotes: evidence for medieval sheep-farming', *Medieval Archaeology* 34, 152.

46 E. Lamond (1890), *Walter of Henley*, 31.

47 G. E. Fussell (1936), *Robert Loder's Farm Accounts*, 40.

48 M. Bailey (2007), 'The sheep accounts of Norwich Cathedral Priory 1484–1534', in *Poverty and Wealth; Sheep Taxation and Charity*, Norwich, Norwich Record Society 71, 13.

those of ewes while wool from young sheep was little regarded. Robert Carpenter, the bailiff already mentioned, wrote c.1260 that the expected fleece weights were 3 lb (1.36 kg) for wethers, 2.25 lb (1 kg) for ewes and 1.5 lb (0.68 kg) for hoggs. These fleece weights would strike a modern sheep farmer as very modest; lowland short wool sheep are expected to have fleeces of 4–5.5 lb (1.81–2.27 kg) and upland sheep 2–3.5 lb (0.91–1.58 kg). Nevertheless they exceed the usual estimates of fleece weights in our period. A study of the flocks of the Bishop of Winchester from 1208–1454 produces a mean fleece weight of around 1.4 lb (0.63 kg) for most years while in some years affected by scab, weights fell as low as 0.87–1.2 lb (0.39–0.54 kg). The heaviest fleeces were around 2.4 lb (2.09 kg) with the best maxima being 3.6 lb (1.63 kg) and 4.55 lb (2.06 kg). It is, however, notable that the fleeces that were most highly valued throughout our period, the short fine wool known as Lemster Ore produced on the Welsh Marches, varied little in weight over the years and still usually weighed less than 2 lb (0.91 kg) in the nineteenth century. The small hardy sheep which grazed the hills of Shropshire at this time had little in common with the heavy fleeced merino sheep of later periods.

There is also evidence that the quality of the wool and the weight of fleeces were severely affected at the end of the thirteenth century by the spread of a virulent form of sheep scab in English flocks. A similar widespread fall in fleece weights has also been identified from around 1370 into the fifteenth century. These falls in fleece weight are evident not only in the flocks of the Bishop of Winchester for which there is a long run of evidence but also in flocks in Kent, Essex and Sussex belonging to the Archbishop of Canterbury. It has been suggested that another cause as well as epidemic disease may have been a noticeable drop in average temperatures with especially harsh winters becoming more common.[49] The sheep scab epidemic has in fact been identified as a major 'biological catastrophe' while the colder climate of the fifteenth century has been seen as the start of the so-called Little Ice Age.[50] Despite these depressing figures and the more hostile environment which wool producers had to contend with, other factors, especially the lower cost of labour and the greater availability of pasture, worked in their favour allowing wool production to continue to be profitable for many years to come.

Sheep farming in medieval times was not, however, even at the peak of the wool trade in the early fourteenth century, the most important activity on their property for most landowners. The production of foodstuffs, principally grain, whether for consumption on the estate or for sale, always occupied pride of place. The possibility of a local or more widespread famine was not a remote danger but a disaster which could occur with very little warning. The years of hunger in England and other nearby

---

49 M. J. Stephenson (1988), 'Wool yields in the medieval economy', *EcHR* 41, 368–91.

50 P. Slavin (2015), 'Flogging a dead cow: coping with animal panzootic on the eve of the Black Death', in A. J. Brown, A. Burn and R. Doherty, eds, *Crises in Economic and Social History; a Comparative Perspective*, Woodbridge: Boydell, 111–35.

countries at the beginning of the fourteenth century (1315–1317), possibly caused by the climatic disruption following the eruption of Mount Tarawera in distant New Zealand, are only the most striking example of this. Nevertheless the care of sheep was undertaken with care and attention to detail as will be apparent from looking at a selection of accounts kept by important landowners. It is to this evidence that we will turn in the next chapter.

Chapter 2

Estate Accounts; Monasteries and the Production of Wool

The sources

The most plentiful evidence of the way sheep-farming was conducted in practice comes from the accounts and other documents kept by the holders of large estates. In the thirteenth century, when documents like this begin to appear, only those with extensive landholdings had the need or the resources to produce such records. The earliest of those which survive are predominantly from the estates of the wealthiest bishops and other ecclesiastical landowners; continuity of ownership and the consequent careful preservation of written records were much easier to ensure when land was in the hands of a bishopric or monastery immune from many of the changes in ownership which could overtake noble estates. This means that it is possible to find long series of documents relating to episcopal lands which allow the fortunes of a particular activity like sheep-farming to be followed over a considerable period of time. The records of lands owned by monastic houses were originally kept as assiduously as those owned by the princes of the church but their survival is much more problematic and patchy because of the upheavals and destruction following the dissolution of monastic foundations in the 1530s.

Long series of estate accounts are least common for estates in the hands of noble families. These lands might be lost by forfeiture to the crown following attainder for political reasons; they would then usually be granted to a different family with little if any interest in the archives of its predecessors. If male heirs failed, the inheritance would be divided among heiresses with the lands coming into other hands following their marriage. With the change in ownership the archives of the former owners were only too likely to be lost.

The value of the records of both noble and ecclesiastical estates for our purposes is also affected by changes over our period in the ways in which large estates were organised. If a large part of the estate was directly farmed by the owner as demesne lands, rather than leased to tenants, then the accounts and other documents kept by reeves and bailiffs very often contain precise details of the flocks of sheep and other stock on the land, and the way in which they were managed. There may also be details of the extent of the estates, buildings including both the costs of maintenance and new construction, and the wages and duties of demesne officials like reeves and employees like shepherds. If much of the land was in the hands of tenants, such detailed information was no longer needed by the landowner and was no longer collected; the landowner was most interested in his rent roll and leases not in the details of the stock kept. In England this change became very marked in the later fourteenth and fifteenth centuries. Many estates were leased to tenants including their pastures and sheep walks. Small numbers of documents relating to tenanted farms or those held by people lower down the social scale only begin to survive from the later part of our period. The surviving document series are also not evenly spread throughout the country. Unfortunately not all the best wool-producing areas are included. There is, for example, virtually no material of this kind from the area around Leominster, the source of the far-famed 'lemster ore' acknowledged to be the best wool produced in England.

Norwich Cathedral Priory

The form of some accounts also causes some problems. In some religious houses responsibility for different aspects of stock management was split between different officials because of the nature of the administration of that religious house. For example, at Norwich Cathedral Priory, both the Master Cellarer and the Cellarer had responsibility for certain manors and the flocks kept on them. Nevertheless, unlike Bury St Edmunds, where the Abbot managed the manors and flocks held in his name completely independently, as did the Cellarer, at Norwich accounts were kept which listed all the sheep in the possession of the priory irrespective of which official was responsible for them. At this large Benedictine house, the surviving records, which run with gaps from the end of the fourteenth century to the Dissolution, show that the extensive pasture lands and sheep flocks of the priory, spread across a number of manors, were as a rule treated as one unit for accounting purposes.[1] The shepherd on each manor was expected to supply a list of all the beasts in his charge once a year usually around St Andrew's Day (30 November).

On the manor of Newton, not far from Castle Acre, in 1489 there was a total of 63 rams, 419 wethers, 62 ewes and 4 lambs. At the beginning of the year when this particular shepherd had taken over this flock, there had been 112 rams, 483 wethers, 35 ewes and 49 young stock (yearlings). During the year 103 sheep were sold, 1 was given away and 24 died.[2] The sheep accounts of all the priory manors were then collated in an overall account, examples of which survive for 1494 and 1495. These show that at Newton, at these later dates, there were 403 wethers in the first year and 453 in the following year. Wether numbers in this instance did not vary greatly over these five years. The priory as a whole owned 6473 sheep in 1494, made up of 1806

---

1 M. Bailey, ed. (2007), 'The sheep accounts of Norwich Cathedral Priory, 1484–1534,' in *Poverty and Wealth: Sheep, Taxation and Charities,* Norwich, Norfolk Record Society 71, 5–17.

2 *Ibid.,* 24–5.

wethers, 27 rams, 2833 ewes, 477 yearlings and 1330 lambs. The overall total increased by nearly 700 in the following year with notable rises in the number of wethers, ewes and lambs.[3]

The aim was to record the number of sheep at the start of a year in each category, along with the changes that took place, births, deaths from whatever cause, sales and the like. The statement at the end of the year listed the animals which 'remained' in the flock. There was, however, little mention of money either received or spent since the calculation of costs or profits was not the concern of these accounts. The fact that the profitability of sheep farming increased in the first decades of the sixteenth century and that this became of much greater concern to the priory is clear from the survival of income and expenditure accounts from the 1520s. There is no evidence that this type of account was kept in earlier periods. In the accounts from 1525–1526 and 1526–1527, it was recorded that the priory made a clear profit from the sale of both wool and sheep of £78 0s 3½d in the first year and £65 5s 0½d in the second.

The 'sheep' or stock accounts provide other information apart from the numbers of sheep in each category on each manor. Those from the manor of Newton for the year November 1489–November 1490, already mentioned, reveal that some sheep had been slaughtered for 'the hospitality of the prior' and that others had died from disease. Looking at the overall figures on this manor – 63 rams, 419 wethers, 62 ewes, 4 lambs – it seems highly likely that this flock was intended principally for the production of wool. The almost equal numbers of ewes and rams is, however, very unusual. It may imply that there was a separate ram flock kept on this manor which might be moved as required to other manors to cover the ewes in a large breeding flock. Clearly the care of new stock bred 'in house' was not a major concern at Newton. Lambs were probably sent to another manor after weaning as so few remained on this manor at the end of the year.

The figures for another manor, Sedgeford, provide more evidence that stock was often bought in to replace losses. On that manor 200 wethers were bought in from Thorpe market but only 40 came as 'home-reared' stock from Hindringham. Hindringham clearly specialised in rearing young stock since another account for all the Norwich manors for 1493 lists 883 lambs on that manor with very few adult sheep. Money was also expended by the priory on renting extra pasture, the wages and clothing of the shepherds, washing and shearing the sheep and the usual hurdles for sheepfolds, grease, tar and ruddling for marking the sheep.[4]

Norfolk shared with some other areas of East Anglia a particular system of pastoral agriculture known as the 'foldcourse'. In this system, which developed on the light sandy soils of the Breckland and the area along the Norfolk coast, the dung of sheep was essential to fertilise the soil to produce good crops of grain. Thus the large flocks of the major landowners were pastured in the autumn after harvest and through the

3 *Ibid.*, 67–8.

4 M. Bailey (2007), 'Sheep accounts', 87–9.

winter before the sowing of spring wheat on the stubble in the open fields of the villages or on land lying fallow. In the summer they were moved to the heaths or commons. Each landowner would control the 'foldcourse' (the lands which could be grazed and which would be dunged) allotted by tradition to his demesne. The villagers benefitted from this system since the sheep were folded overnight on their portion of the open fields as well as on the lord's and thus their fields were also dunged. The sheep folds (in this case those made of hurdles) were moved regularly so that the valuable fertilising dung was spread more or less evenly over a village lands.

Villagers might also have the benefit of running so-called 'cullet' sheep of their own with the lord's flock. The Norfolk Priory flocks followed this regime on at least some of its manors. The account for Heigham and Sedgeford for 1489–1490 have a separate entry for 'cullet' sheep which included in the case of Sedgeford wethers, ewes, hoggs and rams.[5] The system could work well but depended on good will and co-operation between the landlords and the villagers.[6]

The estates of the Bishop of Winchester and Winchester Cathedral Priory

The magnificent series of account rolls for the estates of the wealthiest bishopric in England, however, provide ample evidence for the way sheep flocks were managed on the bishop's manors. The series runs from 1208–1209 to 1454–1455 on rolls and up to 1710–1711 in registers.[7] There are gaps for some years for some manors in the early period but no other series offers anything like the same continuity of coverage. Such an enormous amount of information does create its own problems. How can it be usefully sampled; how can any one manor be considered 'typical'? The way in which an estate of around 60 manors was managed must necessarily differ from the way in which two or three manors, a much more usual holding, were looked after. This is true but handled with care the material provides invaluable information of how sheep flocks were managed.

The core of the Bishop's lands lay in Hampshire, intermingled with the estates of the cathedral priory at Winchester which are also well documented. A comparison between the two estates has revealed some differences between the aims of those responsible for their management. It has been claimed that the Bishop's main consideration was the amount of money which could be generated from his holdings; they could be called 'federated grain factories producing largely for cash'.[8] Winchester priory on the other hand lived on the produce from the manorial farms; large amounts

---

5 M. Bailey (2007) 'Sheep accounts', 25–6.

6 K. J. Allison (1957), 'The sheep-corn husbandry of Norfolk in the sixteenth and seventeenth centuries', *Agricultural History Review* 5, 12–30.

7 M. Page (2002), *The Medieval Bishops of Winchester. Estate, Archive and Administration*, Winchester, Hampshire County Council, Hampshire Papers 24.

8 J. Hare (2006), 'The Bishop and the prior: demesne agriculture in medieval Hampshire,' *Agricultural History Review* 54, 187–212, 189.

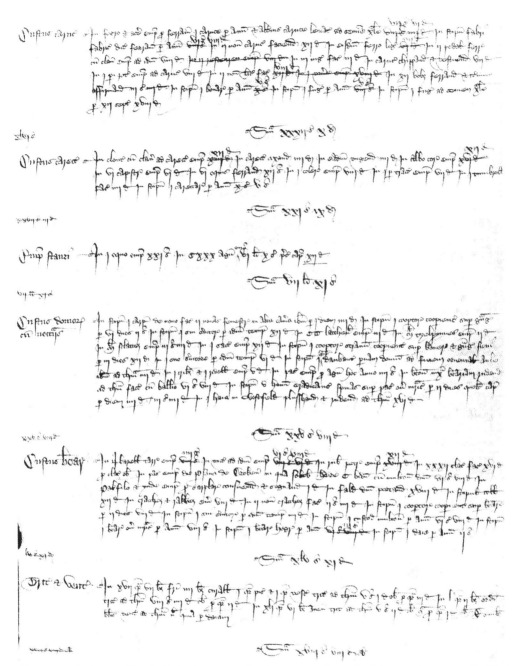

Figure 8. Winchester Pipe Roll; draft account for the manor of Droxford (Hampshire Record Office)

of grain, meat and cheese, including that made from sheep's milk, were produced for the sustenance of the monks. In a quirk of medieval legal practice, the livestock on the farms of the bishopric was also part of the personal possessions of each bishop. On his death his successor could choose whether or not to purchase it from his executors, something which could have a noticeable effect on the size of sheep flocks. There were no such abrupt changes for the priory. Apart from this, however, and perhaps more interest on the part of the priory in the production of sheep's milk, the differences in the way each managed their estates as a whole do not extend to the large flocks of sheep on both estates.

These were largely kept on the downland pastures in Hampshire and Wiltshire and, while their wool was not that held in the highest regard by merchants, it sold well. In the thirteenth century the bishop's flocks consisted normally of over 20,000 beasts and peaked at around 30,000 between 1258 and 1273; after the Black Death there was an immediate decline to around 14,000 sheep but the average rose again to some 33,000 in 1388–1397.[9] The increased leasing of lands and flocks to tenants in the fifteenth century makes it more difficult to be sure of numbers but it is clear that sheep farming was still important with flocks of around 1000 animals on some manors. It is also clear that on the bishop's lands direct involvement in sheep farming continued for longer than the direct production of cereals on demesne lands. On the priory lands flock sizes tended to be more stable with less variation in size than those of the bishop averaging around 20,000 beasts in the first half of the fourteenth century.

In Hampshire, over the whole period, only those of the bishop were larger.[10] Overall the surviving records of both estates give the impression that flock masters were conservative in their outlook and methods. On both estates sheep-houses or *bercaria* were common, providing shelter for the flocks in winter. Breeding ewes were kept separately from the wethers (castrated males) whose fleeces were heavier and the main source of the wool clip. Lambs once weaned would also be kept in a separate flock. Extra feed was also provided in winter particularly for the ewes and lambs. Animals were also routinely moved from one manor to another as required to replace stock lost through disease or for ease of management.

The extensive nature of the data from the Winchester Pipe Rolls makes it possible to look in detail at individual manors. Ashmansworth was a small manor on the downs south of Newbury. The surrounding hills are used to this day to pasture sheep. In 1208–1209 it had a breeding flock of over 250 ewes. These produced 237 lambs; after accounting for tithe and losses due to death 181 were transferred to the neighbouring manor of Highclere at the end of the summer. Two hundred and ten coarse fleeces were also sent to Highclere which ran a wether flock and seems to have acted as a collecting centre for wool, along with 163 sheep's milk cheeses. A new sheepfold was

---

9 M. Page (2003), 'The technology of medieval sheep farming: some evidence from Crawley, Hampshire 1208–1349', *Agricultural History Review* 51, 137–54, 141.

10 J. Hare (2006), 'The Bishop and the prior', 203.

built at Ashmansworth at a cost of 6s 2d. Small sums of money also came in from the sale of the skins of dead lambs and sheep.[11] Fifty wethers were bought in to replace these losses after shearing. The shepherd, John, seems to have been blamed for the deaths and was fined 6d for neglecting his charges. Money was spent on grease to protect the fleeces and for new wattle hurdles around the sheepfold. At the end of the accounting period, the wether flock numbered over 300 while there were 246 weaned lambs in a separate flock with its own keeper. The final tally of the produce of the flocks included 237 fleeces delivered to the reeve at Highclere at the end of the shearing, 249 lambs' fleeces and 11 sheepskins from sheep that died from murrain.[12]

At the beginning of the fifteenth century, in 1409–1410, while the arable land at Ashmansworth was now leased, the flock was still directly managed by the bishopric. Not much had changed from the early fourteenth century. The main flock of wethers was larger, a total of 497 animals. Hoggs were bought in as replacement stock; some from the bishop's manor at Overton (82) and some from Alresford (21). Money was spent on grease, tar and red ochre to treat scab and mark the sheep while hay was provided for winter feed at a cost of 6s 8d. Finally 525 fleeces were delivered to the treasurer at Wolvesey most from the wethers and a small amount from the hoggs. Twenty sheepskins from dead animals were also sold.[13]

To the north of Ashmansworth lies the much larger manor of Witney centred on the Windrush valley at the foot of the Cotswolds. On these hill pastures was produced some of the finest English wool, much sought after by foreign merchants. The year 1208–1209 was a very bad one for the flocks on this manor, however; nearly 300 sheep, the majority of them breeding ewes were sold because of their poor condition. In total 212 animals, a mixture of ewes, wethers and hogs died with their skins sold for the pittance of 36s 1½d. Only 210 fleeces and 82 lambs' fleeces were sold for a reasonable price.[14]

By 1301–1302 the enterprise, clearly run on commercial lines, was in better heart. Two shepherds were employed each receiving the stipend of 5s a year. The manor contained two fulling mills so that at least part of the process of making woollen cloth was carried on locally. Extra milk was provided for the lambs and large quantities of grease, as well as verdigris and vinegar were bought as medicaments for the sheep and to treat the fleeces. Murrain still caused some losses in the flock but at the end of the summer this totalled around 450 adult beasts. The ewe flock had produced 143 lambs; 40 had suffered from illness, 11 went in tithe and 1 to the shepherd as his due, so that 91 had been successfully reared.[15]

---

11 H. G. Barstow, trans. (1998), *1208–1209, Pipe Roll of the Bishopric of Winchester*, Chandlers Ford: privately printed.

12 H. G. Barstow (1998), *Pipe Roll of the Bishopric of Winchester*, 128–32.

13 M. Page, ed. (1999), *The Pipe Roll of the Bishopric of Winchester, 1409–1410*, Winchester: Hampshire County Council for the Hampshire Record Society, 252–6.

14 H. G. Barstow (1998), *1208–1209, Pipe Roll of the Bishopric of Winchester*, 38–44.

15 M. Page (1996), *The Pipe Roll of the Bishopric of Winchester; 1301-2*, 132–42.

By 1409–1410 the demesne had been leased, much of it to Roger Put who was also employed at 6s 8d per year to supervise the sheep. Money was spent re-thatching the sheepcote and the barn and also on making stalls and partitions for the wethers. Tar, grease and red ochre were again bought in while the cost of washing and shearing no fewer than 731 sheep came to 10s. The keeper of the lambs received a bonus and also a specialist was brought in to weigh the wool and arrange its delivery to one Henry London. He was the attorney of no less a personage than Richard Whittington. A total of 2360 fleeces were sent from Witney to London which must have included wool collected from neighbouring flocks as well as some held over from the preceding year. The accounts state that 884 fleeces 'remained' (i.e. were unsold at the accounting date) but no explanation is given for this.[16]

The Priory's stock-book for Michaelmas to Michaelmas 1390–1391, a unique survival, shows a similar variation between manors. The size of flocks varied from 275 at Sutton to 1900 at the priory manor at Overton, with no sheep at all at Wroughton. Wethers, ewes, lambs and rams were accounted for separately with wethers making up nearly half of the overall total of 20,367 on the whole estate.

There was a degree of specialisation in the way the flocks were managed. Crondal on the western end of the North Downs was the home of a breeding flock of 254 sheep served by seven rams. Many of the lambs born there were driven across country, a distance of about 30 miles (48 km), before Michaelmas, to the large manor of Easton near Winchester which carried a flock of 1854 sheep. Other new young stock for Easton came from Silkstead near Hursley, while some of the year old hoggs were sent as far away as Mapledurham in the Thames valley.[17] This is a journey of over 40 miles (64 km), not easy to accomplish driving a flock of sheep. Similarly 40 rams from the bishop's manor of Fareham were sent to Crawley in 1220–1221, a distance of around 32 miles (51 km). The motivation for the movement of quite large numbers of sheep over appreciable distances is not always clear but it does indicate that on large estates there seem to have been active estate-wide management policies. These policies also seem to reflect the methods advocated by writers like Walter of Henley.

Other religious houses

The same kind of active management of sheep which constituted a large part of the income-producing assets of a religious house can be seen in other monastic accounts. Not all, however, found it easy or even possible to run a big enterprise for a long period. The Benedictine house of Croyland in the fens took steps to set up a centralised administration to deal with its considerable flocks, dispersed on outlying estates. From 1276 it organised separate accounting regime for all these flocks known

---

16 *Ibid.*, 94, 96.

17 J. Hare (2006), 'The Bishop and the prior', 203–5.

Figure 9. Ruins of Croyland Abbey (photo: Thoraldson, Creative Commons CC BY-SA 3.0)

as *Bidentes Hoylandie*.[18] Some of the extensive pastures of this house were on recently reclaimed fen land near the abbey itself while it also had manors further north in Lincolnshire and in Cambridgeshire. The enterprise was highly profitable providing as much as 20% of Abbey's total income and a very important element in its cash flow. The head shepherd was in charge and ensured that all wool was sent to the mother house after shearing in the summer with fells from culled sheep or dead lambs following in the autumn. The wool was stored in a central wool-house ready for sale. By 1322, however, Croyland had more or less entirely withdrawn from sheep farming and wool production. This was probably due to horrific losses from disease reaching 3033 in 1314 out of a total flock of 10,961 animals. This scale of losses from disease may have been caused by a recurrence of the devastating epidemic of scab which hit flocks in many parts of England 1279–1281.[19]

In 1321 the Croyland manor of Staundon had a flock of 477 wethers of which 240 died before they could be shorn. A flock of nearly 13,000 beasts in 1314 now comprised less than 500.[20] In 1322 the abbey was no longer actively trading in wool. It has also been suggested that as well as the incidence of disease another element in the collapse of wool production by Croyland Abbey was the rising water table in the fens. This caused catastrophic flooding in the fenland manors, something which was blamed for the higher levels of disease, usually called simply 'murrain', among the flocks. There was clearly a lack of grazing with more than £31 spent on hay in 1314 when, in previous years, amounts of around 12–15s had been spent on supplementary feeding. There is also evidence that the nearby estates of both Ramsey and Peterborough Abbeys suffered in the same way. The sale of wool was a welcome source of cash but there were also attendant and in this case perhaps unforeseeable risks.

Cistercian monasteries

The Cistercian order, or the White Monks so-called from the colour of their habits, is perhaps the institution most often popularly associated with the wool trade in the middle ages. Was this order more successful as a major wool producer than Croyland? The first English house, Waverley Abbey in Surrey, had a flock capable of producing 14 sacks of wool, according to Pegoletti, with the best wool valued at 25 marks per sack. Their principal foundations in northern England, Rievaulx Abbey near Helmsley in north Yorkshire, and the nearby Fountains, Jervaulx and Byland Abbeys, were all in areas where arable farming was difficult but pasture for sheep flocks was plentiful. Although this part of the world was not usually considered by

18 F. M. Page (1929), '*Bidentes Hoylandiae*: a medieval sheep farm', *Economic Journal* 1, 602–13.

19 P. Slavin (2015), 'Flogging a dead cow: coping with Animal Panzootic on the Eve of the Black Death,' in A. T. Brown, A. Burn and R. Doherty, eds, *Crises in Economic and Social History*, Boydell: Woodbridge, 111.

20 M. Stephenson (1987), 'The productivity of medieval sheep on the Great Estates 1100–1500', unpublished PhD: Cambridge, 136–41.

medieval wool merchants as producing the best wools, Pegoletti's list makes clear that these houses produced far more wool than other monasteries and that the quality was above average. Fountains, he estimated would produce 76 sacks of wool in an average year with the best wool fetching 21 marks per sack; the best wool of Byland, Jervaulx and Rievaulx was worth around 17 marks and all three houses could produce 50–60 sacks of wool per year. No other monastic houses came anywhere near these totals.[21] There is, however, little source material which provides detailed information about the way the monks approached the business of caring for their flocks. There is more information about their business methods as traders which will be discussed below. At the order's peak there were 86 houses in England and others in both Scotland and Wales.

The Cistercians' reputed fondness for remote, even wild, locations with access to moorland grazing is often linked to their interest in sheep farming. The northern abbeys, however, were largely founded in areas which had suffered very badly from the devastation and depopulation of northern England in the aftermath of the Norman Conquest. These lands, (often called 'waste' in documents) were not uncultivatable, but relatively empty of settlements and peasant cultivators. This suited the way in which outlying lands belonging to the Cistercians were organised as granges, small settlements where a few professed monks and lay brothers lived and worked, not based on a village, something well-suited to sheep farming.[22] Rievaulx probably fed its flocks in the high moorland pastures in summer bringing them down to the valleys in winter. Something similar, a form of transhumance, was probably also done by some of the Welsh Cistercian houses, including Aberconway, which had pasture rights over a large area of high ground.[23]

There are no reliable series of figures for the number of sheep kept by any particular house at any particular date as there are for the Winchester manors. A rough estimate for the early fourteenth century can be made by taking the number of woolsacks that an abbey was thought capable of producing, in Pegolotti's list, and multiplying it by the number of fleeces that such sacks customarily contained. This was not a universally accepted number but was frequently expected to be about 260. The total arrived at cannot be other than a 'best guess' but this method does allow comparisons to be made between houses. The four most important northern Cistercian houses, Byland, Jervaulx, Rievaulx and Fountains, using this calculation, all had flocks of over 13,000 sheep, with Fountains having nearly 19,000. Some of the more southerly houses had very much smaller numbers of sheep but their best wool commanded higher prices. Thame in Oxfordshire, Kirksted in Lincolnshire, Waverley in Surrey and

21 A. Evans, ed. (1936), *Francesco Balducci Pegoletti, La Pratica della Mercatura,* Cambridge MA, Medieval Academy of America, 258–69.

22 R. A. Donkin (1969), 'The Cistercian Order and the settlement of northern England', *Geographical Review* 59, 403–16.

23 R. A. Donkin (1958), 'Cistercian sheep-farming and wool sales in the thirteenth century', *Agricultural History Review* 6, 2–8.

Figure 10. Rievaulx Abbey seen through trees (Creative Commons CC BY-SA 3.0)

Tintern in Monmouthshire, could all apparently expect over 24 marks per sack while the northern abbeys could expect 15–17½ marks. Only one of the houses belonging to other religious orders which traded with Pegolotti's employers, the Bardi of Florence, could ask more than 20 marks for a sack of wool, the Premonstratensian monastery of St Catherine at Lincoln, with 22½ marks, being charged for their best wool.[24]

There are scattered references in other documents which point to the good reputation of the Cistercians as sheep farmers. The steward of the Bishop of Chichester in the 1220s wrote to the Bishop pointing out that, since a purchase of sheep was intended, a good place to find quality beasts was the Cistercian abbey of Vaudey in Lincolnshire. The steward was on good terms with one of the brothers there who would also advise him on the care of the bishop's sheep. The monks at Fountains also used medicaments in much the same way as the shepherds of the bishop of Winchester.[25]

The relatively high prices paid for wool from Cistercian houses, according to Pegoletti's list, even when the monastery was situated in an area with a reputation for lower quality wools, was probably a result of the way in which the monks prepared the

24 A. Evans (1936), *Francesco Balducci Pegoletti*, 260, 262, 264.

25 R. A. Donkin (1958), 'Cistercian sheep-farming', 3.

Figure 11. Fountains Abbey (photo: Mike Peel, Creative Commons CC 4.0)

wool before sale. Great care was apparently paid to washing the sheep before shearing and then sorting the fleeces. Pipewell, a Cistercian house in Rockingham forest in the Midlands, was contracted in 1291 to ensure that the wool left the 'sheepfolds well washed dry and cleaned'. The wools were also routinely sorted into the various qualities, while Fountains, in 1276, had to ensure that Florentine buyers received only good wool with 'loks' (clippings), 'god et card' (tangled coarse wool), black and grey wool and any sheepskin carefully removed.[26] Both weighing and packing into woolsacks were often done at the monasteries at their expense, sometimes by officials supplied by the merchants. By the end of the twelfth century, the most successful producers on the east coast often had property including warehouses in the towns and ports linked to the wool trade. Monastic houses in the midlands were clearly sending wool in bulk to King's Lynn and Norwich, while those in Lancashire and South Yorkshire were sending consignments to Boston and Lincoln.[27]

There is no reason to suppose that the Cistercian houses gradually ceased to be dominant as wool producers by the middle of the fourteenth century because of some loss of expertise or general change of methods in sheep farming. External factors were probably very influential, one being the financial chaos and bankruptcies

---

26 *Ibid.* 6.

27 R. A. Donkin (1969), 'The Cistercian Order', 415–16.

resulting from failed contracts with foreign merchants affecting some of the largest houses, which will be discussed below. Another was the pressure put upon monastic communities by the high death rate and low levels of recruitment following the Black Death in 1348 and the recurrence of plague in later years. Many of the lands of the abbeys and their flocks were leased to lay tenants and no longer managed as a vast estate. There was, therefore, no further need for detailed accounting of the management of the sheep flocks.

This pattern of expenditure is also apparent on the estates of the Bishop of Worcester. Those on the Cotswolds, near the Winchester manor of Witney, produced high quality wools which sold well to Italian merchants. In the fourteenth century, the flocks were directly managed as one unit with all the sheep for shearing being driven to Blockley where the local brook was very suitable for washing the animals. In 1384 3126 sheep were shorn here. This level of activity continued into the fifteenth century but by *c.*1450 the bishop ceased to manage his own flocks with all the pasture leased and the sheep sold by 1458.[28]

There seem to be few if any marked differences in farming practice between the earlier accounts of the Winchester estates, the *Bidentes Hoylandiae,* the accounts of the Cistercians and those kept by Norwich Priory and the Bishop of Worcester which cover the period from the early thirteenth to the mid-sixteenth century. Change came very slowly in the conservative world of sheep farming.

Lands held by laymen

Documents relating to the Duchy of Lancaster's estates in south Yorkshire, the extensive Honour of Pickering, in many ways show a similar farming system in operation to that on the monastic lands. Although much of the demesne arable land was leased to farmers from the early fourteenth century, the pasture lands and the sheep flocks were managed directly till 1434. Like the monastic orders sheep farming was organised centrally for this estate with one official in overall charge. The aim was to produce wool with wethers making up the majority of sheep on the estate and only relatively small numbers of breeding ewes. In the 1320s around 1300 fleeces were sent to market on a regular basis. Four shepherds were regularly employed with extra labour at busy times like shearing and washing. The fleeces were collected at a wool house in Pickering and were graded into the usual classes of clean, refuse and lockets. Clearly the estate had a good reputation among the visiting wool merchants from Hull, Beverley and York since the wool fetched higher prices than that from nearby areas like Thornton and Kirkdale. The flocks seem to have been moved on a seasonal basis between the pastures on the High Moor in the summer and those on lower ground around Dalby in the winter. The rich grassland in the Vale of Pickering

---

28 E. B. Fryde (1996), *Peasants and Landlords in Later Medieval England c.1380–c.1525,* Stroud, Sutton, 91–4.

itself was, however, reserved for the stud farm producing high quality horses which was another major enterprise.[29]

Later, towards the end of the fifteenth and the first years of the sixteenth century, a rather different regime was in operation on the Duchy lands a little further south in Derbyshire. Here the majority of the estate was leased to small peasant farmers who ran small flocks of 60–80 sheep. Larger flocks of around 500 beasts were pastured up on the High Peak.[30] Not surprisingly the popularity of sheep-farming was affected by the prices paid for wool; when prices were high or rising, as happened around 1510–1520 the Duchy court was faced with loud complaints of the overstocking of the common grazing by those who had no right to do so. In March 1517, a group of tenants on the manor of Elton, not far from Matlock, complained vigorously that over a thousand head of sheep largely owned by a family called Old had been intruded onto the common at Brassington, south of Elton, without any right. The testimony in the resulting inquiry by one Thomas Taylor who was over 71 years old and had lived on the manor for over 27 years, stated that the 'more at Brassyn ton is overlayd with Catell'. The tenants' rights were confirmed in the Coucher Book of the estate with the villagers of Elton paying 14s 8d each for their right to pasture their stock on the 'moor heath and waste at Brassington'.[31]

There was nothing unusual in tenants or leaseholders with perhaps only small holdings of arable land increasing the number of their livestock as much as possible in times of high prices for wool. It is hard to find any good figures for the number of sheep in peasant hands but as has been pointed out the total of 46,382 sacks of wool exported and paying customs in 1304–1305, the peak year, equates at the usual reckoning of 260 fleeces per sack to a national sheep flock of 12 million animals. A similar calculation in 1449–1450 suggests that the fleeces of over 4 million sheep were exported but by this time exports of woollen cloth reached 38,531 cloths of assize. This very roughly would equate to the wool produced by 2,330,000 sheep. This takes no account of wool woven into cloth which was used in England itself. The national sheep flock had perhaps declined to some 8 million animals or thereabouts,[32] somewhat less proportionately than the population in the years after the Black Death. Even given the extremely tentative nature of these figures it is clear that although the flocks kept by large landowners were very considerable they would have been at least equalled and probably surpassed by those of the lesser gentry and the peasantry.

There is, however, one set of accounts which does throw some light on the way at least one enterprising member of the gentry managed his investment in pastoral

29 B. Waites (1977), 'Pastoral farming on the Duchy of Lancaster's Pickering Estate in the fourteenth and fifteenth centuries,' *Yorkshire Archaeological Journal* 49, 77–80.

30 I. S. W. Blanchard (1971), *The Duchy of Lancaster's estates in Derbyshire, 1485–1540*, Derby, Derbyshire Archaeological Society, Record Series 3.

31 *Ibid.*, 44.

32 Figures for the total of wool sacks and cloths of excise exported come from E. M. Carus-Wilson and O. Coleman (1963), *England's Export Trade 1275–1547*, Oxford: Clarendon, 62, 97.

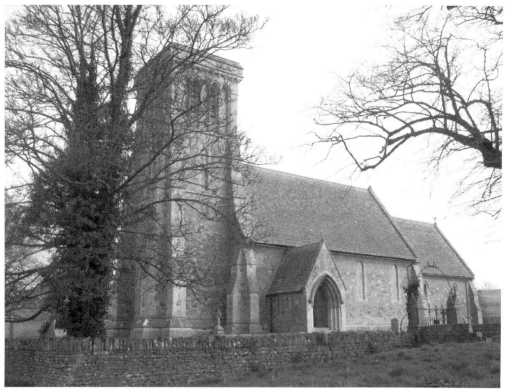

Figure 12. Sevenhampton Church (photo: Robert Cutts, Creative Commons CC 2.0 generic)

farming at much the same time that the Cistercian monasteries in the North of England and some of the monastic houses in Lincolnshire were also seeking to reap the benefits of producing wool in some quantity. These are the accounts of the manor of Sevenhampton in the Vale of the White Horse in Wiltshire, which run from 1270 to 1288. This was part of the extensive land holdings of Adam de Stratton, a member of a family originally holding a small estate by knight service, who made a very successful career in the Exchequer first as a clerk and finally as Chamberlain in the Exchequer of Receipt. He was also in charge of the works at Westminster for the King and, on the side as it were, operated as a financier and source of loans to such an extent that he became known as the 'Christian usurer'. One final string to his bow was as financial controller of all the lands of the immensely rich Isabel de Forz, Countess of Aumale.

It was through this connection that he acquired the manor of Sevenhampton. Given the nature of his business it is perhaps not surprising that he was eventually accused of corruption, his misdeeds including forging charters of the Abbey of Bermondsey in order to take over some lands. When his possessions were investigated £12,500 in bullion was said to have been found in coffers in his house, a truly enormous sum of money. He died as a convicted felon in the Tower of London. From our point of view his fall from grace is convenient since his lands were forfeit to the crown in 1289 and the records of this manor consequently preserved in the royal archives. It is perhaps not surprising given his background that the surviving records which are 'fair copies' are very well written in court hand, perhaps by a clerk sent down from London. He is personally not typical of a non-noble landowner in the late thirteenth century but his records are worth comparing with those of larger estates.[33]

There was no resident lord at Sevenhampton so the manor was run to produce income. While in de Stratton's control the sheep flock was expanded considerably reaching 1001 beasts in 1279 and then fluctuating because of the effects of scab on the flock. The reeve's accounts for the year 1286–1287, when the manor had been run on what might be called commercial lines for some years, show that receipts from the sheep enterprise were healthy. Apart from the rent of a cottage for the shepherd at 6d for a half year, £19 19s 9½d came from the sale of 564 good fleeces (£19 12s) and 100 lambs' fleeces (7s 2d) with 7½d from the sale of locks. 43 wethers, 25 ewes and 20 young sheep were also sold. The main expenses were on milk bought to feed lambs (14½d) and the expensive anti-scab ointment (35s 10d).

The stock account provides carefully calculated figures for the flocks on the manor. In this year, at the start of the account the wether flock consisted of 260 beasts; this had declined to 248; 32 had died, 43 were sold and 69 young sheep had been added from the home-bred flock of hoggs. The number of rams remained steady at two while the ewe flock grew from 217 to 232 by the end of the year (24 died, 25 sold, young home bred additions 65). Similar details are given of the young stock and also of lambs born during the year, an important statistic for a manor where stock was not routinely bought in. In this case, in this year, 211 lambs were born although 29 ewes were sterile, 85 died, the tithe amounted to 14 animals and one was given to the shepherd as his due. The final total noted that 102 lambs survived, of which only one was male.[34] The total survivals in the previous year had been 163. Deaths are said to be due to *morina* (murrain or disease) but could have been due to diseases such as scouring which particularly affects newborn lambs; scab is not necessarily implied. Despite these problems, however, all the wool and wool fells from both adult and young sheep was sold in this particular year. As well as increasing the size of the sheep flocks, Adam of Stratton also invested in buildings on this manor; two new sheepcotes were built including one over 200 ft (61 m) long and another 67 ft (21 m) long. Other new buildings were also intended for cattle. The revenue from livestock farming as a whole on this manor including both cattle and sheep rose from over £6 in 1270 to over £55 in 1279.[35]

---

33 M. W. Farr, ed. (1959), *Accounts and Surveys of the Wiltshire lands of Adam of Stratton*, Devizes, Wiltshire Archaeological Society, xiv–xxiii.

34 M. W. Farr, ed. (1959), *Accounts and Surveys,* 174–5. The figures do not quite tally but some lambs from the prior year were transferred to the young stock flocks.

35 M. J. Stevenson (1987), 'The productivity of medieval sheep', 169–70.

Sheep farming in East Anglia and elsewhere in the late fifteenth and early sixteenth centuries

There is no doubt that by the middle of the fifteenth century the generality of landholders whatever their social status, were swayed by commercial considerations when organising their agricultural enterprises. Much also depended on very local considerations of soil type and climate. Passing references in estate documents make clear that John Hopton, a Suffolk landowner, had quite considerable flocks on two of his manors. At Blythburgh near the coast where his manor included rough grazing and marshy land along the estuary of the Blyth, he was running a flock of 700 sheep in 1435, 586 in 1454–1455 and 721 in 1478.[36] This operation, however, was dwarfed by the flock kept by Sir Roger Townshend over the boundary in Norfolk. Townshend had around 6000–8000 sheep on his lands in the 1470–1480s. This had grown to a flock of over 12,000 by 1490 producing a profit of over £200 a year. Townshend not only employed a special manager for his flocks or 'sheep reeve' but also took a deep personal interest in the running of this mighty enterprise. The personal notes he made at the end of a sheep account for Michaelmas 1482–1483 have already been noted. Apart from comments on the work of his shepherds he also recorded that he would be paid 21s for the skins of culled sheep, (the number is not given) and the old ewes would fetch £5–7. He may have been a hard master to satisfy since his final note in this memorandum was that we must see these things amended 'or befall ouste'.[37]

By 1516 the flocks managed by Roger Townshend's heir were even larger with 18,000 sheep pastured on the family lands. This figure had fallen back to around 5,000 by the latter half of the sixteenth century. The Townshend family like most owners of large numbers of sheep followed the time-honoured practice of keeping separate flocks of ewes and wethers. These were organised on the foldcourse system, already mentioned, as were the great majority of flocks in Breckland and the northern coastal parts of Norfolk. By the sixteenth century this system was causing problems from villagers because of the size of many landlords' flocks. As certain 'poor inhabitants' of Norfolk declared in the reign of Elizabeth, 'within euery Towne and vylage is most comonly one ii or iii manors or more and to euery manor a Shepps course or ffouldcourse belonging.' The number of sheep which could be fed on a particular foldcourse had been tightly controlled in the past. Most would have sufficient feed for only around 300–400 beasts. The petition went on to explain how the gentry no longer fulfilled their obligations under the system, causing great harm to the villagers. Their beasts could not feed on the stubble fields and the fallow lands in the winter as they had the right to do. The available land was 'oueronne with sheppe'.

---

36 C. Richmond (1981), *John Hopton, a Fifteenth Century Suffolk Gentleman,* Cambridge; Cambridge University Press, 98.

37 C. E. Moreton and C. Richmond (2000), 'Beware of grazing on foul mornings'; a gentleman's husbandry notes,' *Norfolk Archaeology* 43, 500–3.

Figure 13. Fields near Burton Dassett in the snow (Creative Commons CC BY-SA 3.0)

The landlords also enclosed their land in the common fields but still expected to have the right to pasture their flocks on the remaining unenclosed portions belonging to villagers. The same thing happened in the summer grazing on the commons; by putting too many sheep on this land the landlords deprived the villagers of the ability to feed their own beasts. The number of cullet sheep allowed could also be reduced by the landlord or this practice might be forbidden altogether. The foldcourse system had worked reasonably well in the past but was under increasing pressure by the middle of the sixteenth century. It tended to be eroded bit by bit as the larger landlords gradually re-organised their holdings and adopted new methods. In some places fold courses were not finally removed until the parliamentary Enclosure Acts of the eighteenth century.[38]

The fortuitous survival of the account book for 1501–1520, in the archives of Westminster Abbey, of a wool merchant and grazier based in Moreton-in-Marsh in the Cotswolds has allowed Christopher Dyer to create a detailed picture of sheep farming practices in the late fifteenth and early sixteenth centuries in that part of the world. The deep and prolonged drop in population in this area which continued from the time of the Black Death to around the third decade of the sixteenth century meant that many settlements which had thrived in the thirteenth century dwindled to tiny hamlets or disappeared altogether. This meant that, unlike the situation in East Anglia, ambitious and energetic tenants or families of the lower gentry could increase their holdings by taking over vacant land. It was also possible easily to enclose what had previously been demesne land and open fields in deserted villages as pastures often known as 'leasows'.

---

38 K. J. Allison (1957), 'The sheep-corn husbandry of Norfolk', 12–30.

The owner of the account book, John Heritage, came from a part of the country where the effects of this drop in population were particularly noticeable. All around his base in Moreton-in-Marsh, extending beyond Chipping Campden to the north and Chipping Norton to the south, engrossing had taken place or abandoned open fields had been enclosed. One example is the valley of Lark Stoke which today has but one house with only three other villages in a 2 mile (3.5 km) radius; in the fourteenth century there were 11 villages and hamlets in the same area. Heritage owned sheep himself and rented pastures including leasows mostly within 8 miles (2.5 m) or so of Moreton-in-Marsh. His most important grazing was at Burton Dassett between Banbury and Leamington and at Ditchford just north of Moreton or on the heath at Moreton. He also made temporary short term-arrangements with landholders in neighbouring villages including Compton and Wolford.

The total number of his sheep between 1504 and 1510 varied between 1000 and 2000, with most kept in flocks of between 200 and 800. His shepherds were relatively well paid and also had the right to run their own animals with Heritage's. He successfully bred new stock with little need to buy in wethers from other owners. Judging from the figures for 1509, the only ones available, his flocks were well cared for, since in that year the fleeces sold averaged 1.83 lb (0.82 kg) in weight. (The mean for the whole period 1208–1450 on the Winchester estates was 1.35 lb (0.61 kg).[39]

The core of his business, however, was as wool merchant or 'brogger' collecting wool from producers all over his part of the world and storing it in his wool-house for sale to clothiers or other merchants. Looking at his accounts with their details of purchases made year by year it is possible to get a much clearer idea of how sheep were being kept in this period in this part of the Cotswolds where the best English wool was produced. It seems that despite the time it must have taken to ride from village to village making small bargains he was content to buy wool in small parcels from peasants who had at most fewer than ten sheep. One particular example is the widow Maud Pyper who sold him as little as 11 lb (5 kg) of wool in a single year. Most of his suppliers had 60–90 adult animals.[40] This would accord very well with what is known about the number of sheep (the stint) tenants with holdings of a yardland or virgate or a little more, an average amount, would be allowed to graze on the common pastures. Heritage did make deals with 'gentlemen' graziers with larger flocks but the bulk of his business was with small producers. The wool money would have been a boon for such men and their families helping to pay rents and taxes and provide some extra disposable income for occasional luxuries.

Over the whole period it is true to say, however, that the methods of sheep-farming changed little. A shepherd on the Bishop of Winchester's Hampshire estates in the early thirteenth century would have found himself at home with the regime on any of the

39 C. Dyer (2012), *A Country Merchant, 1495–1520; Trading and Farming at the End of the Middle Ages,* Oxford, Oxford University Press, 132–63.

40 *Ibid.,* 157.

Figure 14. The tomb of John Hopton in Blythburgh Church (photo: author)

gentry owned sheep-walks on the Cotswolds in the mid-sixteenth century. The way flocks were organised with wethers kept separately from ewes, the lambing rates, and fleece weights would all have been what he might have expected three hundred years earlier taking one year with another. There was apparently no startling innovation in medications for sheep or deeper understanding of breeding techniques. It is not surprising that much of Walter of Henley's advice to the owners of flocks written around 1276 also appeared in *The Book of Husbandry by Master Fitzherbert* published in 1534.

Yet it is also the case that good sheep management in matters of detail could make a difference to the profitability of a flock. Some changes in lambing rates and in fleece weights could be due to bad weather; a run of cold winters (something which seems to have occurred in the 1430s) could impact on the health of sheep, particularly ewes about to lamb. Other matters, however, were in the control of the shepherd. Were the sheep fed adequately in winter with suitable fodder? Were they housed in sheepcotes in good repair? Were the lambs weaned too soon in order to use the ewes' milk for cheese? Were the shepherds overburdened by flocks too large for one man to manage and with inadequate help at lambing or shearing? The answers to all these questions could impact on the productivity of sheep-farming in our period. Sometimes it might be the case that less winter fodder was provided because a conscious decision had been made to reduce costs in a time of falling wool prices. Similarly pastures might become overstocked in a response to rising prices. Wool was produced mainly for sale, unlike arable crops of which a proportion would have been for home consumption in all but the largest estates. The state of the market was always an important factor in determining flock management.[41] This will be discussed along with other aspects of the trade in wool in the next section.

---

41 D. Stone (2003), 'The productivity and management of sheep in late medieval England,' *Agricultural History Review* 51, 1–22.

Part 2

Trade

Chapter 3

Producers and Traders *c*.1250–*c*.1350

Once wool was traded across considerable distances and was no longer only used locally to allay the basic needs of the people for warm coverings and clothes, the organisation of the trade in this essential commodity became gradually more complex and sophisticated. Exactly when this process began is not clear. The fact that Charlemagne wrote to King Offa of Mercia complaining of a decline in the quality of English cloaks (presumably made of wool) has been taken as evidence of an export trade in the early eighth century. There is very little other written evidence of this apart from a clause setting a fixed price for wool in a law code dating from the reign of Edgar (959–963).[1]

After the Conquest when Richard I was captured by his enemies while returning from the Third Crusade in 1193–1194, it is often stated that his ransom was paid in around 50,000 sacks of wool, which, if true would contain the fleeces of about 10–13 million sheep.[2] The entire clip for the year of the most important wool producers was certainly requisitioned by the royal government for this purpose. By the reign of his brother and successor King John, the export of English wool was sufficiently important to the weavers in the Low Countries to be used as a useful economic lever to influence the policies of their ruler.[3]

The overall pattern of trade and the major customers for English wool in fact varied little over the period with which we are concerned. The Low Countries and the major cloth-making towns of Flanders were the primary market. Also important were similar towns in northern Italy; the best quality English wool was sought by the members of

---

1 T. H. Lloyd (1977), *The English Wool Trade in the Middle Ages,* Cambridge: Cambridge University Press, 1.

2 A. R. Bell, C. Brooks and P. R. Dryburgh (2007), *The English Wool Market, c.1230–1327,* Cambridge: Cambridge University Press, 8. The calculation of the number of shorn sheep needed to produce this quantity of wool is based on the assumption that around 200–260 fleeces were needed to fill each woolsack of around 364 lb (165 kg). The average weight of the fleece of medieval sheep cannot be accurately calculated but was around 1.4 lb (0.63 kg). The weight of medieval fleeces is discussed in D. Postles, (1980), 'Fleece weights and the wool supply, *c*.1250–*c*.1350', *Textile History* 12, 96–103.

3 T. H. Lloyd (1977), *English Wool Trade,* 6–8.

the Arte della Lana in Florence and Italian merchants trading all over Western Europe and the Mediterranean, like Francesco Datini in Prato.

The dominance of Italian trading companies in banking both for rulers and for merchants also increased their prominence in the wool trade because of the importance of credit dealings in the way it operated. The amount of wool which was also used in England itself to make cloth increased greatly throughout our period but is perhaps the least easy to quantify.

Legislation from the reign of Richard I had set out the prescribed dimensions of so-called cloths of assize. There are records, the so-called aulnage accounts, dating from the reign of Edward III, which contain details of the subsidy payable to the Crown on such cloths. These are generally considered to be so unreliable, however, that they cannot be used for any meaningful statistical purposes.[4] The amount of cloth which was not exported can therefore only be estimated with the aid, it must be admitted, of a certain amount of guesswork. The amount of cloth exported, however, was recorded, in much the same way as exports of raw wool, as soon as the cloth custom and an additional *ad valorem* duty were imposed in 1347. The combined totals for exports of raw wools, woolfells and woollen cloth are reasonably reliable.

The total amount of wool produced in England, however, can only be estimated largely on a 'best guess' basis because of the uncertainty regarding the amount sold within the country itself or used as 'home-spun' within families. As well as looking at what statistics are available, the way business was conducted, the regulations which governed the wool trade and its economic success will be discussed in this chapter. Where possible the careers of notable individuals engaged in the trade will also be discussed.

The sources

Documentary evidence survives in much greater quantities from the end of the thirteenth century. Much of it, however, is either patchy in nature, relating to particular wool producers and merchants, or consists of official tax related documents which contain few personal details. We have, for example, a body of evidence relating to the activities of Cistercian and other monasteries as wool traders mainly in the thirteenth and early fourteenth centuries (see Chapter 2).[5]

A fruitful personal source is the surviving papers of a family of London wool merchants, the Celys, in the late fifteenth century.[6] The main official source is

---

4 E. M. Carus-Wilson (1954), 'The Aulnage Accounts: a criticism', in E. M. Carus-Wilson, *Medieval Merchant Venturers,* London: Methuen, 279–91.

5 A. R. Bell *et al.,* (2007), *The English Wool Market.* This book discusses the material collected in the same authors', (2006), *Advance Contracts for the sale of Wool, 1200–1327,* Kew: List and Index Society 315.

6 A. Hanham (1975), *The Cely Letters, 1472–1488,* London: Oxford University Press for the Early English Text Society; (1985), *The Celys and their World; an English Merchant Family of the Fifteenth Century,* Cambridge: Cambridge University Press.

the surviving documentation of the export duties imposed on the export of wool beginning with the Great and Ancient Custom of 1275.[7] This duty of half a mark (6s 8d) per woolsack[8] and other duties on hides and leather was the first step in a system which was frequently altered and which was inevitably entangled in all manner of political needs and economic circumstances.

These duties provided the Crown with an elastic and relatively secure source of income; they were easy to collect and hard to avoid, the ideal form of taxation in any century. Collectors were appointed for each head port[9] with the obligation to send a full annual account to the Exchequer detailing the wool exported on which duty was charged in their area of responsibility.

Books or rolls sent up to the Exchequer by each accountant gave details of each cargo although there seems to have been no standard formula. Unfortunately, few of the books which contain much information about individual shippers and cargoes survive; the rolls have somewhat less detailed information overall but provide a certain amount of information about individual cargoes. These documents were used by exchequer clerks to provide the data incorporated in the final version of the accounts, the enrolled customs accounts. These came into being after 1275 and were originally a special section of the Pipe Rolls, the record of all the regular sources of crown income which were first compiled in the early twelfth century. The customs accounts were separated into a series of their own in 1323 largely because of their bulk and the consequent difficulties in consulting the very unwieldy Pipe Rolls.

The customs rolls provide totals of exports in various categories and the money due, arranged by port, but only include details of individual merchants or cargoes when these were exempt from customs for some reason. These enrolled accounts form an almost continuous series from the reign of Edward II till the first years of James I.

The survival of the particulars (the detailed accounts, whether books or rolls) is much more problematic with many gaps in the sequence.[10] Information relating to the wool trade can also be found in other classes of official documents including the memoranda rolls while some port towns, notably Southampton and Exeter,

---

7 The duty replaced an earlier aid charged on trade agreed with merchants; it was negotiated with the leading merchants and granted formally in parliament.

8 The question of the weight of a woolsack is dealt with in detail in T.H. Lloyd (1972), 'The medieval wool-sack: a study in economic history', *Textile History* 3, 92–3.

9 The affairs of small nearby ports were dealt with at the head port, the most important port in a particular area.

10 The particulars of account, both books and rolls are in class E122 in the National Archives. The Pipe rolls are to be found in class E372 and the enrolled customs accounts in class E364. Detailed information about records relating to the customs is in the NA research guide http://www.nationalarchives.gov.uk/records/research-guides/medieval-customs-accounts.html (consulted 21/04/2015).

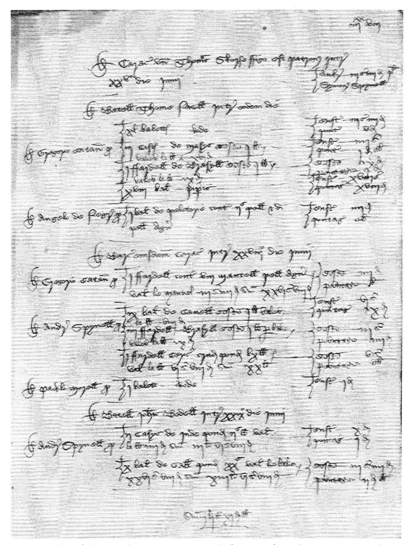

Figure 15. Folio of the Southampton Port Book for 1440 (Southampton Record Series)

also have some surviving records of the local dues imposed on trade through these ports.

Raw wool had to be prepared for the market. The need to sort the clip into the different qualities expected by buyers has already been explained. The wool also had to be wound and packed into canvas sarplers for transport to ports or local markets by packhorses, mules or in carts. After the introduction of permanent customs duties, on arrival at the port, the sarplers of wool for export had to be examined by the customers and stamped with a seal or cocket to show that the dues had been paid or accounted for. Sarplers were distinct from the 'woolsack' which was a measure of weight as well

Figure 16. The Wool House or store in Southampton (Creative Commons CC BY-SA 3.0)

as a container. Although the weight was defined in the Statute of Westminster in 1351 as 364 lb *avoir-dupois* or 26 stones of 14 lb (164.89 kg), there were a great many other measures of weight used for wool as well as other goods at the time. The stone of 14 lb (6.34 kg), for example, was by no means universally accepted.

Modern historians calculating the rise and fall of the wool price in the medieval period have attempted to convert their figures as far as possible to correspond with the 1351 standard but the variation should be kept in mind when looking at contemporary lists.[11] Only by the later fifteenth century was the standard 26 stone woolsack widely accepted. Other details of the way the customs administration worked in the fourteenth and fifteenth centuries are fairly clear. The whole trade was closely regulated both by the Crown and from the last decades of the fourteenth century also by the rules of the Company of the Staple a fellowship of merchants which had monopoly control of the majority of the export trade in wool. In the twelfth and thirteenth centuries such information is much harder to come by but it is reasonable to assume that much of the process was not greatly different from that in later years.

---

11 T. H. Lloyd (1972), 'The medieval wool sack', 92–9.

9 10 11 12 1

Figure 17. A medieval weight used for weighing wool (photo: Portable Antiquities Scheme/British Museum, Creative Commons CC 2.0 generic)

The role of monasteries *c.*1270–1340

Visitors to the impressive ruins of the best known Cistercian monasteries especially Rievaulx and Jervaulx in Yorkshire and Tintern in the Wye valley, are often left with the impression that these were immensely wealthy institutions and that much of this wealth came from the sale of the wool produced by the huge flocks of these houses. Moreover it is also often assumed that these houses dominated the wool trade, at least in the thirteenth and early fourteenth centuries, and were thus a major source of the wealth of England. One early source of this assumption is probably the fact that the enormous ransom, already mentioned, demanded for the release of Richard I after he had been captured on his way home from the Crusades was largely put together by the crown confiscating the entire wool clip for 1193 of English Cistercian and Premonstratensian houses.

Another early indication of the involvement of Cistercian houses in the wool trade is a list of the debts owed to William Cade, a Flemish moneylender from St Omer, dating from around 1166. This mentions two monasteries and four lay landowners, including the de Vesci and the Counts of Aumale.[12] The two monasteries in the list, Louth Park (founded in 1139) and Roche (founded in 1147) were both members of the Cistercian order. One was situated in Lincolnshire and the second near Maltby in south Yorkshire, both areas well known for wool production.

This list seems to show that these houses were trading in wool with an alien merchant only some twenty years or so after their foundation. The debts also plausibly seem to relate to the system of a merchant paying in advance for wool; the debts were incurred because the amount of wool agreed had not been delivered to the merchant at the time the list was drawn up. This system of a merchant whether denizen or alien contracting in advance for the purchase of wool, probably visiting the producer himself or sending an agent to view samples seems to have originated in the very earliest days of the export trade in wool. From its very beginnings, credit was an essential feature of the system and clearly involved a high degree of trust between the parties to any deal.

---

12   H. Jenkinson (1913), 'William Cade, a Financier of the Twelfth Century,' *EHR* 28, 209–27 contains a full transcript of the list of debts. T. H. Lloyd (1977), *The English Wool Trade*, 289.

About seventy-five years later, the accounts of Beaulieu Abbey for the year September 1269 to September 1270, clearly show how this Cistercian house organised the production of wool. Like all houses of this order Beaulieu possessed 'granges' or outlying estates which might be at some distance from the abbey itself; these were usually managed by lay brothers with the produce intended for sale or for use in the abbey. Beaulieu possessed an important grange at Faringdon which ran a large flock of sheep. Although Faringdon was over 70 miles (*c.*113 km) from Beaulieu, all the wool produced there was sent to the Abbey for disposal. The Abbey also paid all the shepherds employed and all the expenses of washing the flock, shearing the sheep and the maintenance of the sheepcotes. There was a large central depot or 'bercaria' where the wool from all the Abbey's properties was collected, graded and packed for sale. For the year in question the wool clip from the entire Abbey flock sold for £147 16s 11d with most coming from the sale of good wool and the remainder from medium wool and locks.[13]

The extent of the involvement of monastic houses in general and the Cistercian order in particular in the wool trade becomes clear in the various surviving lists of wool prices drawn up in the late thirteenth and early fourteenth centuries. Looking at a list made in Douai *c.*1270 of wool producing abbeys in England, this includes 41 Cistercian houses, 3 Augustinian, 3 Gilbertines, 2 Premonstratensian, 1 Benedictine and 1 Carthusian.[14] Pegoletti's *La Pratica della Mercatura,* a manual of advice for would-be Italian merchants written *c.*1320, lists 171 English abbeys, plus 15 in Scotland and 8 in Wales which had wool for sale. Of these all the Scots and Welsh houses and 82 of those in England were Cistercian. Augustinian and Benedictine houses numbered 34, the Premonstratensians 22 and the Gilbertines 17.[15]

Later price lists differentiate between the quality and price of wool produced in English counties and wool-producing regions without specifying individual producers whether lay or ecclesiastical. Two lists were produced in the mid-fourteenth century at a time when Edward III was deeply involved in the direct sale of wool for the benefit of the Crown. The first, from 1337, makes the produce of Hereford and Shropshire the most expensive with that from the Border counties the least desirable. In the similar list, put together by the Commons in the parliament of 1343, wools from Shropshire and Lincoln were valued at 14 marks per sack while those from Devon and Cornwall (not included in 1337) had the lowest values.

In the fifteenth century the lists included in a parliamentary petition of 1454 and the *Noumbre of Weyghtes,* a handbook for merchants at the Calais staple dating from *c.*1475, differ slightly as to which was the most expensive wool and which was the least

---

13 S. F. Hockey, ed. (1975), *The Accounts of Beaulieu Abbey.* London: Royal Historical Society Camden 4th Series 16, 163–70.

14 The Douai schedule is discussed in J. Munro (1994), 'Wool price schedules and the qualities of English wools in the later middle ages *c.*1270–1499', *Textiles Towns and Trade,* Aldershot: Variorum, 119–69.

15 A. Evans ed. (1935), *La Pratica della Mercatura,* Cambridge, MA: Medieval Academy of America.

desirable but the names of the growers were similarly not included. In general there was general agreement that the most expensive wool came from the Welsh Marches while the area producing the cheapest and presumably worst quality varied more over time; Durham in 1337, Cornwall in 1343 and Sussex in 1454.[16]

Cistercian houses, wherever they were located, were able to benefit from their good reputation for preparing the wool for sale to a high standard. Even more of an advantage to overseas merchants was the fact that their wool was, as we have seen at Beaulieu, usually collected at a central store near the Abbey concerned where it could be inspected and samples easily examined. Wool from peasant flocks, which may have made up a large proportion of what was available, was more difficult to access unless a middleman or broker was involved. The time-consuming travelling to buy small quantities of wool, one sack or less in some cases, at markets or from individuals, was best carried out by local men.

Monasteries also became involved in trade like this assembling *collecta* (wools collected from neighbouring owners of flocks) for sale with their own produce, usually at a somewhat lower price. The evidence for the extent to which some of the best known Cistercian houses added *collecta* to their own produce comes from the records of the Exchequer, both the Memoranda Rolls which include recognisances of debts, and the records of litigation in the Exchequer court.[17]

These records also reveal the complications of the way this part of the wool trade was financed in the thirteenth and early fourteenth centuries and the consequences of this for the monasteries which had become wool producers on a large scale. The root of the system was contracts for the advance sale of a part or the whole of a wool clip. The buyer would contract with the producer, often in the spring, to buy an agreed number of sacks of wool of the specified quality with delivery after the sheep had been shorn. Either a proportion of the price or the whole amount would be paid in advance sometimes on the day the contract was signed. The contracts fulfilled the need of the purchasers for an assured supply of good wool and that of the sellers for ready money for all their everyday needs and also in some cases for building projects and the like. The surviving documents are either straightforward records of the existence of the debt or more complex accounts of the litigation and other complications to which these contracts gave rise.

A detailed study of the records has revealed much about the relationship between the merchants and the producers and the way this particular aspect of the wool trade worked; it must, however, be emphasised that the surviving documents relate only to a very small percentage of the total trade in wool during the whole period covered (1200–1327) with most material coming from the last years of the thirteenth

16 T. H. Lloyd (1973), *The Movement of Wool Prices in Medieval England*, Cambridge: Cambridge University Press for the Economic History Society; 70–1 has tables for comparative prices for different areas in the different price schedules.

17 The recognisances are to be found in TNA Kew E159 and E368, the Memoranda rolls of the Exchequer, and the Plea Rolls, E13.

century. Two hundred and fifteen surviving contracts have been studied closely; 113 concern monastic houses and 102 laymen. Of the religious orders, 77 contracts relate to Cistercian producers, 19 to Augustinians, while Benedictines, Cluniacs, and Premonstratensians were each involved in 7–9 instances. Lay producers were only involved in a minority of small contracts.[18] The total amount of wool mentioned in all the contracts studied comes to around 5400 woolsacks. The great majority of this was contracted for in the years after 1281 when an average of over 26,000 sacks of wool per year was exported from England; this figure, moreover, takes no account of wool which was not exported but was supplied to English consumers.[19]

Despite this, individual cases can still reveal much of interest about the wool trade as a whole. Virtually all the contracts were with Italian merchants; 74 with Florentines, 78 with Lucchese, 4 with a company based in Piacenza and 1 with a merchant from Pistoia. The late thirteenth and early fourteenth centuries is of course the period when the English crown was closely involved with financial arrangements with Italian trading companies who were thoroughly familiar with sophisticated financial dealings.

The Riccardi of Lucca were the most deeply involved with no fewer than 78 agreements with monastic houses while the Frescobaldi of Florence held 28.[20] The only other merchant company or national group with more than ten contracts were the merchants from Cahors in south-west France with 14 contracts in the manuscripts studied who seem to have had a particularly close link with the Cistercian house at Pipewell in Northamptonshire.[21] The Italians were buying wool, most of it of the highest quality, to supply the cloth-making industry in their home town. The need to ensure a continuity of supply to the cloth workers at a time when wool producers were grappling with the sudden outbreak of scab in their flocks, something which reduced both the quantity and the quality of the wool on the market, may have made Italian merchants particularly keen to sign advance contracts after around 1275.

The debt records or recognisances from the 1280s seem to show the Abbey of Rievaulx, renowned for the quality of its wools, trying to profit from competition between the Riccardi of Lucca and the Mozzi of Florence for its wools. In 1286 the Mozzi contracted to take 168 sacks of the best wool at the rate of 18 sacks or 20 stones of wool for 9 years with payment of the total sum in advance. The following year the abbey also agreed to provide 24 sacks to the Riccardi, 18 of the best wool, 2 of medium quality and 4 of the possibly inferior *collecta*. By 1289 the Abbey owed on advance

---

18 A. R. Bell, C. Brooks and P. R. Dryburgh (2007), *The English Wool Market c.1230–1327,* Cambridge: Cambridge University Press, 11–67.

19 D. Jenkins, ed. (2003), *Cambridge History of Western Textiles* I, Cambridge: Cambridge University Press, 304–5.

20 A. R. Bell *et al.* (2007), *The English Wool Market*, 20.

21 *Ibid.*, The Cahorsins' trading relationship with Pipewell Abbey is treated in detail in chapter 3.

contracts £1582 to the Mozzi, 250 marks to the Frescobaldi, and £1600 to the Cerchi Bianci, both of Florence.[22]

These merchant companies saw their connections with the Abbey in a commercial light. They had no need of the spiritual services of the Abbey; this need was fulfilled by religious houses nearer home in Italy. The monks had a need for ready money for the everyday running of a large community as well as for any building projects. In effect 'mortgaging' their wool clip in advance was, apparently, a relatively easy way of satisfying their needs.

It was also, however, a road to a growing mountain of debt. In 1291 the abbot of Rievaulx was given permission to disperse the community to other houses; all available income was needed to pay the merchants. Even guests could no longer be accommodated at the Abbey. The Chapter General of the Cistercian Order gave them special exemption from the obligation of hospitality to travellers for three years because of the dire financial situation in which Rievaulx found itself. There is no clear evidence for the size of the Rievaulx flocks and how this may have varied over the years. Pegoletti's list states that Rievaulx produced 60 sacks per year but this may be much too high with another estimate suggesting that 21 sacks per year is more realistic.

The contract with the Mozzi was finally fulfilled after a considerable delay (their contract specified that they had absolute priority over all other debtors). The Abbey did eventually weather the crisis but continued to have 'cash flow' problems which could only be mitigated by further loans; most, however, in the early fourteenth century were provided by local landowners who appreciated and valued the spiritual benefits deriving from support of the Abbey and were bound to it by local loyalties and obligations.

Other Cistercian abbeys found themselves in a similar position with regard to debts; the General Chapter of the order was well aware of the problem and struggled to control it by at first forbidding all advance sales of wool as early as 1151, a regulation which proved to be unenforceable. Indebtedness was almost the inevitable consequence of the deeply felt need to expand the resources of a religious house so that the monks had the ability 'to worship God in a more splendid manner'.[23]

The agonised plea of the recently deposed abbot of Pipewell in 1323, written on a spare leaf of the abbey cartulary makes all too clear the consequences of becoming too deeply involved in advance dealings in wool:

> Remember dearest brethren and reverend fathers that by the said recognisances and due to seven years of dearth and common murrain of beasts the goods of the house of Pipewell had been so exhausted that nothing remained for the meagre sustenance of

---

22 *Ibid.*, 51–2. A mark was worth 13s 4d, two-thirds of a pound sterling.

23 E. Jamroziak (2003), 'Rievaulx Abbey as a wool producer in the late thirteenth century: Cistercians, sheep and debts', *Northern History* 40, 197–218.

the monks: sometimes they sat in the refectory for three or four days with only black bread and potage, at other times they wandered from market to market to buy bread and this they patiently endured. I, the wretch and sinner who have occupied the place of abbot, therefore counsel, ask implore and warn in as much as I am able lest another abbot fall so deeply into the hands of the Lombard that they heed the French maxim 'leger est aprendre mes fort est a rendre'.[24]

Pipewell's problems began in the last decades of the thirteenth century, like those of other abbeys dealing in wool. The Abbey had a good reputation for its produce and also for careful preparation of the wool for sale. It was also well situated for access to markets and the major wool exporting port of Boston. Even though its finances were already in some disarray, in 1288 it entered into a contract for the sale of its wool clip with a group of merchants from Cahors, led by William Servat, an experienced merchant and banker with close connections to the crown. Under the terms of this agreement the monastery would receive large sums in advance payments, and would supply a total of 360 sacks of wool over 15 years divided annually into 9 sacks of good wool, 3 of medium wool, 7 of locks and 5 of *tayller* (presumably of the lowest quality, though all grades would be free of matted wool and other impurities). This amount of wool presupposes, it has been calculated, access to a flock of 5,500 sheep; there are no details of size of the Pipewell flocks at this date but the amount of pasture in their possession and also the estimates in Pegoletti's list imply a maximum of 3,000 sheep. Not surprisingly the abbey fell behind on the deliveries to Servat and his colleagues almost immediately and the contract was re-negotiated in 1291. The terms were in some ways harsher with the merchants claiming the right to 2 sacks a year without payment because of the abbey's 'trespasses and damages' against them. The contract, however, also contained a scheme to set up a flock owned in equal shares by the monks and the merchants to be maintained by the abbey which would have the right to all natural increase in the number of sheep. This may have been an attempt to support the abbey after the flocks had suffered badly from the epidemics of scab and murrain very prevalent at this time.

Despite this and other attempts to settle the debts resulting from the failure to fulfil this agreement the problem was never finally resolved. The list of recognisances in the abbey cartulary made some time after 1314 includes a total of £2,400 owed to various debtors. The last is a bond for £213 and 22 sacks of wool still owed to William Servat. The abbey's need for ready money, the effect of disease on the flocks, the demands for taxes by the crown, the ups and downs of the wool market itself had prevented successive abbots from ever being able to clear all their obligations.

There had been periods when the abbey finances had improved. In the time of the abbacy of Andrew de Royewell in the first years of the fourteenth century the community felt able to build extensively including a new church and chapter house. The abbey was also able to build up its holdings of livestock having a large herd of

---

24 A. R. Bell *et al.* (2007), *The English Wool Market*, 68.

milking cows, another of draught oxen, and 2,000 sheep and 144 lambs in 1308. The good times did not last, however, and further debts were incurred after 1314, some with factors working for the Bardi company of Florence. The bleak years of terrible weather and harvest failures between c.1315–1319 made paying off debts whether in cash or by supplying wool a daunting task. Expedients like selling off some of the abbey's possessions or selling leases on some of the abbey lands to laymen brought little relief. The community was finally dispersed for a period of at least three years in August 1323; just four months after William of Lawford had written his sorrowful plea in the cartulary.[25]

It is very easy to blame the system of advance sales for the financial problems of some at least of the monasteries which were heavily involved in the wool trade. Rievaulx and Pipewell were not the only ones which became overburdened with debts in this way. Should we, therefore, conclude that the idea that the sale of wool made the monks wealthy is a myth? Or that some monasteries were profligate and badly managed squandering the money they earned through over-grandiose building schemes? Either conclusion is perhaps an over-simplification. It is perhaps true that the role of monasteries especially Cistercian houses in the wool trade as a whole has been over-emphasised.

For a variety of reasons their importance as wool producers diminished in the first half of the fourteenth century while earlier their importance in the thirteenth century in this regard is to some extent a result of the nature of much of the surviving evidence. The granges of the Cistercians in their heyday supported large flocks of sheep as did the demesne lands of the secular clergy and the most important lay landlords. The move away from the direct exploitation of their lands to leasing lands to tenants affected religious houses as well as other landlords and thus made them the landlords of tenant farmers rather than direct producers of wool.

The fact that Italian merchant companies in particular traded extensively with monastic houses, something which is set out in detail in Pegoletti's price list, has also, perhaps, led to the neglect of the fact that there was as much business to be done with noble laymen and smaller producers at fairs and markets. Monastic houses also, of course, did not see trade and the making of profits as their main *raison d'être*. They needed money as a means to an end, which was not the accumulation of wealth but the worship of God. To this end they needed money to maintain the fabric and life of the monastery but also to glorify God by providing a worthy setting for His worship.

They had, moreover, obligations to relieve the poor and sick and provide shelter for travellers whether of high or low degree. They also suffered from the fact that the crown in England, for much of the thirteenth and fourteenth centuries, accepted the truth of their wealth and imposed heavy taxes especially in time of war. The widespread problems caused by epidemics of scab from c.1270 and other diseases and episodes of bad weather were as much a problem for monastic sheep farmers as for all

---

25 A. R. Bell *et al.* (2007), *The English Wool Market*, chapter 3. 'A case study of Pipewell Abbey.'

others in these years. Advance payments for the sale of wool seemed to offer a way out of their 'cash flow' problems but for some houses became the origin of a cycle of debt from which escape was very difficult.

Middlemen and merchants

We have been able to look at the wool-dealing practices of religious houses in the late thirteenth and early fourteenth centuries in some detail because of the number of records which have survived of their advance contracts for the sale of wool. New research into the same group of sources, with the addition of the records of debts certificated under the system set up by the Statutes of Acton Burrell (1283) and the Statute of Westminster (1285) and the Hundred Rolls, particularly for the important wool producing area of Lincolnshire and adjacent counties has revealed more details of the way wool was traded in this part of the country, in much the same period, the late thirteenth century and the first decades of the fourteenth century.[26]

Monastic houses of all sizes were heavily engaged in the trade but, as well as having close links with the leading Italian merchant houses, they also disposed of wool through local merchants often based in Lincoln itself. Most of the wool was exported via Boston although, at times when exports were officially restricted, smaller creeks and out of the way ports might also be used to escape the danger of official scrutiny.

The certificates under the Statute Merchant regime are particularly useful for the light they throw on the trading activities of local men. One example is the group of traders from Leicestershire who, in 1287, are recorded as owing four members of the Riccardi of Lucca merchant house the sum of 348 marks, probably because of the failure to deliver wool to the Italians already paid for. Another group of traders and producers, clustered around Alkborough in the northwest of Lincolnshire, seems to have acted in the same way as middlemen or brokers.

In 1285 two brothers, Robert and Reginald de Camera sold the Riccardi wool worth £180; they received a further £156 over the next four years from the Frescobaldi. This represented the sale of considerable quantities of wool. The two had clearly been in business for some time since in 1275, as recorded in the Hundred Roll enquiry they had supplied 142 sacks of wool at Hull over a period of three years 'to the use of Reginald of Piacenza'.

Not all middlemen active at this period dealt in large shipments. The certificates under the Statute Merchant also show Lincoln traders buying up wool in small quantities from local people. For example William of Heapham of Lincoln was happy to buy half a sack of wool worth 100s from one Richard of Thoresby. Somewhat later, in 1291, Adam Cokerel, the bailiff of Lincoln at the time, was contracted to supply the

---

26 I am grateful to Dr Alan Kissane and Dr Paul Dryburgh for sight of their currently unpublished paper on the medieval wool trade in Lincolnshire, and for sharing some of their research findings with me. This and the following paragraph are based on their findings.

Riccardi of Lucca with 6 sacks of good wool, *collecta* from both Lindsey and Kesteven, which he had probably bought up in the Lincoln wool market.

The involvement of local men in the wool trade in Lincoln then increased rapidly; by 1310–1311 there were 41 identified wool traders in the city of Lincoln varying from one trading in only 3 sacks of wool to another dealing in over 200. By this time there is also evidence that some merchants had acquired land and moved into the production of wool. This applies to Stephen de Stonham who had acquired former Templar lands at Willoughton and Temple Bruer. He appears in the certificate registers as frequently lending money to other local landowners but it is likely that these were in effect advance payment for wool.

Increasingly in the fourteenth century the former domination of the wool market by foreign merchants, whether Italians or Flemings, lessened. Actions by the English Crown made it more difficult for foreign merchants to deal directly with producers. A much greater proportion of sales were arranged through English merchants some probably acting as factors for foreigners. Particularly from the reign of Edward III, with the overall aim of raising large sums of money to finance the king's wars, attempts were made to regulate the sale of wool. No one method proved entirely successful but a variety of approaches was used. The customs system was manipulated to try and increase the overall sums of money flowing to the crown. Taxes in wool rather than on wool were introduced, while the king also intervened directly in the market by becoming for a brief period what has been called a 'woolmonger extraordinary'.[27] The ordinary operations of merchants were also affected and probably made more difficult by regulations like export bans and the establishment of staple towns at various places at home and abroad. The records of the Commons in Parliament are not surprisingly full of the plaints of wool men and also their increasingly complex negotiations with the king in attempts to mitigate some of the problems. The interests of wool merchants become more prominent than those of wool producers.

Some understanding of the relationship between merchants and wool producers in the mid-fourteenth century can, however, be gained by looking at some of the few surviving wool accounts of an individual merchant. Those of William de la Pole of Hull, an exceptional man, described in the Meaux chronicle as 'second to no English merchant' are particularly enlightening.[28] He was an unscrupulous man and intent on rising in society to such good effect that his son Michael became a celebrated knight and eventually a peer, serving with in the armies of both the Black Prince and John of Gaunt.[29] William de la Pole was also an expert businessman. His main route to power and influence was as

---

27 T. H. Lloyd (1977), *The English Wool Trade*, chapter 5, 144–92.

28 E. A. Bond (1866–68) ed., *Chronica Monasterii de Melsa, a Fundatione Usque ad Annum 1396, Auctore Thoma de Burton, Abbate. Accedit Continuatio ad Annum 1406, Rerum Britannicarum medii aevi scriptores (Chronicles and Memorials of Great Britain and Ireland during the Middle Ages*, London, Longmans: Green and Co.; Reader and Dyer, 3, Account of Sir William de la Pole, 48.

29 *ODNB* entries for Sir William de la Pole (d.1366) and Michael de la Pole, first Earl of Suffolk (1330–1389).

a leading provider of finance to Edward III, something which will be discussed in part 3 of this book. Here we are concerned with a small group of wool accounts which provide useful information of the way he organised his business and his dealing in wool.

The accounts come from 1337. In this year the king with the help of prominent merchants including Pole had organised the English Wool Company, the profits of which would finance the king's war against France and subsidise his allies in the Netherlands. The scheme as a whole was a failure but the accounts kept by Pole are illuminating. They relate to wool bought in Lindsey in Lincolnshire, Yorkshire, and Nottingham. No particular suppliers are named but it is clear that all the wool, an overall total of 350 sacks, had been acquired by his agents travelling through their allocated district buying it parcel by parcel probably from a wide range of producers, a method very similar to that which was in use *c.*1310–1311, mentioned above.

The wool was delivered to Lincoln, York or Nottingham. Only in Yorkshire is more information given of where the wool was bought. Richmond, Northallerton and Myton on Swale are mentioned with the possibility that the wool was bought in markets held in these places or were the base from which de la Pole's agents set out to collect wool. The accounts carefully break down the expenses; for example, for carriage, renting storage space, food and drink for the workers, and for packing the wool. All the expenses are reduced to the common unit of the cost per woolsack, thus making it easy for de la Pole to calculate the overall expenditure.

De la Pole's partner in the English Wool Company, the London merchant and alderman Reginald Conduit, does not follow any systematic plan in his accounts; sometimes not mentioning unit costs, sometimes using 'sarpler' as a unit (though it was not a standard measure) and sometimes the woolsack. A careful comparison of de la Pole's accounts with those of other merchants, as well as Conduit, reveal him to have been an exceptionally canny businessman. He clearly had trained his buying agents well so that he was able to get good wools at a lower price than his rivals and treated the agents generously. Pole's brokers or *broggers* received as their pay an average of 3s 4d per sack collected while Conduit's men got only 3s having bought from the producers at somewhat higher prices than those paid by Pole's men.

We can also trace the journey of consignments from the collecting point to the port used for export. The Lindsey wools were taken by cart or packhorse to Lincoln itself; then by cart to Barton on Humber where they were loaded into boats and taken across the estuary to Hull. At Hull some of the wools needed to be repacked with losses occurring from deterioration in the condition of the wool. The last stage was the final transport of the woolsacks from storage at Hull again into boats which would take them to be loaded in the waiting 'great ships' which clearly could not tie up at wharfs but were at anchor in the harbour. The Yorkshire wool came down the Ouse to Hull and that from Nottingham having been collected at Blythe, went to Hull by water from Bawtry by way of a tributary of the Trent.[30]

---

30 E. B. Fryde (1964), *The Wool Accounts of William de la Pole: a Study of Some Aspects of the English Wool Trade at the Start of the Hundred Years War,* York: St Antony's Press, 15–20.

Nothing in the accounts, however, hints at the difficulties which wool merchants (whether those with influence in high places and access to large sums of money or those in a much smaller way of business) faced because of the intervention of the crown in their affairs. Probably because it was more or less taken for granted by those in authority at the time that one of the few sources of wealth which could be relatively easily put at the service of the crown and the realm was the wool trade, this intervention in its varied forms became an increasing burden both for individuals and for the trade as a whole.

Chapter 4

The Direct Intervention of the Crown

Prises and taxes

In 1337, the wool listed in de la Pole's accounts was destined for Dordrecht and was part of a scheme which makes plain the way the crown regarded the wool trade as a relatively easily available source of ready money. Edward III was following the precedent set by his grandfather Edward I. In 1294, Edward I was faced with the possibility of renewed war with France at a time when his finances were at a low ebb following years of warfare in Wales and on the borders of Gascony. His attempted solution to his urgent need for ready money was to propose to seize the entire wool clip for this year, arrange its transport to markets in the Low Countries for sale and finally to use the proceeds to subsidise his allies in the region. English wool merchants were appalled at this prospect which would disrupt the market and probably ensure their ruin.

The leading merchants, in an assembly called for the purpose of discussing the scheme, came up with the alternative plan of greatly increased duties on the export of wool or a *maltote* at the rate of 40 s. per sack.[1] The source of this idea was later said to be the wealthy and very influential Shropshire wool merchant, Laurence of Ludlow. This man, who had established a flourishing business dealing in the excellent wools of the Welsh Marches, was also, like de la Pole, a money lender on a significant scale and well known to the king who was among his debtors. The scheme was acceptable to the crown. It would produce ready money much more quickly than the sale of the wool crop on the market. From the point of view of the merchants it allowed them to continue to trade with the burden of the new duties, in fact, shifted to the producers in the shape of lower prices for their produce.

The wool fleet sailed in November 1294 after the higher duties had been paid. On board were no fewer than 180 sacks of Laurence's wools, the fleeces of 46,800 sheep. The ships were caught in a storm in the North Sea on the night of 26 November and that carrying Laurence foundered. His body was washed ashore at Aldeburgh. The annalist of Dunstable Abbey, one of his suppliers, recorded gleefully, 'because he (Laurence) sinned against the wool growers he was swallowed by the waves in a ship

---

1 T. H. Lloyd (1977), *The English Wool Trade in the Middle Ages*, Cambridge: Cambridge University Press, 74–80.

full of wool'.[2] Some of the wool, on the other hand, survived its dunking in the North Sea and, after drying and re-packing, sold for £190.

It is doubtful whether raising the rate of the export duty on raw wool improved royal finances as much as had been anticipated because exports slumped. The *maltote* and the steep fall in wool prices may also have reduced the willingness of the community at large to pay tax and assist the king in what was clearly a dire financial situation. It is certainly the case that a further prise[3] ordered in the early summer of 1297 was rapidly abandoned. There was great reluctance to comply with the purveyors and, in fact, the king lost money over the whole enterprise because the customs revenue collapsed. The wave of unrest occasioned by this episode also created political difficulties for the monarch with the cancellation of the *maltote* added to the ancient custom being the substance of clause 7 of the *Confirmatio Cartarum* which the king was forced to concede in the autumn of 1297.

Despite this discouraging precedent, in 1336 Edward III and his advisors seem to have begun thinking of a new scheme to allow the crown to profit from the wool trade. A ban on exporting wool except by special licence was put in place, together with increases in customs duties. A prise was clearly contemplated since the prices at which wool would be purchased by the royal purveyors were also established and published at Nottingham the following year. In the summer of 1337 the whole scheme was revealed, again after discussion with a merchants' assembly. More or less the whole wool clip for the year would be sold directly by the crown or its agents to pay for the war with France.

This enormous amount of wool (the crown was basing its demands on a total of 30,000 wool sacks of the standard weight being available) consisted partly of wool bought or already owned by the group of 99 merchants involved as purveyors, and partly of wools acquired on behalf of the crown under the right of purveyance. It would be taken to a foreign staple (in fact Dordrecht) where it would be sold by these merchants and the proceeds delivered to the crown's agents.

The group of merchants was headed by William de la Pole and Reginald Conduit and is sometimes described as the English Wool Company (see Chapter 3). There were incentives for wool merchants to be involved in this extraordinary enterprise since those who participated by collecting wool in a county were promised protection from any future prise and from proceedings for debt. Clearly the purveyed wool was not seized from the growers without any promise of payment at all but the producers were obliged to hand over their wool to the purveyors in exchange for personal bonds drawn on the individual merchants concerned, not the more usual royal letters obligatory.

---

2 H. Summerson (2005), 'Most renowned of merchants: the life and occupation of Laurence of Ludlow. (d.1294)', *Midland History* 30, 20–35.

3 A prise was a compulsory purchase of wool by the crown at a price also set by the crown; it was part of the system of purveyance by which the king had the right to obtain supplies on favorable terms.

The first wool ships were ready to sail in late September and October 1337 with cargoes being unloaded in early November. From this point the whole scheme began to go wrong, getting into more and more difficulties, perhaps because the acute royal need for ready cash over-rode all commercial or even equitable considerations.[4] According to Fryde, the biographer of de la Pole, the scheme was 'very ingenious' and with 'real merits' and 'essential soundness'. It collapsed, in his view, because of the 'miscalculations, errors of judgement and short-sighted selfishness of the merchants and some of King's leading agents'.[5]

The members of the English Wool Company had agreed a schedule of advance payments with the king. The first tranche was due on the sailing of the first consignment

Figure 18. Scene of merchants at the quayside from the Hamburg State Book (Creative Commons CC BY-SA 3.0)

with further installments due at Easter and Ascension Day 1338. The royal agents in Dordrecht began to demand large loans from the merchants/purveyors more or less immediately after the ships were unloaded even though no wool had been sold at this point. The merchants naturally objected strongly to this but in the end handed control of what wool had reached Dordrecht to the royal agents in return for a promise of an immediate payment of around £2 per sarpler in cash. The royal agents meanwhile complained bitterly at the small amount of wool reaching Dordrecht – about a third of what had been required. They may also have realised that a great deal had in fact been smuggled out of England paying neither customs nor being sold for the king's benefit.

---

4 T. H. Lloyd (1977), *The English Wool Trade*, 144–50.

5 E. B. Fryde (1988), *William de la Pole: Merchant and King's Banker (†1366),* London: Hambledon Press, 56.

The merchants, unlike the growers, received indentures binding the king to pay the value of the wool over and above the cash payment above at some future date but trust between the parties was gravely dented by these events. There was no likelihood that these bonds could be redeemed in the near future, something which, of course, made it even more unlikely that the growers would receive any rapid payment for their wool. The growers equally had many complaints about the way the purveyance had been operated with frequent accusations of forced sales, bribery and other abuses. Any feelings of trust between the merchant community and the king's agents were now almost non-existent.

The king's need for ready money, however, was still urgent. In his view, in the spring of 1338, he was still 'owed' 20,000 sacks of wool, the balance of what should have been delivered in the autumn and winter of 1337–1338. His solution to the problem was to order a further levy of wool already shorn to be collected with immediate effect. The disaffection of the merchant community and the distrust of wool growers were made plain in the fact that this 'loan' raised only 1867 sacks of wool.

The king hoped to be able to get round the hostility of English merchants to his schemes by turning to his Italian bankers and creditors, the Bardi and Peruzzi, agreeing with them favourable terms for the sale of wool exported in the summer in return for an immediate loan.

This agreement also ran into trouble and in July 1338, the Great Council agreed with the king that the amount of wool still outstanding from the original 30,000 sacks originally demanded should be collected from all those who paid the fifteenth and tenth, the tax on the value of moveable property granted by Parliament. There was no intention to pay for this levy; it was clearly a tax in kind. Not all taxpayers in fact possessed wool so some were forced to buy it to fulfil the levy, a somewhat paradoxical result. Some of the levy was also assigned to major royal creditors and thus did nothing to relive the royal shortage of ready money.

Throughout most of 1339, despite the fact that nearly 8,000 sacks of royal wool reached the market, the king was, in fact, living from hand to mouth in a state of virtual bankruptcy. Over the winter of 1339–1340 the king, the nobility and the House of Commons in Parliament (in January and March 1340) negotiated for some way of combining the relief of the king's dire financial situation with the redress of their grievances. A grant of the ninth lamb, fleece and sheaf was suggested in return for the important concession that the rate of customs dues would henceforward only be decided in a full parliament, not in any other assembly. The Commons then agreed new rates. Until Whitsun 1341 customs dues would include a subsidy of 33s 4d in addition to the ancient custom of 6s 8d making a total of 40s. Aliens would also have to pay the so-called new custom as a further addition.[6]

The proceeds of a levy like the ninth based on agricultural produce would only come in slowly throughout the farming year. It would have done little to relieve the king's

---

6 T. H. Lloyd (1977), *The English Wool Trade,* 151–8.

immediate needs even if collecting it had proved to be simple and straightforward which was unlikely. By midsummer the king was desperate for a loan to be paid in wool as an advance on the proceeds of the levy. A ban on all private buying and selling of wool was put in place with merchants offered inducements to buy royal wool if they would advance ready money to the king in Flanders and elsewhere overseas. It was promised that open sale of wool would be permitted at the usual rates of duty after Michaelmas.

Despite the king having initially requested 20,000 sacks of wool very little was forthcoming; in some parts of the country no wool at all could be found by the assessors. Resistance to the assessors was widespread. The promise of open sales in the autumn was forgotten; only those with licences, usually those who had purchased royal wool, were allowed to export. The near-total failure of this loan brought the king painfully face to face with the dilemma he faced in attempting to manipulate the overseas market for English wool to gain allies and finance his war with France. If he attempted direct intervention in the market by way of a levy, or a purveyance or prise of wool together with a ban on private trading he was in danger of losing the support of both the woolgrowers and the merchants while the revenue from the customs was rapidly reduced. Selling wool also did not produce large sums in cash quickly (the market had always operated on payment in installments and quite lengthy credit terms and was not geared to producing quick cash returns). Requiring merchants to provide loans in advance of sales or raising the rates of customs duties depended on the state of the markets overseas and could run into problems not only of mounting royal debts secured on future customs payments but of possible non-co-operation from merchants or great increases in smuggling and export of uncustomed wool. The idea that the wool trade could be used as an ever-ready source of royal finance clearly had serious flaws.

Despite these disappointments, however, Edward III made one final attempt to profit directly from the sale of wool. In the parliament which met in April 1341 it was decided that both the levy of one-ninth and the subsequent loan would be suspended. In their place would be a tax in wool payable by the laity and the most important lords spiritual; of the total of 30,000 sacks required, 20,000 would be collected by August 1341 and the remainder by August 1342. Anyone who had paid part or all of the suspended levies would be reimbursed from this new grant which would be raised by means of a quota on each county.

Perhaps because there was a greater understanding of the pressing need of the king for war finance in the country at large, this tax in wool was the most successful of all those undertaken by Edward III or his predecessors. There were of course problems relating to the county assessments, the weighing of the wool and the possibility of converting the wool requirement into cash. Nevertheless over 18,000 sacks of wool had been handed over to royal agents by August 1341. Much of this was already spoken for being owed to creditors and foreign allies who had been promised wool from the failed levy of 1340. Some 8,300 sacks were accounted for in this way; another 5,649 sacks went to English merchants and finally 1,392 sacks went directly to English treasurers for war or military captains to cover their expenses in the Low Countries.

The pressure from creditors and allies who had not received promised subsidies was relieved by these means but there were still questions over the viability of this approach to the king's financial vulnerability. Exports of wool were allowed only under licence during the winter of 1341–1342. Arrangements to collect the final 10,000 sacks originally agreed were well underway in the spring and summer of 1342 when the crown abruptly and radically changed its policy. In agreement with the merchants, in July the export market was thrown open to all. The reason for this sudden about-turn was evident to anyone connected with the wool trade. Prices for wool had collapsed in the Low Countries. There was little prospect of the crown making any profit from its attempts to create a monopoly out of the export of wool. It now seemed that that the way forward was for the crown to concentrate on maximising the revenue from the duties on exports, leaving trade to the merchants.[7]

There is little doubt that while some of the merchants most deeply engaged in the trade had initially thought, in 1336, that they might be able to profit themselves from the policies of the royal 'woolmonger extraordinary', the whole period 1336–1342 had made life very difficult for both merchants and wool growers. The Dordrecht episode had left merchants holding bonds with no clear redemption date; export bans had been imposed and then modified at short notice. Licences to avoid the bans, which were in any case costly, carried onerous conditions regarding the payment of customs or provision of loans overseas in cash. Levies in wool or taxes in kind had been imposed with different methods of assessment and collection and with power in the hands of a narrow group of wealthy merchants. Vociferous complaints were made to the king and in parliament. In 1341 it was alleged, for example, that the collectors in Sussex were taking about 2–4 cloves from every wool sack by manipulating the weight of sacks in their favour. In Worcestershire the collectors were accused of taking bribes and putting sand in the fleeces.[8]

Proceedings in the Parliament of 1343 hinted at the rift that existed between the wool merchants and the wool growers. The merchants were by this time in favour of increasing the rates of duty on exported wool rather than face the disruption to trade caused by the king's direct involvement in the sale of wool. This was because they could hope to absorb the extra cost of higher duties by paying growers a lower price for their wool. The Commons also contained many members from county constituencies who were themselves either wool producers or who were well aware of the interests of landowners and their tenants and their resistance to any reduction in the price of wool.

The tension between these two groups can be seen in two apparently contradictory petitions granted by the crown in 1343. On the one hand, an extension of the subsidy added to the ancient and new customs on wool to run until 1346 was granted with the proviso that the proceeds would be used to redeem the outstanding Dordrecht

---

7 *Ibid.*, 159–74.

8 *Ibid.*, 161.

bonds, a long-standing demand of wool merchants. On the other hand it was also agreed that a new higher schedule of wool prices should be established to replace that agreed at Nottingham in 1337, a demand that served the interests of the producers. The feeling that merchants had done better out of negotiations with the king than landowners also found expression in a petition which called for the ancient custom of wool to be returned to its long-term level of 6s 8d per sack. It was, the Commons declared, the merchants who had granted the extra subsidy of 33s 4d per sack and this higher level was to 'the burden and misfortune of your commonalty'; moreover it was unreasonable 'for the commonalty to be taxed on their goods by the merchants'. The king replied rather tartly that there was no burden on the commonalty since 'they have set a certain price on the wool throughout the counties' and it was the king's will that 'no wool should be bought below this price on forfeiture of the same wool from the hands of the merchant who so buy it'.[9] There was clearly little if any immediate prospect that the subsidy added to the ancient custom would be removed.

The commonalty also had little reason to trust the king's bland words on the wool price. Some time after this the Abbot of Meaux on the Yorkshire coast explained clearly what effect high export taxes had on wool producers; they cause the price of wool to fall; 'and so it is those who own the wool who pay this tax to the King and not the merchants who appear to make the grant to him; for wools are sold at a lesser price the greater the tax paid to the King for them'.[10]

Nevertheless the future policy of the crown in relation to the wool trade would be largely based on the manipulation of the customs system rather than the use of prises and taxes in kind. With the exception of a grant of 20,000 sacks of wool requested in March 1347 in the aftermath of the victory at Crécy and when the siege of Calais was entering its final phase, the changes in the administration of the customs system were the main means by which the crown intervened in the wool trade from this point.

Customs dues and the staple system

The dues

While a tax of one-tenth on the value of all goods exported was used as a way to raise part of Richard I's ransom in 1194 and John introduced a similar tax of one-fifteenth in 1203, Edward I in 1275 was responsible for the introduction of a system of customs dues collected at the ports on the export of wool, woolfells and hides. This was raised at the rate of half a mark, 6s 8d, on each woolsack, and the same amount on 300 woolfells. This so-called ancient custom (*magna et antiqua custuma*) was paid by all exporting merchants both those accounted to be denizens (the native-born and those who had acquired this status by Letters of Denisation) and aliens (all other foreigners). From

---

9 *Parliament Rolls*; introduction to the parliament of April 1343; item 17 in the report of that parliament.

10 E. Power (1941), *The Wool Trade in English Medieval History*, Oxford: Oxford University Press, 74.

the point of view of the monarch it was a great success; a sum of £43,802 was raised for the crown in the first four years of its operation. This duty in fact continued to be paid until the export of raw wool was prohibited over three hundred years later.

In 1303 as part of the agreement with the community of foreign merchants trading with England which resulted in the *Carta Mercatoria*, giving alien merchants some protection of their right to trade unhindered, goods exported or imported by alien merchants were subject to an additional duty, the so-called New Custom. In the case of wool and woolfells this amounted to an extra 3s 4d per woolsack or 300 woolfells. This was briefly suspended between 1311 and 1322 but was otherwise collected along with the ancient custom.

In addition to these duties extra payments could be added when the need of the crown for extra money became acute. Some of these extra payments have already been discussed. The first was the *maltote* of 1294–1297; later additions known as subsidies were frequently demanded for short periods in the years from 1337–1343 as an aspect of Edward III's efforts to profit from the wool trade to finance his war with France. The subsidy agreed in 1343 of 33s 4d per sack was paid by denizen merchants as well as the ancient custom making a total of 40s while aliens paying both ancient and new customs paid 44s 4d. The rate for denizen merchants including both the customs and subsidy varied between 40s and 44s 4d until the end of the fifteenth century. That for aliens fluctuated more frequently and to a greater extent. At one point in the 1450s it soared to over £5 per sack but more usually it was around 50s from *c*.1370 to *c*.1400 and then around 60s, rising to 76s 8d in the 1470s. Wool merchants also faced small extra payments for things like fixing the coquet (the seal certifying that the customs had been paid) to each woolsack and also local duties payable to the authorities in port towns. 4d per woolsack was payable at Southampton for example, although there was a long list of exemptions.[11]

The requirement to pay customs duties no matter at what level will always create the possibility of smuggling. It is more or less impossible to estimate how common this was in our period and the scale of any losses to royal revenue. Some incidents, which make clear that a hard-pressed merchant would take illegal action if he thought he could get away with it, came to light in subsequent court proceedings. The prominent Yorkshire merchant John Goldbeter successfully managed to prevent the royal agents seizing his wool at Dordrecht in 1337, somehow spiriting it away and selling it to Flemings, something specifically prohibited by the crown. His consignment of 10 sarplers was a small fraction of the 300 which were not accounted for on this infamous occasion but he was the only merchant who apparently not only avoided the royal purveyors but also managed to sell his wool.[12]

---

11 H. S. Cobb (1961), *The Local Port Book of Southampton for 1439–1440,* Southampton: Southampton Records Society V, xvii.

12 E. B. Fryde (1966), *Some Business Transactions of York Merchants, John Goldbeter, William Acastre and Partners 1336–1349,* York: St Antony's Press, 7. CPR 1338–47, 191, CCR 1346–49 187, 241.

The Parliament of 1343 resolved that one of the questions which the members felt should be investigated by the Justices was the extent to which: 'wool woolfells leather and other customable merchandise which has been not been customed or coketted or properly weighed which is discovered being taken out of the realm of England.'[13] Later parliaments in the fifteenth century also presented petitions to the crown for measures to be enforced against smuggling, but by this time the basis of the offence was not only avoiding the duties on wool export but also taking wool to other places than the Staple at Calais. In 1582 alleged smuggling of wool was still irritating the law-abiding leading to a petition addressed to Sir Francis Walsingham detailing cases including the smuggling of uncoketed wool through Malden.[14] This was not a problem with an easy solution, nor is it one where the effects can be easily quantified.

The staple system

The idea of a staple, or an appointed place at which all transactions in a certain nominated commodity must by law take place, was a familiar tool to regulate trade, used quite widely by medieval governments. The idea of free trade, as understood by nineteenth-century liberals or modern economists, was not current at this period. A staple for the sale of wool exported to Flanders was set up by a decree of Edward I in Dort in 1285; later this moved to Bruges. The king's aim was to put pressure on the Flemings to support England in its quarrels with France by restricting their access to English wool, the essential raw material for their cloth industry. This policy was continued by Edward II who used the move of the staple to St Omer in 1313 as a lever to encourage the Flemings to abandon their policy of supporting the Scots against the English.[15] The move also had the support of merchants who feared their wares might be confiscated in Flanders at a time when relations with England were poor.[16]

Staples had clear benefits for a ruler since this simplified the collection of dues or taxes and could also be used as a way to put pressure on other rulers. For merchants and producers, the establishment of a staple had both advantages and disadvantages. Both could be assured that buyers and sellers would be on hand seeking bargains and that trade would have at least a modicum of protection. On the other hand very often the most active and successful merchants could easily squeeze out the 'small men' in such an environment. Moreover, as far as the wool trade was concerned, the location of the staple was a matter of disputes and argument among the various parties involved. This question very easily became entangled in royal policy; if the location was placed

---

13 *Parliament Roll* for 1343. Parliament of Edward III: April 1343.

14 R. H. Tawney and E. Power (1924), *Tudor Economic Documents Illustrating the Economic and Social History of Tudor England*, 3 vols. London: University of London Historical Series, II, 193–8.

15 W. Stanford Reid (1959), 'The Scots and the staple ordinance of 1313,' *Speculum* 34, 598–610.

16 R. L. Baker (1956), 'The establishment of the English wool staple in 1313,' *Speculum* 31, 444–53.

in a town across the Channel, it could be a tool with which to influence the policies of local rulers. This was also a policy which found favour with English wool merchants since it gave them an advantage over alien merchants.

Wool growers on the other hand tended to prefer the nomination of staple towns in England itself. Both merchants and wool producers had representation in parliament and thus could use issues relating to staple policy as a lever when negotiating the granting of taxes with the crown. The twists and turns in staple policy in the latter half of the fourteenth century reflect these concerns. After the final establishment of the Company of the Staple at the end of the century the staple for the wool trade was permanently based in Calais. From around 1399 until the final loss of the town by the English in 1558, the company and the crown had close links which had considerable effects both on the economy of the trade and on the military and strategic concerns of the realm.

Wool staple policy 1343–1399

Before the outbreak of the wars with France, which formed the first phase of the Hundred Years War, several attempts were made to institute a coherent policy for a wool staple and, with it, regulation of the export of wool. The staple at St Omer continued until after the signing of a truce with Flanders in 1323 with some efforts to enforce its use. By the time the truce was signed many merchants were sending their wool to Bruges, the centre of the cloth-manufacturing region of Flanders. In 1326, however, a short-lived attempt was made to establish a number of staple towns in the territories of the English Crown in the British Isles. As well as towns in Ireland and Wales, the list included major English centres including London, Bristol, Norwich and York. The most onerous regulation associated with this ordinance was that, while denizen merchants could contract to buy wool where they liked, their purchases then had to remain on the market for 40 days in a staple town, an obstruction to their freedom to trade. Aliens, on the other hand, could only buy wool in a staple town, and were thus denied direct access to producers. They could, however, export any wool bought at the staple without further delay.

This scheme, which would probably have operated to the benefit of middlemen rather than either denizen or alien merchants or wool growers, lasted only just over a year before being withdrawn by the crown. After winning this concession, some wool merchants, probably those in the largest way of business who stood to lose most from the curtailment of wool exports, agreed to provide a loan for the king. This led to a furious row between merchants from York and those from London but, finally, in 1328 at a parliament held in Northampton, all staples whether at home or abroad were abolished. The convenience of a staple across the Channel for exporting merchants as a place where they could give each other support, establish business contacts and enjoy something of a social life, led to the informal re-establishment of the staple at Bruges. There it remained, with only a brief interruption for other abortive attempts

Figure 19. Bruges; the centre of the medieval wool trade in Flanders (Creative Commons CC BY-SA 3.0 and GNU Free documentation 1.2 Jean-Christophe Benoist)

to set up 'home' staples, in 1333–1334 and 1343 until Edward III took definite steps to reactivate the legislation relating to the wool staple in 1354.[17]

One of several petitions presented in the parliament of 1343 put forward arguments in favour of 'home' staple towns. It was claimed that the price of wool would increase quickly and that there would be fewer losses of wool at sea (or rather by implication the losses would not concern English merchants) and there would be fewer problems with the circulation of 'false' money if the Staple was in England. (This complaint was based on the assertion that the currency used in Bruges was overvalued, leading to losses when it was brought into England.)

The Flemings in Bruges were also interfering with the ability of other foreigners (probably Italians are meant) to buy wool in Bruges and re-export it and, finally, the major Flemish cities of Ghent, Bruges and Ypres were manipulating the staple to their own advantage. If their petition was granted, the higher customs duties already discussed would be accepted. This petition was followed three months later by an agreement reached between the king and 33 English merchants that they would

17 T. H. Lloyd (1977), *op. cit.*, 110–21.

run the customs system for at least the next three years. This arrangement, which involved most of those traders who were already deeply involved in the tangled web of royal finances, rapidly ran into trouble. Wool exports were suspended entirely in 1345 because of the lack of security from commerce raiders for merchant ships in the Channel. The years 1346–1347 saw the war against France reach fever pitch with trade disrupted by the Crécy campaign and the siege of Calais which also created a severe shortage of shipping for trading purposes. In 1348, the year of the Black Death, the trading partnership holding the farm of the customs went bankrupt. The staple for the small amount of wool that did reach the Flemish market was not removed from Bruges, with both denizen and alien merchants consigning goods there, until around Michaelmas 1352.

From this point it became clear that the crown was determined to introduce a new policy for the export of wool and the establishment of staple towns. The new policy was set out in the Ordinance of the Staple which was promulgated at a great council which met in the White Chamber in the Tower of London in late September 1353.[18] This acknowledged that wool was 'the sovereign merchandise and jewel of England' but the profits of the trade had been creamed off by foreigners 'to the great damage and impoverishment of the commonalty' of the realm because the staple was overseas.

New staples would be established in Newcastle upon Tyne, York, Lincoln, Norwich, Westminster, Canterbury, Chichester, Winchester, Exeter and Bristol. There would be one at Carmarthen for Wales; and for Ireland staple towns at Dublin, Waterford, Cork and Drogheda. The wool would be weighed and the staple seal attached at each town and then taken to a nominated port (if not already at a head port like Bristol) where the customs officials would again weigh and seal the sacks. Most importantly, however, only alien merchants would be permitted to export wool. They would be fully covered by 'our [the king's] protection and safe conduct' but would also, of course, pay customs dues and subsidies at the higher 'alien' rate.

The ordinance furthermore set up a new system for enforcing the payment of debts backed up by a special staple court in each town and clauses against the fraudulent use of weights. The provision and letting of warehouses set aside for staple goods was also to be under the control of the mayor of the staple and other worthy burgesses. It seems that the ordinance was generally welcomed by the Commons and the merchant community in general. This was made clear when in the full parliament of the following year the ordinance was reissued at the request of the Commons as a perpetual statute. The technical clauses regarding the collection of debts and protection of foreign merchants, in fact, remained in operation for many years. The location of wool staples in English towns, however, soon ran into trouble as it had done in the past. By 1357 a staple was once more operating at Bruges with denizen merchants allowed to export directly. In 1359 the privileges of this staple were formally recognised but even this arrangement proved no more than temporary. From the point of view of the crown

---

18　*Parliament Rolls*, Parliament of Edward III: September 1353.

there was a new factor to consider; the town of Calais and its maintenance as a fortress outpost of the realm of England on formerly French territory.

Calais and the company of the staple

The town had fallen to the English in the summer of 1347 after a long siege. The cost of defending it and paying the garrison took up a significant proportion of the royal income. In the year May 1359–May 1360 nearly £15,000 from the Treasury and other sources was spent in the town on its defence. In 1371–1372, a typical year for the period, the costs of Calais reached £20,264, more than any other item of royal expenditure apart from the king's own household.[19] The idea of using the boundless riches generated by the wool trade (this view was widely held) to help the crown bear the burden of the support of Calais was clearly put to Edward III and soon got his support.

Discussions with merchants about how to proceed were held in May 1361. The intention to move the staple from Bruges to Calais was proclaimed in the summer of 1362 and became operational in the early spring of 1363 after preparations had been made in Calais probably including the preparation of wool-houses and the like. The Commons expressed some hesitations about the idea in October 1362 informing the king that opinion among their members was divided but clearly finally acquiesced in the proposal.

The plan to be implemented in fact covered rather more than just the setting up of the staple for wool and woolfells. A charter issued in March 1363 set up a new system of government for the town. This would be in the hands of a group of 26 English merchants with two mayors, one to rule the staple and the other to have responsibility for the town. Among these 26 are some familiar names of merchants with court connections. The most striking is probably that of John Wesenham, an East Anglian merchant who had been heavily involved in loans to the king in the 1340s and was at one time a partner of Walter Chiriton one of the unsuccessful farmers of the customs. The scheme proved very rapidly to be unworkable; within six months parliament was ringing to the vocal complaints of traders outside the 'magic circle' of the 26. This group, it was claimed, had manipulated the market to their own advantage, charged excessive fees, which they had diverted to their own use, cornered the property market in the town and in fact had caused 'outrageous damage' to all other merchants.[20] Not surprisingly the new charter for the town of Calais was withdrawn by the king in June of the following year, while the staple would remain organised in the customary way with a mayor and constables with responsibility only for the wool trade. This has sometimes been considered to be the origin of the Company of the Staple which

---

19 D. Grummitt (2008), *The Calais Garrison: War and Military Service in England, 1436–558*, Woodbridge: Boydell, 141.

20 R. L. Baker (1976), 'The government of Calais in 1363', in W. C. Jordan, William C. Jordan, Bruce McNab, Teofilo F. Ruiz, *Order and Innovation in the Middle Ages: Essays in Honor of Joseph R. Strayer*, Princeton: Princeton University Press, 207–14.

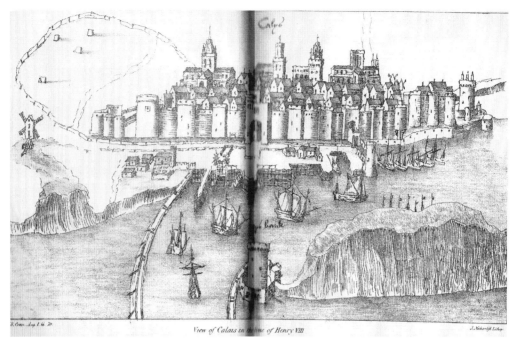

Figure 20. View of Calais from the sea in the early sixteenth century (from J.G. Nichols, ed. 1846, The Chronicles of Calais under Henry VII and Henry VIII*)*

played a very large part in the affairs of both the wool trade and the town of Calais in the fifteenth century. There are good reasons to doubt this.

The company in its heyday was based in Calais; that is, all its papers and its administration were in that town and not in London. When Calais fell to the French in 1558, its muniments and archives disappeared and were presumably destroyed. The only substantial document to escape the catastrophe was the Register of the Company into which all the royal grants and the like relating to the company were copied, beginning at an unknown date in the reign of Edward IV. The Ordinance Book of the company unfortunately exists only in a version made up after the events of 1558. The Register contains entries which give the impression that some sort of an organised company existed at the staple at Bruges as early as 1341 and that it was firmly established at Calais from 1359 (some four years before the staple was announced in 1363).

The confusion about the precise date of the foundation of the company is probably down to the desire of the company in the 1470s to have a respectable and ancient lineage as a major player in English affairs and differing definitions of the word 'company'. This could mean no more than an informal group with common interests making some arrangements for mutual benefits or a regulated company with officers, statutes and the like. The latter certainly existed in the fifteenth century despite the fact that the earliest charter of which a copy survives was issued by Queen Elizabeth.

The founding charter may not have been granted, probably by Henry IV, until after the company settled permanently in Calais.[21]

The group set up in 1364 to run the staple whatever its nature soon faced many difficulties. When the war between France and England was resumed in late 1369 crossing the Channel could be a dangerous voyage for slow and heavily laden wool ships. There were also concerns that Flemish merchants would be unwilling to face the journey to Calais fearing perhaps the loss of their goods and their lives. Perhaps more relevant to the merchants charged with running the staple was the fact that the crown saw the issue of licences to export elsewhere as an easy way to raise money, particularly from traders from southern Europe or the Mediterranean who found Calais anything but convenient as a source of raw wool. A petition in the Parliament of 1373 complaining that the issue of licences was 'to the great loss damage and decrease of profit' of the town and the king, was not favourably received.[22] The petitioners complained that this was contrary to the statute setting up the staple, though by this they may have meant no more than the king's order to do the same rather than the foundation of the Company.

Matters came to a head in the Good Parliament of 1376. The Commons directly accused 'the king's said intimates and others of their faction' of causing the ruin of the staple and contributing to the problems relating to the supply of bullion. The damage had been caused by the issue of licences to those in favour at court or at their instigation. Richard Lyons, the most prominent of those charged with running the staple in 1364, was accused 'of many deceits extortion and other evil deeds' including the unlawful removal of the staple. He had imposed new charges on the export of wool and woolfells and had used the money raised for his own advantage and other financial wrongdoing. Lyons was impeached by the Commons and imprisoned.[23]

The Commons' claim that the Calais Staple had been set up by statute law seems to have been a fiction. The upshot of the events in the Good Parliament, however, served to establish the principle that the location of the wool staple needed the approval of the Commons and moreover confirmed that the Commons had to approve the collection of the all-important subsidy addition to the customs dues on the export of wool.[24]

The outbreak of unrest amounting to civil war in Flanders made the position of a staple at Calais precarious after 1379. The Flemish demand for wool fell drastically while other traders were reluctant to visit a town also affected by the continuing hostilities between England and France. The uncertainty increased in 1381 when Charles V of France was actively preparing an invasion of England. The low point of the trade occurred in 1384 when only 83 sacks of wool were unloaded on the quay

---

21 S. Rose (2008), *Calais: an English Town in France 1347–1558*, Woodbridge: Boydell, 40–6.

22 *Parliament Rolls*, Parliament of Edward III: November 1373.

23 *Ibid.*, Parliament of Edward III: November 1376.

24 T. H. Lloyd (1977), *The English Wool Trade*, 217–24.

at Calais. The wool porters and labourers in the town must have suffered severely from this loss of trade and employment while English wool merchants had, to a large extent, deserted the town and the staple and had taken their cargoes of wool and their trade to Middelburg in Zealand.

Calais seemed about to regain its position in 1389 when a truce was concluded with France, but there was a further period of uncertainty and instability for the long-suffering wool merchants in the following year. Members of the Commons, who spoke for wool producers, put forward a petition requesting the crown to restore the home staples set up by the statute of 1353. Not only was this accepted but the ban on denizens participating in the export trade was resuscitated. Within less than a year, however, this policy was once more abandoned. Denizen merchants regained the right to export but the staple itself continued to suffer from the number of licences issued to send wool to other ports.

This problem was once more brought to royal attention in Henry IV's first parliament in 1401. It may be that the mayor and merchants of Calais who presented the petition felt that the accession of the new king presented an ideal opportunity for them to press their case for the staple. He would be happy to be assured of their support by acceding to their request. The king accepted their plea that the issue of licences to evade the staple was leading to the 'great deflation of the price' of wool and the other commodities at Calais and agreed that letters patent to export elsewhere would be withheld, mentioning particularly the issue of low quality wools from the North (produced 'beyond the water of the Tees').[25]

From this time on the staple for wool and woolfells was located in Calais until the loss of the town in 1558. The Company of the Staple was firmly established and developed as a corporate entity with an indispensable role in the regulation of the wool trade. The details of its relationship with the crown and the company's involvement in the financing and defence of the town of Calais changed over the course of this period. As far as individual wool merchants were concerned, however, it was the beginning of a period of welcome stability after the multitude of changes in not only the location of the staple, but also the regulations which wool merchants were expected to obey.

---

25 *Parliament Rolls*, Parliament of Henry VI: 1401.

Chapter 5

Prices and Quantities

The price of wool

The shepherd mulling over his accounts in Shakespeare's *The Winter's Tale* used a counting board to help his calculations:

> Let me see; every 'leven wether tods, every tod yields pound and odd shilling; fifteen hundred shorn, what wool comes to? ...I cannot do it without counters.

Modern scholars attempting to answer the same question have found it no easy task to determine the price of wool and how it changed over our period, even with the aid of computers. The sources for wool prices are often confusing. We have mentioned various price lists, but these, of course, are advisory and only provide a guide to what might be expected or what the producers hoped for. The sources for the actual prices realised are fragmentary and are not available for all wool producing areas including some of those which were thought of as producing the best wool, like the Welsh Marches.

T. H. Lloyd who published his indispensable *The Movement of Wool Prices in Medieval England* in 1973 carefully explained what sources he had used and how he had to manipulate the data collected in order to arrive at a table of the area means and annual means of wool price for the years 1209–1500. This was a major feature of his study of wool prices in these years. First of all medieval weights and measures were not standardised; a stone, for example, could vary in weight from 6 lb to 28 lb (2.72–12.68 kg); and of course a pound was not always 16 oz (454 g). Prices recorded in manorial and monastic accounts also do not always refer to wool of the same quality.

Apart from the semi-refuse wool, sometimes known as loks, lambs' wool was usually cheaper than that from adult sheep. Old wool was also priced differently from the new season's wool clip. Lloyd's solution to these problems was to convert the diverse weights used in his sources to the stone of 14 lb (6.34 kg) wherever possible. Only the prices for the fleece wool of adult sheep were used, ignoring that of the highest quality where this was priced separately. Because of the regional variation in wool prices, clear from all the extant price lists from that of Pegolotti dating from the early fourteenth century to that included in the treatise called *The Nombre of Weyghtes* of Edward IV's reign, Lloyd established regional mean prices before attempting to calculate an overall mean price for each year. The area means were calculated by taking the mean of prices for the manorial or institutional price series available.

The number of extant price series in the various areas varies widely, however, as does their coverage of the whole period. Lloyd's area 3 included only the price for wool sold by St Swithun's Priory Winchester and extended with some gaps from 1269 to 1348. Other series, which consist solely of data of the centrally negotiated prices obtained by monastic houses or large estates, are those for area 7: Westminster Abbey (1353–1403), 16: Bolton Priory (1288–1325), and 17: the Aumale estates (1262–1326), again with some significant gaps. Another problem with the figures used to calculate the area annual mean price is that, although some areas include quite a large number of different sources of data (area 15 Norfolk, Suffolk and Cambridge includes 31), any individual price series within the group may have been available for quite a short period of time. This has the effect that the area mean in any one year may have been calculated from a much smaller number of sources, perhaps as few as one, as is the case in area 15 between 1397 and 1491.

It is also the case that strictly local conditions might affect a wool producer, such as very poor weather or a virulent outbreak of sheep scab. One example of this might be the manor of Horsley in the Cotswolds whose wool was sold for £5 4s 0d per sack in 1454 when the Commons in Parliament were attempting to fix the price of Cotswold wool at £8 6s 8d per sack. It therefore seems to be the case that these tables give a reasonable idea of the general trends in prices over this period but should be used cautiously if more detailed data is required.

Lloyd's book includes a series of graphs which display the annual mean, maximum and minimum prices for wool over the periods, which demonstrate very clearly the range of the variability and the volatility in wool prices in his chosen period. The maximum wool price figures seem to be particularly subject to quite violent swings. For example a decline of 2s per stone occurred around 1385 and the price more or less halved around 1423. In both cases prices only recovered a little in the succeeding years.

This variability is further illustrated in Table 1 which compares the prices achieved for wool from the Cotswolds, North Buckinghamshire and Oxfordshire, East Anglia and Durham in three different years in which adequate data is available. Since it takes time to build up a flock of sheep even under the most favourable conditions, perhaps buying in new stock rather than relying on natural increase, it is easy to understand the difficulties faced by wool producers. The production of wool was a commercial enterprise aimed at the market but the health of that market and the trends in prices seem to have been very difficult to forecast successfully.

The gaps in the sources also affect some of the figures especially those for annual mean prices. The data for the fifteenth century in particular shows how the erratic survival of price data distorts the annual mean and the resulting trend. For some reason, possibly a greater preponderance of small producers in 'quality' wool areas rather than big estates with good runs of accounts, there are few sources of prices for this kind of wool with those surviving covering only short periods of time.

Table 1. Wool prices in in shillings per stone a) in 1379; b) in 1459 (data for North Bucks and Oxon unavailable for this year) c) in 1496 (data for Cotswolds unavailable for this year). Data from T. H. Lloyd, The Movement of Wool Prices in Medieval England, *1973.*

WOOL PRICES IN 1379 IN SHILLINGS PER STONE

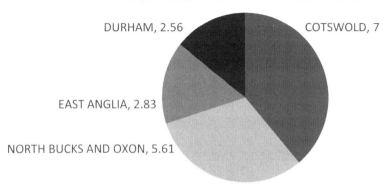

WOOL PRICES IN SHILLINGS PER STONE IN 1459. NO DATA FOR NORTH BUCKS AND OXON

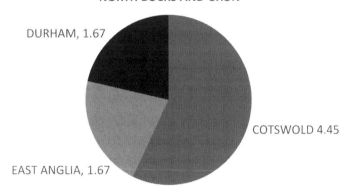

WOOL PRICES IN SHILLINGS PER STONE IN 1496. NO DATA FOR COTSWOLD

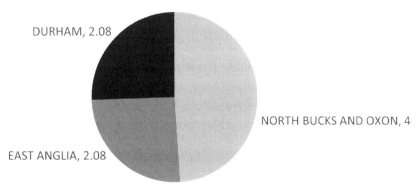

On the other hand there is a very good set of figures for the poor wool area of the north-east of England with more or less no gaps from around 1425 till 1500. This means that the annual mean and the trend line show sudden peaks from a low base in the years when 'quality' wool prices can be found. This is very evident in 1479 and 1481–1482. Similarly in the early fourteenth century the annual mean rises noticeably in the years when no data is available from the poor wool areas.[1] The market for wool in the fourteenth and fifteenth centuries was complex with local issues relating to the quality and reputation of the product, the incidence of diseases like scab, the ease of transport and the quantities available affecting whether farming sheep for wool was profitable or not. These factors, of course, operated independently of the problems caused for both wool producers and merchants by the changes in regulation, taxes and export duties by the crown discussed above.

A lot of attention has also been focused by scholars on the surviving price lists for English wool as well as the wool prices recorded in estate accounts. The earliest, from the late thirteenth and early fourteenth centuries, are largely concerned with wool produced by monastic houses. The best known, that put together by the Italian merchant, Francesco Balducci Pegoletti, is to be found in a trading manual for Florentine merchants generally known as *La Pratica di Mercatura,* covering all that a neophyte merchant needed to know in the first decades of the fourteenth century.

One section dealt with trade with England, something that Pegolotti personally experienced when in London in 1317–1321 in charge of the local office of the great banking and trading house of the Bardi. Apart from noting the customs charges due on wool exported from England, Pegolotti provided a list of monastic houses with wool for sale and the prices to be expected. As discussed in earlier chapters, this list is the source for the areas from which the best wool came at this date and also makes plain the dominant position of Cistercian houses in wool production. Other price lists from the mid-fourteenth century have their origin in the various attempts by the crown to manipulate the wool market in the king's favour. These lists, of course, do not record prices actually paid but either those that might be expected or attempts to set standard, usually minimum, prices, in the case of the lists produced either by parliament or by the crown. Their main value is to provide clear evidence of the value placed by those involved in the trade on wool produced in most counties of England. Although there are minor variations between the lists the consensus is that the wool from Herefordshire, especially Leominster, also known as March wool, was of supreme quality, followed by that from Shropshire and the Cotswolds, Kesteven and Lindsey in Lincoln. The Midland counties also produced good wool of reasonable quality while that from the Scots borders, Devon and Cornwall and East Anglia was least esteemed.

---

1 T. H. Lloyd (1973), *The Movement of Wool Prices in Medieval England,* Cambridge: Cambridge University Press for the Economic History Society, table 1.

Prices at the Calais staple

The last of the lists from the fourteenth century was contained in a petition to parliament in 1357 which, despite being agreed by the Commons, was never put into effect in a statute. No further attempts were made to set wool prices until a petition put forward in the session of the 1453 parliament prorogued to the early month of 1454. At the time Henry VI had succumbed to one of his bouts of mental illness; the Duke of York had been made protector of the kingdom. France had also decisively defeated the remaining English forces in France at the battle of Castillon in the previous summer. The situation in Calais was clearly precarious with trade at a low level.

In these circumstances it is possible that the petition was linked to a feud in the Company of the Staple between those who saw an opportunity to reinforce their control of the wool trade and their opponents. One group of merchants, probably those with the largest share of the available business, wished to reinforce the partition ordinance of 1429 which directed the Staplers to share or partition the moneys raised by the wool trade in proportion to the stocks held by each merchant in the company's wool stores. The crown did not accept the petition, agreeing with those Staplers, who feared 'the grete inconvientz and damages that shuld ensew therof' and the consequent damage to cloth manufacturers. In its place the crown gratefully accepted a loan from the company to pay the garrison of Calais, on the verge of mutiny because of the non-payment of their wages.

The links between the Staplers and the crown will be discussed further in part 3. Here we can note that the schedule of prices attached to the petition, despite the fact that this was not accepted, provides a useful guide to the conditions in the wool trade in the middle of the fifteenth century.

This is reinforced by a list in a manual for English merchants called *The Nombre of Weyghtes.* This was written probably in the reign of Edward IV to offer guidance to those unfamiliar with English overseas trade. The section on the wool trade spends some time on the complex system of weights used. The author warns an inexperienced wool buyer that 'yt is bowght edyr by ye nayle or ye stones or ye todd and als ye sakk. And as amongst husband in the countre it is most used to be sold by ye stone and by ye todde. And betwixt gaderers of ye countre and ye merchants it is most use to be sold by ye sakk.' He also includes a handy list of the price fetched by different grades of wool at the Staple in Calais. As far as the origin of wools is concerned there is little change from the earlier lists; March wools are by far the most expensive priced at £13 6s 8d per sack as weighed in Calais (315 lb/*c*.143 kg); the cheapest was Yorkshire wool at £7 per Calais sack. The great majority of medium to good wool was priced at between £10 6s 8d and £9 3s 4d with the lowest quality from the southern counties and Norfolk at £8 16s 8d to £7 13s 4d all per sack as above.

Not surprisingly the author, clearly himself a Stapler, made no mention of the wools from the Border counties since these were not sold at the Staple but by a statute of 1423, exported from Newcastle upon Tyne to Bruges or Middelburg because of their coarse nature. The author also includes a very useful list of the expenses and charges incurred in the transport of English wool from the Cotswolds to the Staple at Calais or to Southampton. Wool bound for the looms of Italian cities could also legitimately avoid the Staple, being exported by sea from Southampton, and it is clear that the author has a particular interest in trade with Venice. In his list of expenses, transport (overland by cart) to London or Southampton costs 4s per sarpler (2 woolsacks). Other than this he noted the cost of the canvas and other necessaries for the sarplers, all the labour in packing the wool, porterage and petty fees to all those involved; these included 2d for the cocket seal, 4d for marking the sarplers, and 1d for pack thread; 2d to a scrivener for a docket, 6d to porters, 2d for storage at the quay.

The royal custom and subsidy (listed as 'weighing at the crane' that is the royal weigh-beam) came to 53s 4d, the alien merchant rate, giving a clue as to the author's usual contacts in the trade. All these charges are given per sack. He then turns to the extra expenses of the trade to Venice, probably his main interest. In total he calculated that if a sack of Cotswold wool cost £8 originally, further expenses of £3 6s 8d were incurred by the time it was loaded on a galley in Southampton for the voyage through the Straits of Gibraltar to the Adriatic. The freight charge to Venice was £3 4s 2d. Here further charges and taxes were due, ensuring that the original price had more than doubled by the time the wool reached its destination.[2]

Profits per woolsack at Calais are hard to estimate because of the number of variables which could affect the final sale price. The evidence from the Cely letters compared with that in this document makes this clear. It has been calculated that for wool from the Cotswolds, the wool which made up the bulk of the Celys' business, the high price of the best quality wool (known as good Cots) easily absorbed all the costs including taxes and customs dues. Young Cots (lambswool) also sold at a price which allowed for a good profit. Trade in middle Cots, the wool which made up about a quarter of the Cely business, was at best barely profitable, at least in 1470s–1480s. This wool also cost £8 per sack in England and incurred the same costs as 'good' Cots but was usually sold in Calais at a lower price. Alison Hanham's final conclusion was that good Cots bought at £8 per standard wool-sack would realise a profit of 38.4% at Calais while middle Cots would incur a loss of 5%.[3]

The importance of the cloth trade

These figures hint at the growing importance of the export of English made woollen cloth to both wool growers and wool merchants. There is no way of reliably calculating the amount of English cloth exported or the importance of the industry

2 BL MSS. Cotton Vespasian E ix ff86r-109r. A version has been published in A. R. Myers, ed. (1969), *English Historical Documents IV 1327-1485,* London: Eyre and Spottiswode, 1028–9 but the transcription of wool prices is not entirely accurate.

3 A. Hanham (1985), *The Celys and their World: an English Merchant Family of the Fifteenth Century,* Cambridge: Cambridge University Press, 122–9.

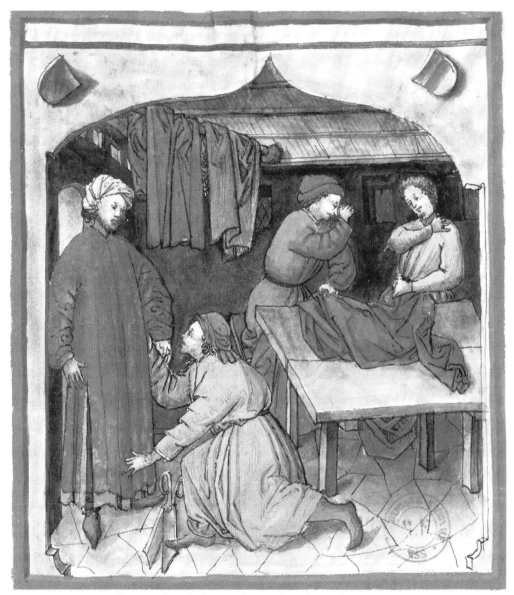

Figure 21. Selling woollen clothing; a late medieval shop (BNF MS Latin 9333 f.103)

as a whole before the first imposition of a duty on all woollen cloth exported in 1347. Before this date a small duty had been imposed in 1303 on the export by alien merchants only of cloths of assize (the standard measurement always used for these taxes). In 1347 a duty was imposed on cloth exported by both denizen and alien merchants; denizens paid 1s 2d per cloth of assize without grain and all aliens 2s 9d for cloth of the same quality; members of the Hanseatic League of trading cities paid the lower rate of 1s per cloth.[4] Perhaps unwittingly this protected English cloth makers from competition from the more expensive imported cloths and also of course gave them a large price advantage in overseas markets, since their raw material was so much cheaper and did not bear the burden of export taxes. It took some time for the export of cloth to take off. In the decade from 1380–1390 the number of cloths exported rose from under 20,000 per year to over 40,000. It varied around this figure until 1480 when it began to rise rapidly in fact reaching a peak of nearly 140,000 in 1546.[5]

It can be argued that the poor prices at Calais for medium quality wool are related to the success of the export trade in English cloth. Cloth makers, particularly those in Flanders, needed the very best English wools for their luxury cloths but found the wools of lesser quality too expensive. The cloth makers of Mechelen in Brabant could by guild regulation use only Leominster wool for their famed *Gulden Aren* cloths. There were similar restrictions on the wool used for the best cloth made in Ghent; the *Dickedinnen* cloths had to be made of fine wool, March wools or those from the Cotswolds or Berkshire.[6]

Many manufacturers were beginning to turn to another source of wool for making everyday cloth in the last decades of the fifteenth century. Wool from Spain was very suitable for the so-called *nouvelles draperies* and allowed them to be produced at a price which compared well with that of English-made cloth. A list of prices attached to the commercial treaty agreed between Henry VII of England and the Archduke Philip the Fair, ruler of the Netherlands, in May 1499 reveals that the best wools were considerably more expensive than in the Stapler's Manual of *c.*1475. The March wools were said to cost between £22 6s 8d and £17 per sack compared with £13 6s 8d in the earlier list. Despite this, the terms of the treaty had included a provision for a general price cut on all English wools of 6s 8d per sack. The price of the 'ordinary' wools from Lincolnshire was certainly lower, listed at £8 6s 8d rather than the £9 16s 8d expected

---

4 A standard cloth of assize measured 24 yd long by 1.5–2 yd wide (22 × 1.39–1.83 m) fulled and finished. Smaller narrower cloths were converted into notional cloths of assize for tax purposes. The tax did take some account of the quality of the cloth; those dyed with the expensive 'grain' scarlet dye paid the most. The totals of cloths exported include cloths of all qualities but not worsteds made in a slightly different way from broadcloth. A standard wool sack would contain enough wool for between 4 and 4.5 cloths of assize.

5 J. H. Munro (2003), 'Medieval woollens: textiles, textile technology and industrial organisation *c.*800-1500,' in D. Jenkins, ed., *The History of Western Textiles* I, Cambridge: Cambridge University Press, 181–2. The figures are to be found in table which converts raw wool exports into broadcloth equivalents in order to estimate the total of wool based products exported from England 1281–1545.

6 J. H. Munro (1994), 'Wool price schedules and the qualities of English Wool in the Later Middle Ages *c.*1290–1499,' in J. Munro (ed), *Textiles Towns and Trade* (1994) Aldershot: Variorum, item III, 153.

Table 2. Wool and cloth exports with combined totals in broadcloth equivalents, 1340-1550. Data from J. H. Munro, 'Medieval Woollens: The Western European Woollen Industries and their Struggle for International Markets, c.1000-1500,' in The Cambridge History of Western Textiles, *2003.*

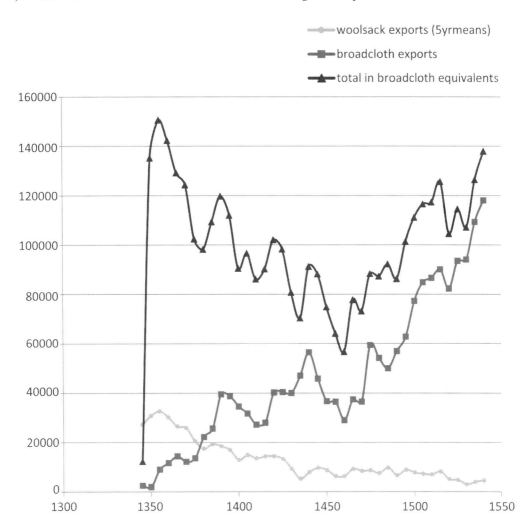

in 1475.[7] It can be argued that the export of raw English wool was now only profitable for the very best quality; much of what was produced was no longer exported but aimed at the booming market for English cloth.

The export of raw wool from England reached its peak in the first years of the fourteenth century. The table compiled by John Munro, already mentioned, makes the general trend obvious; cloth exports rise as those of raw wool decline. Table 2 displays the figures for total raw wool exports and total broadcloth exports as a graph.

---

7 *Ibid.*, 152–4.

Clearly the individuals who suffered from this trend were the members of the Company of the Staple, since the export of raw wool was their reason for existence. The crown also suffered since the taxes and customs dues on raw wool were much higher than those on cloth and the receipts from these had previously been the most elastic and productive part of the royal revenue.

It is much harder to judge the effect of this gradual but radical re-orientation of the market for wool on wool growers. As has been said, these figures do not include wool sold onto the home market, particularly to the clothiers and their agents. Even if much less English wool fed the looms of the Netherlands or of Italian cloth makers like those of Prato, there were still willing buyers in the market who were acting for the clothiers of Suffolk and other English centres of cloth making. The market as a whole, however, had become more complex. The Cistercian monks of the late thirteenth century had to deal with problems like the unexpected spread of sheep scab among their flocks as well as the familiar problems caused by adverse weather or royal tax demands. As far as selling their wool was concerned, however, there seems to have been a well-established system based on their relationship with the merchants houses mainly of northern Italy.

A grazier at the end of the fifteenth or the early years of the sixteenth century was looking at a much more uncertain future. His fortunes were closely linked to those of the cloth trade, whether at home or abroad. The reputation of English wool was still high but new producers threatened its dominance especially in the market for wools of average quality. New techniques in the textile industry were also perhaps better suited to wools of a different type from the short stapled English wools which were essential for the production of the best English heavy broadcloth. Changes in the political world and in the trading system of Europe as a whole had repercussions on the wool trade which could not be controlled, or even much influenced, by wool producers. Fortunately the survival of collections of family papers allow us to look at the careers of some individual wool merchants and the ways in which they attempted to deal with the difficulties they faced.

Chapter 6

Merchants and Clothiers *c.*1400–*c.*1560

The business and personal correspondence and accounts kept by individual merchants and business men and also by some of the Italian merchant companies trading in English wool and English-made cloth allow a much more personalised picture to be painted of the wool trade in the fifteenth and early sixteenth centuries. Three well-known collections of the personal papers of families connected with the wool trade, the land-owning Stonors of Oxfordshire, and the Celys and the Johnsons both with close connections with the Company of the Staple provide evidence of the working of the trade and how it affected the fortunes of these families.[1]

The chance survival of the account books of two members of the Heritage family from the Midlands, John Heritage of Burton Dassett in Warwickshire and Moreton-in-Marsh in Gloucestershire and his son Thomas and some other family documents have allowed a much better understanding of the way of life of men who were both merchants and farmers.[2] It is also possible to get a much closer view of the way Italian merchants, buying wool to export to the Mediterranean, operated in England from their business correspondence and other papers.

This is particularly the case with some of the traders acting for the Datini Company of Prato near Florence at the beginning of the fifteenth century. Their letters and other papers addressed to Francesco Datini survive in the enormous archive of the Fondaco Datini and similarly allow a more personal understanding of this aspect of the wool trade.[3]

Many of the letters and accounts in this archive make plain the high cost of English best quality wool in Italy; in March 1400 English March wool and that from Lindsey was selling in Milan at more than two and a half times the price per 100 lb (45 kg)

---

1 These family papers are to be found in: C. Carpenter, ed. (1996), *Kingsford's Stonor Letters and Papers, 129–1483,* Cambridge: Cambridge University Press; A. Hanham, ed. (1975), *The Cely Letters, 1472–1488,* Oxford: Oxford University Press: B. Winchester, ed. (1953), The Johnson Letters, unpublished PhD, University of London.

2 N. Alcock, ed. (1981), *Warwickshire Grazier and London Skinner*, Oxford: Oxford University Press for the British Academy; C. Dyer, (2012), *A Country Merchant, 1494–1520; Trading and Farming at the End of the Middle Ages,* Oxford: Oxford University Press.

3 Archivo di Stato di Prato; Fondaco di Firenze, Carteggio da Londra, no. 664. This includes all the correspondence mentioned below.

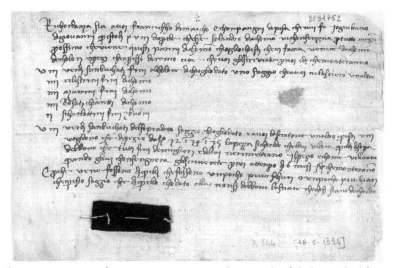

Figure 22. A letter to a customer from Francesco Datini with a sample of cloth attached (Datini Archives)

of wool from Majorca.[4] This high price may have been a factor in Cotswolds wool of about the same quality finding increasing favour with Italian merchants.

A letter to Francesco Datini from his English agents the Cambini of Florence written in June 1400 claimed that this was the case.[5] The Cambini themselves had been buying wool in this area for export to the Datini cloth business in Prato by sea from Southampton for some years by 1400. One of their suppliers was William Grevel of Chipping Campden, described on his tomb in the church there as the 'flower of the wool merchants of all England.'[6] A year after his death in 1401, one of the Cambini remarked in a letter that Grevel had often brought as many as 300 sacks of wool onto the market including wool from the Bishop of Worcester's estates and those of the earl of Warwick.

Francesco Datini also had dealings in England with the company of the Orlandini; both companies obtained supplies not only from merchants like Grevel but also at the big wool fairs held in the Cotswolds after shearing was completed. The most important was at the end of June in Burford while another was held somewhat later at Northleach.[7] The Datini Company which traded all over the Mediterranean also bought English cloth.

A letter from the company of Piero Marchi to Datino dated 5 March 1389 gives details of the consignments which were being imminently shipped to Genoa from

---

4 F. Melis, ed. (1972), *Documenti per la storia economici del secoli xiii–xvi*, Firenze. item 21; letter of 28 March 1400, Giovanni da Pessano to the Datini Company.

5 E. B. Fryde (1996), *Peasants and Landlords in Later Medieval England,* Stroud: Sutton, 90.

6 P. C. Rushen (1911), *History and Antiquities of Chipping Campden,* London: privately published, 20–1.

7 E. B. Fryde (1996), *Peasants and Landlords,* 96.

Figure 23. A statue of Francesco Datini in Prato, his birthplace (photo: Massimilian O Galardi, Creative Commons CC BY-SA 3.0)

Southampton waiting only for clearance by the customs. The goods, white (unfinished) Guildford cloths and striped Essex cloths, were divided among two ships; all the costs incurred in London, on transport to Southampton and in that port were listed including the agent's own expenses. These came in all to 51s 12d for each *ballone* and one *balla* of cloth.[8] It is clear from the Datini company records that their trade with England largely consisted of consignments of medium to low quality English cloths from Guildford or Essex and small quantities of the best wool from the Cotswolds which were destined for the high quality woollen manufacturers of Florence. The cheap English cloths were usually sold on to the Company's associates often either in Spain or in southern France.

A series of letters between the Cambini Company and Datini in 1420–1423 also allow a particularly close view of the wool trade. The Cambini reported in May 1402 that around 800 sacks of wool were due to leave Southampton for Genoa. On this occasion a majority was the best wool including some from the renowned Hailes Abbey flock. The remainder was only of moderate quality and was apparently destined for woollen manufacturers in Lombardy.

By the following month the wool market in the Cotswolds was in disarray; a severe outbreak of scab had drastically reduced the amount of good wool on the market and the price had risen considerably. The reaction of the Cambini and the other Italian merchant companies was to form in effect a cartel to buy up all the good wool on the market. They managed to acquire about 400 sacks of which 300 were loaded onto carracks at Southampton in January 1403. The following summer prices were still high at the Burford fair. Probably at least a proportion of the price demanded had to be paid in cash but as the Cambini told Datini, it was possible to change Florentine gold coins into sterling in Cirencester.[9]

The Celys and the Stonors, merchants of the staple

The importance of Cotswold wool on the export market is also reflected in the correspondence of the Cely family. The Celys were Londoners and members of the Company of the staple at Calais. A large collection of their family papers, principally letters and other documents concerned with their family business but also including items dealing with their personal affairs, came into the hands of the royal courts in the course of a legal dispute in 1489. There they remained until becoming part of the collection at the Public Record Office now the National Archives in Kew.[10] The letters

---

8   F. Melis, ed. (1972), *Documentia*, item 62. Letter of 5 March 1389 from Piero Marchi to Datini, 254.

9   E. B. Fryde (1996), *Peasants and Landlords*, 95, 97.

10 The letters make up vols. 53 and 59 in the class Ancient Correspondence (SC1). There are also seven files of accounts and memoranda which can be found in class C.47 (Chancery Miscellanea) 37/10–16. Some of the letters and a few other documents were printed in an edition by H. E. Malden, (1900), *The Cely Papers; Selections from the Correspondence and*

and other documents provide much evidence of the way the Company of the Staple operated and how the wool trade via Calais was organised in the last decades of the fifteenth century.

Like many other Staplers, the Celys' business was based in London but members of the family, apprentices or other employees, spent a considerable amount of time in Calais. In the Celys' case, the older members of the family, Richard Cely senior and his brother John usually lived in London. Richard's three sons were also involved in the business; Richard junior in London, while George was usually in Calais working with William Cely, their factor and probably a distant relation. The third brother Robert was something of a spendthrift and gambler and left the family business and the Company of the Staple in the early 1480s.

The London end of the business were responsible for buying the raw wool, making sure it was sorted into the various qualities expected by the market, properly packed, and transported to a port. By the 1480s this was overwhelmingly London; between 1333 and 8023 woolsacks left the port each year in the period 1479–1499. Boston exported between just under 1000 and 2338 woolsacks in the same years. Southampton had a relatively steady trade in wool exported by aliens (mostly Italians) averaging around 800 sacks a year while Sandwich, Hull and Ipswich were responsible for a small and generally declining share of the exports.[11] The Celys only rarely shipped cargoes from these ports.

Although some Staplers probably dealt directly with wool producers this could be a tedious and time-consuming way to conduct business. The wool was usually sold by sample, and thus buying from producers would have entailed travelling from place to place after the flocks had been shorn in June, often examining small parcels of wool produced by those with only a few sheep as well as the wool-clip of masters of large flocks. 'Broggers' or brokers, who were increasingly important to the trade in the fifteenth century, would collect all these parcels of wool in a central wool house, in their home town in the Cotswolds or elsewhere, where a London merchant could examine them more conveniently.

Very important in this manner of trade were the packers who sorted, graded and packed the wool. The merchants had to be able to have confidence in their honesty and integrity. This is made clear from the terms of 'thoethe of the woulpackers' in the ordinance *Book of the Company of the Staple* drawn up in 1563 after they had lost most of their earlier records when Calais was captured by the French in 1558. It is very likely that the wording of the oath followed that of the original ordinances. The wool packers had to swear to act without 'fraude collusion or deceipt', acting honestly so that they would not 'cause to be packed or wrapped in the fleces of the woulle earthe,

---

Memoranda of the Cely Family, Merchants of the Staple 1475-1488, London: Camden Third series I. The most recent edition including letters only is A. Hanham (1975), *The Cely Letters, 1472-1488,* Oxford: Oxford University Press for the Early English Text Society.

11   E. M. Carus-Wilson and O. Colman (1963), *England's Export Trade, 1275-1547,* Oxford: Clarendon Press, 68–9.

stones dung or sand'. Similarly all the wools should be clearly named and identified on every sarpler so packed. Thus they should write 'with open greate letters' the origin and quality of the wool, for example 'middle marche' or 'good cottiswold', on each sarpler or other container along with their own surname in such a way that neither could be removed without 'breaking' the container.[12] Generally each sarpler would contain 2 woolsacks by weight.

The Celys mainly dealt with William Midwinter of Northleach and his stepson Thomas Bush. He had large storehouses for the wool he had bought from growers at the markets in Northleach, Chipping Campden and Chipping Norton. One of the Celys would come to examine samples of the stored wools and make his choice of which to buy. The terms of the deal would be set out in an indenture listing the quantity by wool sack, quality and the price. In one dated 28 August 1476 the price for both good and middle wool was £8 15s per sack. The wool was to be delivered to 'the Lead Hall at the King's beam' (the public weigh-beam in London). The wool would be paid for in three installments; the first when it had been weighed, the next at the end of May and the third on 26 August 1477, just under a year after the indenture was drawn up.[13]

This sort of credit arrangement was common although some deals, usually for small parcels, were concluded on cash in hand basis. Both the seller and the buyer were present when the wool was weighed the buyer benefiting from a customary rebate of 28 lb (12.7 kg) per sarpler to allow for the weight of the canvas wrapper and the drying of the wool in transit. It is one of the difficulties when trying to assess the profits made in the wool trade that the expenses incurred by merchants in transporting the wool to market and in dues to officials and the like are very hard to estimate accurately. This is because not all the expenses are fully recorded (this is, for example, usually the case if the wool had to be stored in a rented store before shipping). It is also the case that different systems of weights and measures were used in England from Calais. When the sarplers reached Calais and had been unloaded from the ships, they were all re-weighed according to the Calais system in which a wool sack weighed 315 lb (142.7 kg) not 364 lb (164.9 kg) as in England.

Perhaps more important than this (since Calais weights were well understood and accepted by all Staplers and in fact worked to their advantage) was the 'quality control' operated by officials of the Staple known as collectors. All the wool had to be 'awarded' or certified to be the type and quality signified by the markings on the sarpler. This was done by sample, sometimes by the examination of a sarpler chosen by the collector. William Cely wrote to George Cely in London in September 1487 explaining how he could not get the latest cargo of wool 'awarded' because no 24, the sarpler chosen by the Lieutenant (collector), was found to contain, 'lx mydyll

---

12 E. E. Rich (1937) *The Ordinance Book of the Merchants of the Staple*, Cambridge: Cambridge University Press, 129.

13 A. Hanham (1985), *The Celys and their World, an English Merchant Family of the Fifteenth Century*, Cambridge: Cambridge University Press, 115–16.

fflessys and hyt ys a very gruff wull'.[14] William's reaction to this was to have this wool re-packed in a sarpler numbered 8; presumably one which was marked as low quality. He still, however, needed 2 sarplers of good wool for one of their regular customers, John Lopez, who was willing to pay the standard price at the Place (the Staplers' headquarters) for wool of the agreed quality. The same letter also complains about the current exchange rates, a plaint which comes up very frequently in the correspondence; 'and money goeth now upon the Bourse at 11s 3½d the noble and no other money but *Nenyng* (Burgundian) groats, crowns, Andrew Guilders and Rhenish guilders and the exchange goeth ever the longer worse and worse'.

The problems caused by badly packed and wrongly classified wool not only greatly annoyed the eventual buyer but possibly affected the reputation of the sellers and that of the Staple Company. George Cely, on one occasion in 1480, wrote to his father after meeting a very dissatisfied customer at the Antwerp Whitsun market; 'in the reverence of God, see better to the packing of your wool that shall come, or else your wool is like to lose that name it has had ever affore in time past. I never wist you send coarser wool to Calais for the country than this last was'. The Fellowship (the staple) had been very reluctant to 'award' it as Cotswold produce at all, since the quality was so poor.[15]

Wool was shipped from London to Calais in organised convoys three times a year in spring, in summer after the shearing season and in the autumn. Single vessels might also sail at other times but the convoys of wool ships were often escorted by armed ships carrying soldiers. There was frequently a fear of commerce raiders operating in the Channel which became acute at moments when English relations with Flanders or France were poor. The Celys' own ship, the *Margaret Cely*, undertook this task (known as 'wafting') in 1486 when relations between England and Flanders were tense, carrying not only 28 soldiers but also 'four small serpentines with seven chambers of one making, two greater serpentines with six chambers, three arquebus, two hand guns, six long bows and thirty sheaf of arrows,' together with equipment for making lead bullets for the guns.[16] Richard Cely was always anxious until he heard that the ships from London had docked safely. In November 1481, late in the year for wool shipments, he wrote to George in Calais, 'I trust to God the *Christopher of Rainham* be come to Calais.' He was anxious because he had heard that seven ships from the fleet had not arrived including two known to have lost their rigging in a storm.[17]

The following year in October three ships from the convoy had not arrived; two were stormbound in Sandwich and a third had made it safely to Ostend but only after the whole cargo had been thrown overboard by the master, something that was permitted

---

14 A. Hanham (1975) *The Cely Letters,* letter 234.

15 *Ibid.,* letter 93.

16 *Ibid.,* letter 363.

17 *Ibid.,* letter 137.

under the laws of the sea if the vessel was in danger of foundering.[18] Fortunately, as William Cely reported, the Cely partnership had no wool in this fleet but much of the wool they had bought had reached Calais in bad condition, probably from water damage, a not infrequent problem.

Letters from London to George or William in Calais often recorded how the Celys' wool had been loaded onto the ships in the port. In November 1481 part of a shipment of woolfells in the *Thomas of New Hythe* was placed aft of the mast under the fells being shipped by Thomas Betson, a fellow Stapler. A further letter detailed where wool fells belonging to the Celys were stowed in six other ships; in the *Mary Grace of London* the packs were marked with a C and lay behind the mast.[19] There was probably a lack of ventilation in the holds of the wool-ships since on occasion fells reached Calais damaged by 'burning' or overheating. This happened to 83 in a big shipment of 7000 fells in 1483. They were 'sore blemished as burnt in the ships'.[20]

Selling the wool once it had reached the Staple was not a straightforward business. Since the Staple Company had a monopoly over sales it could and did enforce quite rigorous conditions. The onerous regulations known as the Bullion and Partition ordinances no longer applied[21] since they had been withdrawn in 1443 but the company still controlled sales of wool and woolfells to alien merchants. One of the ways in which this was done was to insist that so-called 'old' wool available at the Staple must be included in sales as well as 'new' wool. It is not at all clear how 'old wool' was defined; Alison Hanham has pointed out that it seemed to vary from season to season presumably according to market conditions and the amount of stock on hand in the wool-houses in Calais.[22] The distinction was important because the Staple regulations specified that a ratio of one to three sarplers of 'old' wool to 'new' wool must be maintained in all bargains. William Cely wrote to George in April 1482 about how this rule impeded trade. He reported that there were many traders from Holland at Calais but, 'as for wool I can sell here none without I had old wool for they can have no old wool but where they buy new wool'. He evidently had no old wool available.[23]

The Celys, like all traders in Calais, also had to deal with the difficulties of exchange between sterling and the various currencies used by their customers. The Staple at Calais had established the rule that selling prices were expressed in marks sterling

---

18 *Ibid.*, letter 198. The right of the master to ditch some of the cargo if the safety of the vessel was threatened can be found in the laws of Oleron which were accepted very widely by medieval ship masters. R. Ward (2009), *The World of the Medieval Shipmaster: Law, Business and the Sea c.1350–c.1450*, Woodbridge: Boydell, 95–7.

19 A. Hanham (1975), *The Cely Letters,* letters 132 and 133.

20 *Ibid.*, letter 212.

21 These are discussed in part 3.

22 *Ibid.*, 134–5.

23 *Ibid.*, letter 156.

(13s 4d) per Calais sack weight but that the total cost of a bargain with a particular customer was calculated in Flemish pounds at the official Staple exchange rate. The price per sack weight was also set by the company. The 'official' Staple exchange rate very often differed from that current at the marts, leading to a form of money of account described in one document as, 'pounds by which wools are bought'. Apart from this a merchant also faced difficulties with the number of different coins minted by different rulers in use in the Low Countries and liable to turn up in any cash bargain. In August 1480 George Cely concluded a sale with a Fleming; he was paid half the cost in cash immediately which amounted to £34 12s 6d Flemish at the rate of 25s 4d Flemish to every £1 sterling. He actually received the following coins;

> 93 Andrews worth 4s 6d each
> 18½ crowns at 5s 4d
> 6 Venetian ducats and 2 salutes at 5s 6d
> 1 Rhenish gulden a 4s 4d
> 5 Utrecht gulden at 4s
> And £8 0s 2d in double briquettes at 4½d

All these coins had to be weighed and examined to make sure that they were 'good' (not clipped or otherwise tampered with and containing the correct amount of bullion). George's final calculation was that he had received £37 5s 8d Flemish; he provided change for his customer in 12 *guilhelmus* valued at 4s 4d each and a further 14d in small coins.[24]

The proportion of the price which was held over to a later date was usually collected at one of the big annual fairs or *marts* in the Netherlands. These were held four times a year, in the winter (cold mart), at Easter (Pask mart) at Whitsuntide (Synchon or Pinxster mart) and in the autumn round about St Bamis' day (Balms or Bamis mart) at Antwerp or Bergen op Zoom. Much of the settling of debts was done by endorsing bills of exchange to another merchant or banker or by assigning debts. Carrying bullion back to Calais along roads which were not always secure from raiders of various kinds could be a dangerous undertaking. In March 1478 the authorities at Leyden wrote to the Staple Company at Calais asking if, 'our townsmen may be free to deposit their money in Bruges and to do their trade in the staple of Calais with bills of exchange as was wont to be done in times past their payments to be done in Bruges.'[25] The

---

24 A. Hanham (1985), *The Celys and their World,* 179. The transaction can be found at TNA C47/15 fol.11. Andrews were Burgundian gold coins with a St Andrew's cross on the obverse. Crowns were probably French gold coins, Gulden gold coins struck by either the ruler of the Rhineland or the Bishop of Utrecht. Double briquettes were Burgundian silver coins. A *gulielmus* was a coin minted by William IV of Holland.

25 E. Power (1933), 'The wool trade in the fifteenth century,' in E. Power and M. M. Postan, eds, *Studies in English Trade in the Fifteenth Century,* London: Routledge, 67, quoting from N. W. Posthumus (1910–22), *Bronnen tot de Geschiedenis van der Leidsche Textielnijverheid.*

company in fact agreed to this concession except as far as payment for wool fells was concerned.

This might look as if the risk was merely transferred to the Staplers bringing cash back to Calais but, in fact, by this date it was normal business practice for a Stapler in Bruges to use any bills or cash he had received in the town to finance bills drawn on London merchants importing goods obtained at the marts to England. This suited both parties since the English importers needed Flemish currency to buy goods in Bruges or elsewhere while the Stapler needed English money in London to purchase wool from producers. The Cely papers include many examples of this kind of deal and also record the existence in Bruges of specialist moneychanger/bankers known as *wisselaers.* In 1479 George Cely sold 1000 fells to one Richard Starkey and received two obligations, one payable in May and the other in November. George presented the first in May to Starkey; he 'wrote him upon' (the phrase used), that is endorsed the bill to a wisseler. George then wrote 'upon' (endorsed) the bill received by the wisseler in favour of an English merchant William Welbeck to be paid in London. George took back to Calais a relatively small sum in cash to pay outstanding customs charges.[26]

One of the Celys' most regular customers was Juan or John de Lopez of Bruges. Lopez, a Spaniard, was a permanent resident of Bruges, a member of a closely linked group of merchants trading between Spain, England, Calais and the Low Countries. In the 1470s Lopez was a factor for the Pardo family company in Bruges. This family from Burgos was very active in trade in wool. One Juan Pardo was in London in 1484 where he was closely associated with another Spaniard, Pedro de Salamanca. In the early sixteenth century, the family as a whole, had a trading network linking Bruges, Rouen, Lisbon and Seville.[27]

The Celys sold Juan a very large consignment of wool and wool fells in April 1486 in a deal which led to litigation in the mayor's court in London.[28] Lopez preferred to pay for wools bought from the Celys by bills in London drawn on Pedro Valladolid (whose surname appears in the Cely letters as Bayle or Bayle et Delyt and other varied spellings). Later Valladolid was replaced by Pedro de Salamanca as Lopez' agent in London. Lopez in Bruges often acted in partnership with Gomez de Soria, one of the most respected merchants in the city who lived in splendour in the *Hotel de Mâle,* also known as the *House of Seven Towers* in the High Street.

The scale of the trading links between Lopez and the Celys is clear from the first mention of his name in the surviving collection of letters and other papers. In 1478 he bought, with Flemish partners, over 88 sacks of wool costing more than £1000. Another shipment in in July of the same year included both good and middle Cots,

26 A. Hanham (1985), *The Celys and their World,* 189.

27 W. Childs (1978), *Anglo-Castilian Trade in the Later Middle Ages,* Manchester: Manchester University Press, 73, 181, 194, 231.

28 A. Hanham (1985), *op. cit.,* 341–2.

much to the pleasure of Richard senior in London.[29] In 1483, a bargain with Lopez got into difficulties because the tense political situation in England after Richard III had taken the throne had made it very difficult to maintain a reliable exchange of letters between Calais and London. Lopez had assured William that he would pay his debts by bills drawn on his London agent, Valladolid, but this could only happen when the relevant letter arrived from London to authorise the deal going ahead. In these circumstances William in Calais would not permit any further sales to Lopez except by ready money. In another letter of the same date, 13 November, he also informed George that he had indeed told Lopez he must set up this payment and had even visited him in Bruges but all to no avail until communications were restored.

By early December he could report that one of Lopez' Flemish partners had confirmed that the letter to Valladolid had been written asking him to give the Celys in London, 'as much money as he might spare'. By January the matter was still not settled, even with Lopez claiming that he had 'sent over £2000 in letters of payment'. William informed the Cely brothers that Lopez wanted to buy more wool at the usual discount but he would not agree unless it was all paid for in ready money. About three weeks later, at the end of January, William's view of Lopez had changed. In a letter dated 29 January he pointed out that Lopez was very well thought of at Calais and that his man, Wyllykyn, was in the town and was sure to buy a lot of wool. Even so less than two weeks later he was still concerned about the way any new bargain with Lopez would be financed. Wyllykyn had claimed that any payment would be made in England by bills drawn upon Valladolid but he (William) would look for other buyers unless he received clear directions from London that he should deal with Lopez.

The next step in this saga was that Lopez' Flemish partner Gisbert van Wynsbarge arrived in Calais. After asking if the vital letter from the Celys in London had arrived (it had not) he then wished to buy all the remaining Cotswold wool paid for by a letter of payment at pleasure for the whole sum, redeemable either in England or in Calais as the Celys wished. William was not to be swayed by this deal and still demanded cash or a clear mandate from his employers. In a letter of 24 February William reported that further assurances had been given that £500 sterling in bills had been sent to England to Valladolid. William now at last began to think he was being told the truth. Five days later the deal was finally concluded.

First of all a letter arrived from London dated 16 February agreeing to the sale with payment half at London before Easter and the remainder within three months of the delivery of the wool. An earlier letter had been delayed by going first to Bruges with others for Lopez. William was left in some difficulty by this since he had already promised the wool to another customer but at last the deal went through with the necessary bills drawn up. Even at the last moment William remained somewhat cautious about the whole affair. He, however, reminded the Celys that Lopez and his

29 A. Hanham (1975), *op. cit.*, letters 26, 31.

partner were *fast* (dependable) men and that Valladolid had promised that no matter what happened he would honour the bills.[30]

The tangled story of this deal illustrates the difficulty of doing business when communications were both unreliable and slow. It also shows how well used and understood was the system of bills and letters of payment. Finally, business and trade depended greatly on trust and an individual's reputation. To be regarded as *fast men* was something to be jealously guarded.

Another problem was how politics could affect trade, something made clear in the tangled story of dealing between the Celys and Lopez in 1487–1488. In a letter dated 12 September 1487 from William to George and Richard, William reported that as the Merchant Adventurers had warned, there was 'no intercourse, league nor amity ... between the King our sovereign lord and the King of the Romans' (the Emperor). The exchange rate was very poor and Calais was suffering from a 'great plague of sickness'. William Cely, however, told George that 'John *Lowppys*' (as he called him) was 'long sore after your coming that he might make a bargain with you for your wools. He desireth to have two sarplers to prove it by till your mastership come'. William was only too keen for the deal to go through 'since the market was very slack here'.

There were still some problems with bills of exchange with Lopez claiming that a bill had already been paid to George in England while William claimed to have the bill 'by me still'. He is sending George 'enclosed in this letter a bill of the copy of John de Lopez book of such parcels as he saith he hath paid to see if your reckoning and his agree'. By November the situation in the Low Counties was even more insecure. William explained that he 'was never in so great jeopardy coming out of Flanders in my life for men of war lying by the way waiting for English men'.

In Bruges he had clearly met Lopez who had advised him that, 'he should write to your mastership to understand ... he adviseth you to bestow your money in *grosse wares* (that is not spices) now betimes at this Bamis mart; in such wares as your mastership thinketh will be best at London whether it be madder wax or fustians but I trow madder be best'. Lopez also advised that the goods should be shipped in Spanish vessels and in the name of Gomez de Soria to avoid any danger of seizure by those working for the Emperor. He finally reports that Lopez and de Soria will invest their own money as well as Cely's in this venture which will be the 'best ways to make over your money for the exchange is right nought'. By December it was not clear if Lopez had set up this deal, but his wools had been impounded by the garrison of Gravenynge to be held until the Emperor paid their overdue wages. Even so, by 16th of that month Lopez had the money ready for Cely but, as William laments, 'I know no way how to make it you (for you to get it) without great loss' since the exchange 'goeth very ill'.

By February Lopez had more to worry about than this. Bruges was in open rebellion against the Emperor, with the gates shut and the market place full of the burgesses in

---

30 The tangled story of the bargain between Lopez and the Celys in 1483 will be found in A. Hanham (1975), *The Cely Letters,* letters 201-2, 204-13, 215, 217, 220 and 222.

harness (armour). William goes on to hope that some agreement will in fact be made at Bruges between the various parties and should that happen Lopez' man was waiting at Calais to conclude matters and arrange payment. The last surviving letter from William to George dated 12 March 1488 reveals that this was a somewhat optimistic view of things. Things were still 'in mischief' in Flanders but happily Lopez had managed to bribe his way out of trouble, unlike one unfortunate Thomas Spycer who had become entangled in the unrest and who was arrested and beheaded by the forces of the Emperor.[31]

Life as a wool merchant at Calais in the late fifteenth century was not, however, completely dominated by the intricacies of the market and the need to try and satisfy both the demands of customers and the rules of the Company of the Staple, in a somewhat unstable political climate. The letters of the Celys and their associates also make clear that life for a young man in Calais could be somewhat more relaxed than the life of a City family of some standing in London itself. Trips to Bruges to stay at the inns, the *Shepys Clawe* (*Sheep's Hoof*) or the *Star* were convivial and relaxed; George may also have stayed with Lopez in what was probably greater luxury. In Calais itself George had a group of friends and colleagues and shared rented rooms with some of them. He and his unmarried friends were challenged to an archery match by the *weddyd* men in the place called the Pane outside Calais in August 1478 the prize being a good dinner (cost 12d per man).[32] Apart from events like this the young Staplers and apprentices also formed relationships with women in the town. Among the letters is a declaration of love for George in French by one Clare, while he also had a longer relationship with a woman called Margery who may have borne him at least two children.[33]

In England, by the end of the 1470s, the Celys had an estate in Essex, Bretts Place in Aveley, as well as a house in Mincing Lane in the City and some other landed property in the east of England. It is hard, however, to be sure how profitable was their wool business.[34] The lack of any continuous set of accounts makes any estimate largely conjectural; the letters make clear that there were occasions when they were in great need of ready money with creditors pressing and funds from credit sales coming in slowly and irregularly. It is also the case that the survival of the letters and papers is due to the fact that George died in debt to Richard junior and the subsequent litigation. Richard senior left a sum of money to St Olave's Hart Street, the church attended by the Cely family, to help build the steeple and make an altar for St Stephen in the church but, in the absence of a surviving will, it is not known how large his total estate was and if there were any other charitable bequests.[35] George's will[36] was admitted to

31 The events in this paragraph are described in A. Hanham (1975), *The Cely Letters,* letters 234–5, 237–9, 241 and 243.

32 *Ibid.,* 29.

33 S. Rose (2008), *Calais an English Town,* 105–6.

34 Alison Hanham has discussed this issue in detail in *The Celys and their World,* 164–202.

35 A. Hanham (1985), *The Celys and their World,* 255.

36 PCC 8 Horne.

Figure 24. St Olave's, Hart Street, London, the church attended by the Cely family (photo: author)

probate in 1496, some seven years after it was written, shortly before he died in 1489. The delay was probably because of the legal action by Richard junior. When the will was written, George had lands in Essex which were left to provide for his children. The only other items of real value were his share in the *Margaret Cely* and a jewel said to be 'had of King Richard'.[37]

Richard junior's will dated July 1493[38] makes mention of this jewel (valued at £100) which was clearly one of the points at issue between the brothers. Richard, however, died in debt to his wife's family. He had been forced to transfer his lands in London and Essex to the Rawsons, his in-laws, shortly before his death. Other land was sold by his executors to pay his creditors.[39] Even if the Cely business had done reasonably well in the 1470s and early 1480s it had clearly run into trouble by at least 1487–1488.

It has been argued that the purchase of the *Margaret Cely* was an attempt to extend their interests from the wool trade to shipping and involvement in the wine trade to

---

37 Presumably Richard III is meant; there is no information about how the Celys might have acquired such a jewel from the King.

38 PCC 25 Dogett.

39 A. Hanham (1985), *The Celys and their World*, 412–4.

Bordeaux because of the many disruptions to the trade in wool in the 1480s.[40] What we know or can surmise about the fortunes of the Celys is perhaps a warning not to assume that all wool merchants ended their days as wealthy men. In the fifteenth century the combined effects of the attitude of the crown to the trade, the political situation in the Low Countries and the policies and regulations of the Company of the Staple made trading in wool a complex and often uncertain business. Profits could be made but much hard and persistent work, a good relationship with and understanding of the difficulties of wool-producers and the ability to steer a course through the twists and turns of the financial markets of the day were all needed to achieve this much desired end.

There is fortunately another Stapler active at the same time as the Celys whose business affairs can be compared with those of this family. This is Thomas Betson. Our knowledge of his life comes from another collection of papers surviving because of a family's involvement in litigation. These papers relate to the affairs of the Stonors, a gentry family living in the Chilterns on the border of Oxfordshire and Buckinghamshire. The Stonors were well established in their neighbourhood and owned lands not only nearby but in other parts of southern England including Devon. William Stonor followed his father, Thomas, in the management of this considerable property on the latter's death in 1474 when William was 24 and unmarried. A letter from his brother hints that considerable negotiations were in train for a suitable match. These were probably successful for in 1475 William married Elizabeth Ryche, a very wealthy widow.

The marriage brought William into contact with Thomas Betson. Elizabeth's wealth was not due to inheriting lands from a family of noble or gentle status but because she had survived two husbands who were successful London merchants, as was her own father. Her first husband, Thomas Ryche, probably died in 1471 leaving her with three daughters and a son. Not long after his demise she married another merchant, John Fenn, by whom she had two more children. Fenn's factor and former apprentice was Thomas Betson, who had managed Fenn's interest in the wool trade and was himself a member of the Company of the Staple. Within a very short time after the marriage of William and Elizabeth, William had also become a member of the company by purchase and was actively trading wool to Calais with Betson as his partner.[41]

Much of the interest in Betson as far as the Stonor Papers are concerned has centred on his marriage to Elizabeth's daughter, Katherine, in 1478 because of the gentle teasing affection shown in his letters to his young future bride.[42] More important here is the light thrown on the operation of the wool trade by the partnership of William and Thomas. Elizabeth as a widow had considerable resources in liquid capital which could be profitably employed in the wool trade. In Betson, soon to be her son-in-law,

---

40 *Ibid.*, 361.

41 A. Hanham (2005), 'The Stonors and Thomas Betson; some neglected evidence', *The Ricardian* 15, 33–52.

42 E. Power (1924 reprinted 1937), 'Thomas Betson: a merchant of the staple in the fifteenth century,' in E. Power, *Medieval People,* London: Penguin, 123–57.

Figure 25. Chapel of Stonor House, the house and the estate (photo: Robert Harding, Alamy Stock Photo)

she had a friend and close associate experienced in the trade and with all the necessary connections in Calais, London and the marts in Flanders.

Elizabeth's widow's portion of one-third from Fenn's estate came to the large sum of £1500.[43] She had other funds inherited from Ryche and control of her children's legacies while they were minors. It has been suggested that the Stonors, as the owners of extensive estates including properties in good wool-producing areas such as their two manors in the Cotswolds, Condicote and Bourton, were themselves graziers and wool producers on a large scale. There is little evidence to support this.[44] None of the accounts or other estate documents found among the papers relates to large flocks; the largest seems to be a flock of 249 sheep and 168 lambs at Horton Kirby in Kent in 1469. Kentish wool was not sought after at this time and this flock may have been primarily kept to produce mutton for urban butchers. Some sheep were also leased, probably to tenants; this happened at Nuneham in Oxfordshire where one Simon Cooke leased 50 sheep in 1400.[45] It seems more likely that William Stonor took advantage of his control

43 A. Hanham (2005), 'The Stonors', 35.

44 C. Carpenter, ed. (1996), *Kingsford's Stonor Letters*, xxviii, hereafter *The Stonor Letters*.

45 E. Noble (2009), *The World of the Stonors: a Gentry Society*, Woodbridge: Boydell, 94–5.

of his wife's liquid capital to buy wool from broggers in the Cotswolds for export to Calais. On his part it was an investment and business opportunity which he probably hoped might produce better returns than his estates.

Two letters in 1476 concern a transaction relating to wool. In the first, dated 12 April, Betson informed Stonor that a consignment of wool had been loaded for shipment to Calais.[46] A second one from Betson's servant resident in Calais, Thomas Henham, dated 1 May, included the good news that the wool had all arrived and was in good condition. Most of the wool was fine Cots (Cotswold 30 sarplers) with smaller amounts of medium Cots, fine young Cots and finally one sarpler of 'refuse', a total of 51 sarplers.[47] This represented an investment on a considerable scale; around 1476 wool prices were low at about 5s per stone with fine Cots rather more, about 8s. This amount of wool, the equivalent roughly speaking of 150 wool sacks, would have a value of *c*.£1000.[48]

The Stonor/Betson partnership operated on the usual system of the purchaser paying about one-third of the total due on the striking of the bargain and the remainder in two installments at six-month intervals. This is clear from the account of a sale to two merchants from Bruges of four sarplers of fine Cots wool in July 1478. Stonor's agent in Calais, Thomas Howlake, received an initial payment of £62 6s 7g (g=groat) (Flemish) and would collect £59 13g in the following January and July.[49]

It may well be the case that Stonor's attempt to profit from the trade in wool was not as successful as he had hoped. When Elizabeth Stonor died in 1479 the partnership seems to have come to an abrupt end. Betson was heavily in debt to Stonor in 1480 when a long list of his obligations, drawn up in March, included one debt of over £700 and four others of £100.[50] In 1482 in a letter from his agent in London, Richard Page, Stonor was advised to make sure that Betson paid the £1200 still outstanding in cash not goods, as Stonor had no need to be 'incumbered with wares at will not be your profit'.[51] Stonor showed no further interest in the wool trade after his wife's death as far as we know. The remainder of his life was devoted to advancing both socially and financially through two successive marriages to wealthy widows from the gentry and nobility and becoming involved in affairs at court. The path to riches for this gentleman did not lie through investment in the wool trade.

In the second half of the fifteenth century it was possible through hard work, persistence and experience to trade profitably in wool but it was no easy path to riches. The export trade to the Low Countries was controlled by the Company of the

---

46 *The Stonor Letters,* letter 161.

47 *The Stonor Letters,* letter 163.

48 A sarpler usually contained about 2½ wool sacks by weight; a woolsack weighed 26 stone; this is of course a pretty crude estimate of the total value of the wool.

49 *The Stonor Letters,* letter 223.

50 *Ibid.,* letter 264.

51 *Ibid.,* letter 322.

Staple but was not without competitors. Italian merchants still dominated the licensed export of wool by sea largely to Florence or Venice. The expanding cloth industry in England itself bought up an ever increasing amount of the wool clip to feed the looms of the clothiers based in southern England. The reputation of the best English wool was still very high among those producing the best quality luxury cloths in the Low Countries, but wool from the flocks of Spain was also finding a ready market among the manufacturers of worsted type cloths and the so-called 'new draperies'.

Looming over difficulties of this kind were also the intricacies of financial dealings in a trade which had always been largely based on credit; the intervention of political disputes between rulers could severely disrupt both the free passage of goods and the operation of fairs at which exchange dealings were largely conducted. The anxieties expressed in a letter written by William Cely from Calais to Richard and George in London in February 1487 were very understandable. He explained that 'the season is such in Bruges now that no man there hath no leisure to go about any things pertaining merchandise'. Furthermore he said, 'touching making over of money at Bruges by exchange or other ways of conveyance in ready money or fine gold there can be none till this heat be over'. By March matters were still in turmoil in Flanders and William reported to London that, 'such men as be of any substance in Bruges ... stealeth daily away and goeth to Middelburg in Zealand'. Trying to trade in times like this required strong nerves and perhaps also an optimistic temperament.[52] It is not surprising that the Celys attempted to diversify their business activities by buying the *Margaret Cely* and entering the wine trade to Bordeaux. Even so their partnership ended mired in debt and litigation.

Broggers and merchants in the sixteenth century

Traders in wool in the sixteenth century faced equally difficult conditions. In the first half of the century competition from the makers of woollen cloth for supplies of raw wool grew fiercer. The total number of woolsacks exported fell steadily from the beginning of the century and became ever more concentrated on the port of London. While Boston and Southampton continued to export small quantities on a regular basis up to the 1540s trade in raw wool through ports in the west of England had ceased; that through Sandwich, Hull and Ipswich was also greatly reduced. The trade of London fluctuated from year to year but averaged around 3500–4000 sacks *per annum*. For the whole country the average total of wool exported for the years 1540–1547 was 5025 sacks. Cloth exports including worsteds averaged c.124, 750 standard cloths of assize per annum.[53] This total implies (if it is calculated that one standard wool sack contained the wool needed to make 4½ cloths), that this number of cloths was equivalent to the export of 28,790 sacks of raw wool.

---

52 A. Hanham (1975), *The Cely letters,* letters 241 and 243.

53 P. J. Bowden (1962), *The Wool Trade in Tudor and Stuart England*, London: Macmillan, 37.

London was the prime exporter of cloth as of wool but Ipswich, Hull, Exeter, Bristol and Southampton also had a respectable share of the trade. The problem with these calculations, if trying to estimate total English wool production, is that no allowance is made, as before, for the amount of wool used to make cloth for the home market. There are no reliable figures for the production or consumption of cloth for sale in England.

Eileen Power attempted to produce figures which are included in her lectures on the wool trade. Her figures are based on the assumption that the import of foreign made woollen cloth in the early fourteenth century (for which the customs accounts provide information) satisfied the demand for new cloth in England at the time since home-based manufacture was negligible. The reverse was the case in the mid-fifteenth century; imports of cloth were very low while English clothiers were supplying the home market. In her view the totals produced by adding the 'wool content' of imported cloth to the figures for exported wool in the early fourteenth century show a large fall in the production of English wool in the fifteenth cenrury from the peak reached in the first years of the fourteenth century. Power also postulates a corresponding reduction in the size of English sheep flocks.[54]

A more recent study by John Oldland, however, takes a more optimistic view. He argues that the figures for cloth produced and exported are under-estimated; the customs officials in the sixteenth century who made up the rolls of the customs accounts used the length of a broadcloth, decreed by statute to be 24 yd (22 m), as the standard measure for charging duties. Clothiers, however, produced cloths with bigger dimensions, sometimes as much as 40 yd (36.5 m) long. A standard kersey cloth was treated for customs purposes as equivalent to one-third of a standard broadcloth in size but cloths of this type were similarly under-estimated.

Agricultural evidence, particularly the increasing conversion of arable to pasture in this period, also supports the idea that the decline in the number of sheep was far less than that suggested earlier. In Oldland's view, the combination of this evidence with that of cloth exports, contemporaneous changes in fashion, and the types of cloth manufactured suggests that wool production was not as badly affected by the fall in population after the Black Death as has been supposed and was, in fact, increasing by around 1550.[55]

Wool-growers in the first half of the sixteenth century profited from a strong demand for their product. Merchants whose main business was the export of raw wool, that is, merchants who were members of the Company of the Staple, faced a rather more uncertain and complex situation. Competition with clothiers at home for the best wool and from Spanish wool in the markets in the Low Countries was one aspect of this. Another was all the familiar problems with credit transactions and

---

54 E. Power (1941), *The Wool Trade*, 36–7.

55 J. Oldland (2014), 'Wool and cloth production in late medieval and early Tudor England', *EcHR* 67, 25–47.

political changes which continued to impact on Staplers making the trade unstable and even precarious at times.

We are fortunate that some business accounts of two related wool broggers based in the Cotswolds and Warwickshire, and many private and business letters and some accounts of John Johnson, a member of the Company of the Staple, have survived. These allow us to understand how they attempted to prosper in the wool trade and adapted to the difficulties they encountered in this period.

The earliest of this collection of documents is an account book kept by John Heritage which covers the years 1501–1520; it was found at the end of the twentieth century in the Muniments Room of Westminster Abbey by an historian of music, probably looking for something quite different.[56] Heritage was born in the village of Burton Dassett in Warwickshire. He carried on his business as a wool merchant in Moreton-in-Marsh in Gloucestershire, where his wife's family was based (see page 42). Other documents relating to the family, such as wills, leases and other legal documents, have been found in both central and local archives. These make plain that he would have been described by his contemporaries as a yeoman, a man of considerable means but not of gentle or noble status. He was not only a merchant but also a grazier and occasional moneylender with substantial flocks of sheep reared on rented lands.

His father, Roger Heritage, had left him a substantial property, a holding of more than 200 acres (81 ha) of arable and more land put down to pasture leased from the lords of the manor of Burton Dassett. Roger had traded in all kinds of agricultural produce, including the wool clip from 860 sheep. His inventory on death revealed him to be the head of a considerable establishment with no fewer than eight surviving children and six servants, that is paid employees, including a shepherd and other agricultural workers. John's marriage to Joan Palmer linked him to a family well known in Moreton-in-Marsh with a very similar background.

John seems to be almost the stereotype of the enterprising commercially minded 'modern' man of the sixteenth century who lived in a different world from the equally stereotypical medieval peasant employed in little more than subsistence agriculture. These are of course over-simplifications which easily flourish in the absence of much detailed information about individuals and their lives. John himself, his family and his way of life, have, however, been fully described and placed in the context of the first half of the sixteenth century in England by Christopher Dyer.[57] Here we are primarily concerned to understand how he conducted business as a wool merchant. For this his account book is a uniquely valuable source.

It was opened in 1501 when John had been running the property inherited from his father for 6 years and had been trading in wool in Moreton since 1498. The book is based not on double-entry book-keeping but on a simple charge and discharge

---

56 *Westminster Abbey Muniments* 12258.

57 C. Dyer (2012), *A Country Merchant 1495–1520: Trading and Farming at the End of the Middle Ages*, Oxford: Oxford University Press.

system. Each year begins on a new page with careful listing of each supplier from whom he bought wool. Payments began with 'earnest money' handed over at the time of striking the bargain, usually at some time between March and May, that is before shearing had taken place. Payments of further installments were spread out over the year with the date and place of payment carefully noted.

Wool was sold in 'tods' as the writer of the *Nombre of weyghtes* had earlier reminded a merchant new to the trade. Entries are sometimes not complete, perhaps because John relied on his excellent memory for some details, but totals are provided for the amount of wool bought each year, its cost and the total sum laid out in earnest money.

The wool was bought from a wide range of suppliers and also included that from Heritage's own flocks. This varied between three and eight woolsacks per annum in the years 1501–1518. Between 1501 and 1509 he acquired from other suppliers an average of around 40 sacks of wool per year, with 1506 being his best year when he had 58 sacks to sell. After 1509–1519 he reduced his involvement in the trade, dealing in fewer than 20 sacks a year, with as few as nine in 1515.[58] In the first year covered by his account book, 1501–1502, Heritage bought quite a large amount of wool from members of the gentry with substantial landholdings. Notably one purchase involved 8 sacks of wool (about 1600 fleeces) produced by William Greville of Upper Lemington. In later years, however, Heritage bought largely from graziers like himself who leased demesne lands or from small-scale producers with flocks of only around 100 sheep. One possible reason for this shift away from trading directly with the gentry may be the competition that he faced from other broggers who could offer better terms to sellers of this status or, conversely, that Heritage found he was able to drive harder bargains with less sophisticated producers.

There is no doubt that a great deal of haggling went on before a bargain was concluded. What price would be offered for the consignment? What proportion of the wool offered was low quality, particularly the despised 'remys'? Was some sort of rebate offered to deal with this? How much could be offered as earnest money? How quickly would the full price be paid and in how many installments? All these matters would be hotly debated; the account book often includes a note of where money changed hands making plain that a wool merchant was constantly on the move from village to village, meeting his suppliers in the fields or at markets or even by chance.

The centre of Heritage's trade was his wool house in Moreton where the wool was delivered, stored and most was made ready for the journey to London and onward sale to a Stapler. It seems few if any London merchants rode up to the Cotswolds or other wool-producing areas to deal directly with local merchants on their home territory as they had done in the days of the Celys.

Heritage sold small quantities of wool to local clothiers, much of it of a quality too poor to be acceptable to the Staplers for sale in Calais. In 1502–1503 Robert Paycocke of Coggeshall in Essex, bought more than two sacks of 'remys' wool all destined for

---

58 C. Dyer (2012), *A Country Merchant,* appendix 2 tables of gathered wool, 228–9.

the highly successful industry making low grade woollen cloth which was based in this village. The better wool destined for the London market was wound, packed into large canvas sarplers and sent by cart down to London, passing through Chipping Norton and High Wycombe on the way. Once in London Heritage is known to have done business with several merchants, one at least being a member of the wealthy Spring family of Lavenham in Suffolk, as famous as clothiers as the Paycocks.

The final details of any deal would have been concluded after the weighing of the woolsacks at the King's Beam in Cornhill. Any Stapler buying from Heritage would have made up a cargo of wool to be shipped to Calais from parcels of wool purchased from a range of suppliers; this would also have routinely been divided among several ships for the Channel crossing, a long-standing practice in the trade.

All this activity was kept in motion by credit, just as it had been from the very beginnings of the export trade. Heritage needed ready money as earnest money to seal a bargain and equally expected to receive cash in similar circumstance when he sold wool on to a Stapler. The remainder of the price would be paid in installments. If installments were not paid on time, if the market was slow with few buyers, if the exchange in Flanders turned against the Staplers, trouble loomed. Heritage and his colleagues lived from hand to mouth, running very hard to keep still or, more properly, to avoid defaulting on their debts. It was hard to build up even a small reserve of ready money; it was necessary as well as prudent to take advantage of any opportunities offered to make a profit. Heritage did not allow the carts he had hired to return to the Cotswolds empty but loaded them up with all manner of saleable goods for the market in Moreton. Some were bulky; herrings and other salt fish, the tar used by shepherds; others were more costly luxuries perhaps pre-ordered by the more prosperous burgesses of Moreton.[59]

One difficulty that Heritage had to deal with was that, unlike the traders in Calais or the marts in Flanders and the City of London, most of his business was conducted on a cash basis with small installments paid by him usually in person to the supplier. Bills of exchange and obligations endorsed and passed from hand to hand were not much used in his dealings with small wool producers. The coinage in circulation in England at the beginning of the sixteenth century was based around the silver penny, frequently cut into halves or quarters for everyday transactions. Gold coins could be used for larger transactions. Barter or payments in kind were also frequent and on more than one occasion he settled debts in sheep. The goods bought in London would also be paid for in the same way.[60]

It is not easy to calculate whether Heritage's trading was profitable. There are figures for the amount he spent each year on wool but none for his receipts and expenses. The amount spent was around £300 per year in 1501–1509 with 1506 being the peak at £410. After 1508 he seems to have reduced his involvement in the trade

---

59 C. Dyer (2012), *A Country Merchant 1495–1520*, 114–9.

60 *Ibid.*, 120–3.

spending something nearer £100 per year in 1512–1517. Taking into account all his expenses, the profit on the sale of wool worth £300, using the price per tod current in the London market, may have amounted to about 9.3%, a percentage similar to that in the butchery trade at the same time.

Heritage also made money from his activities as a grazier which may have realised a bigger profit than his business as a brogger. It is not, however, clear why he reduced his wool trading at a time when prices were rising strongly but it may be connected with failing health and lack of energy to conduct this stressful and uncertain business.[61] Although not much is known about his later years, he seems to have moved to London to a house in Cripplegate, leaving his pasture land, flocks and herds to be managed by servants. No will survives to allow an estimate of his possessions at the end of his life.[62]

Some further light on the fortunes of the wool trade in the same area is shed by the account book originally kept by his son Thomas. Thomas was well educated, perhaps at the grammar school at either Chipping Campden or Chipping Norton. When he was around 16 years old he was apprenticed to a London skinner and became a member of the Skinners' Company, the main business of which was the sale of furs as well as more common-or-garden hides and skins. Although a skinner by trade, Thomas became something of a general merchant with widespread interests buying and selling goods of all kinds including Spanish iron. He also inherited the property at Burton Dassett where he had a flock of at least 600 sheep as well as a large herd of cattle.

Much like his father he collected wool for sale from the surrounding villages and also had property in Moreton-in-Marsh. He died in 1541, leaving a widow, Millicent, who later married Peter Temple, a member of a merchant family in Witney already connected by marriage with the Heritages. This man took over the family land holdings at Burton Dassett, and became a grazier as well as a brogger like his predecessors. He also began to write up his accounts, scattered through Thomas's book on blank leaves.[63] These provide a clear picture of his activities particularly after he moved to Warwickshire in 1543. He had an active and profitable business based on raising and fattening cattle as well as that concerned with sheep and wool. His marriage to Millicent, bringing with it her considerable land holdings, allowed him to change his way of life. He had trained as a lawyer at Lincoln's Inn and seemed set on a career in the law but from the early 1540s he built up land holdings, the origins of the great estates of his descendants, the Temples of Stowe.

From his accounts it is possible to get some idea of the structure of his business and the relative profitability of different aspects of it. It is even possible to reach a

---

61 *Ibid.*, 126–30.

62 *Ibid.*, 36.

63 The MS of the account book is Huntington Library MSST 36. It has been edited and published by N. W. Alcock (1981), *Warwickshire Grazier and London Skinner 1532–1555*, Oxford: Oxford University Press for the British Academy.

reasonably reliable conclusion regarding his income in the years 1545–1551 from both his sheep flocks and the sale of wool. Sheep and lambs were sold to other graziers; for example, John Spencer of Wormleighton bought 230 couple of sheep in 1546. They were also sold to butchers to feed the increasing demand for mutton and lamb in London.[64]

The price rose steadily over the period doubling between 1544 and the late 1550s; this was a period of increasing inflation but, even so, Temple's income from this source increased in real as well as monetary terms. His known costs between 1545 and 1551 amounted to £307 18s 10d to set against an income of just under £995. These costs relate to the purchase of extra stock and do not cover all his expenses, including the wages of shepherds, the lease of pasture and small items like the tar medicaments needed against scab. In the same period his income from the sale of wool amounted to £1180, a considerable sum. He also included in his accounts, however, some predictions of what he estimated his future income both from the sale of sheep and the sale of wool would amount to. He calculated that by the late 1550s the income from selling stock would be larger than that from selling wool. One prediction put sheep sales as producing £430 and wool only £327.[65] The size and composition of his flocks at this time are recorded; one count totalled 4820 animals.[66]

The greater part of the wool sold by Temple came from his own flocks. Both the number of sheep shorn and the price paid for their wool varied from year to year. In 1548–1550, prices were high (from 22s 0d to 25s 4d per tod). In these years Temple's flock probably included over 2500 sheep; their wool sold for £246 19s in 1548, 291 in 1549 and 180 in 1550. In the same years Temple also greatly increased the amount of wool he bought from other producers. In 1548 he set out on a tour through villages, mostly to the north of his home at Burton Dassett; in around ten days he visited no fewer than 27 villages and contracted to buy wool from 65 villagers. All these contracts involved the payment of earnest money to the producers; he spent a total of £285, in this way, paying the price of 19s 10d per tod for the wool (no mention is made of difference in quality). If he later sold the wool bought at the same price as his own (22s per tod) his profit would have been £31 before expenses.

He did much the same the following year but thereafter only bought the odd consignment of wool from other producers. He does not explain this sudden but short-lived change in the nature of his business becoming briefly a much more active wool broker rather than a grazier. We can speculate that he found it not worth his while. The need to lay out ready money on advance sales and earnest money may have been a deterrent, especially as this was needed in the spring while money from his sales of stock and of wool would have been most plentiful in summer and autumn. It would

64 N. W. Alcock (1981) *Warwickshire Grazier*, 82.

65 N. W. Alcock (1981) *Warwickshire Grazier.* These figures can be found in table 3.2, p. 80: numbers of sheep bought and sold: receipts and costs.

66 *Ibid.*, 98–9.

also have been tedious and exhausting to ride from village to village and haggle over the quality of the wool offered and the price to be paid.

A possible motive driving him to increase his wool broking business in these years may be connected with the ambitious new house which Temple began to build in the summer of 1548. This was mainly constructed of the local stone, but had glazed windows, even in the kitchen, as well as two chimneys. It was clearly a substantial building. A deed drawn up in 1578 in favour of his widow, when her son John had taken over most of the house, mentions that she had the use of 'two chambers, one studye newly builded under the gallerye and one maydes chamber at the stayre head wherin a presse nowe standeth'. Some extra income from wool sales would have been welcome while the building work was in progress.[67]

There is more information in the accounts about the merchants to whom Temple sold his wool clip. Some went to his brother Robert who had a successful cloth-making business in Witney from the 1520s till around 1555.[68] Most of the remainder was sold to members of the Company of the Staple for sale in Calais. Among them was Anthony Cave, a close associate of John and Otwell Johnson, whose letters provide an even more detailed picture of the wool trade at this period than Temple's accounts. Two others, also London merchants of note, were Stephen Kyrton and Richard Whettell.[69] Both lived in Lime Street ward in the City very near the house owned by Cave but used as their counting-house by the Johnsons.[70] They were probably friends as well as business colleagues and neighbours.

After 1550 Peter Temple gradually gave up using the account book which has allowed us to understand his dealing in sheep and in wool. It is clear that his business as a grazier continued to be successful but his main interest was no longer in the day-to-day management of his extensive agricultural business but in building up his landholdings. He was intent on making the transition from wealthy yeoman to gentleman with all the social prestige that went with this change of status. While he purchased interests, often in former crown land acquired from the Augmentations Office, spread over a wide area, the transaction which included manorial powers and signified his becoming a landowner rather than a tenant concerned Burton Dassett. In 1557–1560 he was able to buy one-third of the manor from the Dannett family. The rent roll was considerable (£253 per annum) but it was the social prestige which made this purchase so attractive, perhaps along with the desire to have ownership of the land which had been the origin of his fortunes as a grazier. By 1590 his son John was also able to buy the freehold of lands at Stowe. By 1577 Peter Temple had already been

---

67 *Ibid.*, 195–202.

68 *Ibid.*, 9–10.

69 J. Stow (1908), 'Limestreete warde', in C. L. Kingsford ed., *A Survey of London. Reprinted From the Text of 1603,* Oxford: Clarendon Press, 150–63. *British History Online* http://www.british-history.ac.uk/no-series/survey-of-london-stow/1603/pp150-63 [accessed 17 May 2016].

70 B. Winchester (1955), *Tudor Family Portrait,* London: Jonathan Cape, 210–11.

described as 'esquire' in a deed; the family had in modern parlance 'made it'.[71] The well-known words of a Nottinghamshire merchant, that 'the shepe hath payed for all' applied to him and his heirs but was it the sheep rather than their wool which was the source of his fortune?

The Johnson brothers; John, Otwell and Richard

The Johnson papers constitute a much larger and more complex source than the account book which passed from the Heritage to the Temple family. The main body of the collection comprises nearly 1000 letters, including at least two of the letter books in which merchants copied their correspondence for later reference. There are also some business, personal and household accounts. The main body of the papers covers the years 1542–1552, although there are some earlier items and others which relate to the later period of John Johnson's life. Like the earlier Cely papers all this became part of the National Archives because of legal proceedings. In the case of the Johnsons, their papers were handed over to the Privy Council and the Lord Chancellor after John Johnson became insolvent and faced a series of legal actions following his bankruptcy and that of his associates. The papers, especially the letters, provide a detailed and humane view of both the business and the personal lives of the family especially of John and his brother Otwell. A small selection of the documents was included in the published *Calendars of Letters and Papers Foreign and Domestic of the reign of Henry VIII* but the majority have never been printed. They have, however, been transcribed and edited by Barbara Winchester in volumes 2–4 of her 1953 London PhD thesis, 'The letters of John Johnson, 1542–1552'.[72] Much of the material in volume 1 of the thesis, a long introduction to the letters, was published in her book, *Tudor Family Portrait* which emphasised the personal aspects of the documents.[73]

John Johnson came from a merchant family, probably originally of Flemish origin, with strong links to the wool trade, to Calais and to the company of the Staple. His uncle William had been an Alderman of Calais at the time of the meeting between

---

71 N. W. Alcock (1981), *Warwickshire Grazier* 231–35, 246.

72 The originals of the main body of the letters can be found in TNA Kew, SP46/5, SP46/6 and SP46/7. The transcriptions by Barbara Winchester occupy vols. 2–4 of her thesis and are there numbered from 1-946. A selection is also included in the volumes of *Letters and Papers Foreign and Domestic of the Reign of Henry VIII*. References to the letters will use the page numbering from the thesis rather than the folio numbers in the volumes of State Papers since there is on occasion more than one letter on a folio. All the letters included in the volumes of *Letters and Papers ...* are included in the thesis volumes. The papers relating to Johnson's activities after his bankruptcy are mainly preserved in the collection of State Papers in the National Archives and will be referenced individually. The most complete set of accounts is the double-entry ledger for Christmas 1534 to 25 March 1538 which is calendared in *L&P* xix i 300 and xix ii App.7. It is TNA SP1/185 ff.100–27 and SP1/196 ff.97–225.

73 B. Winchester (1955), *Tudor Family Portrait*, London: Jonathan Cape.

Henry VIII and Francis I at the Field of the Cloth of Gold just outside Guines in 1517. Both William and his brother Richard traded in cloth and wool and were modestly successful. Richard apprenticed John, the eldest of his three sons, to Antony Cave, a well-to-do merchant, grazier and Stapler based at Tickford in Buckinghamshire. Not only was Cave a rising man in his own right, he also had links of one kind or another with some of the most important families in the area. Johnson could hardly have been more fortunate in his father's choice of master. Johnson was provided with a good education, being fluent in French and well versed in double-entry bookkeeping. He also became a devout Protestant at a time of religious turmoil in England.

His marriage to Cave's niece Sabine Saunders, a member of a large family which lived at Sibbertoft in Northamptonshire, increased his links with the countryside of the south Midlands and with perhaps the most vital element in contemporary English society. Sabine's youngest brother, Ambrose, was also apprenticed to Antony Cave, two others were lawyers while she was closest to Laurence, a well-known Protestant divine with a strongly spiritual cast of mind who suffered martyrdom in the reign of Queen Mary. Coming from such a background John Johnson was in a good position both to build up his resources through trade and to establish himself as a landowner and gentleman with wide lands and large flocks and herds.

John Johnson's interest in trade centred on the family partnership which was well established by 1542. This linked Antony Cave at first with John Johnson and his brother Otwell; later Ambrose Saunders and Richard Johnson were also closely involved. The partnership's London base was Cave's house in Lime Street where Otwell also lived with his family. Antony Cave was a Stapler as well as free of the Draper's Company. The Johnson brothers were also freemen of the same company; John by redemption in 1534, Otwell by apprenticeship in 1541 (and a freeman of the City of London in 1542) and Richard in 1549. John was also a Stapler. The family and their mentor Cave organised their trade in wool in such a way that Antony Cave seldom left his country home at Tickford; the collection of wool from his own flocks and those of other producers in the countryside around was in the hands of John and later, as the business became more successful, other local men employed by John to do this work. Otwell, who was in the service of Sir John Cage, Comptroller of the King's Household and Constable of the Tower as well as a merchant, ran the counting house and wool store in Lime Street. His letters make clear his expertise as an administrator and accountant. The youngest brother, Richard, after completing his apprenticeship with Cave, lived in Calais from 1547 where he married Margaret Mattrys, whose family owned more than 300 acres (121 ha) in the Pale and other property in Calais as well.[74]

After his marriage John and his wife first lived at Polebrook near Oundle, in the parsonage house rented from the incumbent. In 1544, the family moved

---

74 B. Winchester (1953), 'Johnson Letters', 23, 30–1, 37, 43. This thesis is cited from this point as Winchester, thesis.

Figure 26. Glapthorn Church, Northamptonshire (photo: Church Wardens of Glapthorn reproduced by permission)

to Glapthorn Manor, a few miles away, also rented this time from Sir Thomas Brudenell. This was a substantial property with extensive gardens. John made this his home, making great efforts to build up substantial land holdings, all on leases of various kinds in the surrounding villages. It was also the centre from which his wool-buying and collecting business was conducted. Letters record how he attempted to buy wool from the gentry with large flocks as well as in much smaller parcels from villagers with a few sheep. One letter shows him asking Sir Thomas Brudenell for his business adding the inducement that advance payment would be possible.

'Yf your mastership have made no-promes of your wullis.
of this yeare., or that ye intend not to ship them to
the Staple yaurself I praie you (if it please you) let me
be your marchaimt as well for that wull ye have in Cotsold
as elswher, and I shal. be content to geve you as reasonable
a price as the 'tyme, do requier or as moefte as anny other
man will. Besydes thatt if it please you to have parte of your' monne
afforehaund, I wyll provyde it for you.[75]

A good general idea of the way in which Johnson collected wool from smaller producers is provided by a copy of his brother-in-law's book of expenses (his 'reconynge') which was included in the papers taken over by the Privy Council. Robert Saunders had acted as John's agent in 1543 buying up wool in all the villages around his home at Flore which lies between Daventry and Northampton. Some was bought in very small parcels like the 4 tods supplied by the vicar of Flore or the 2 tods which a man from Haddon 'carried to Flore'. The largest supplier was one 'Lucas of Thoreseby' who sold Robert 42 tods. In all he bought 24 sacks of wool worth £206 6s 8d for John, under a third of the total of £728 3s 9d which John spent on buying wool in this particular year.[76] Villagers selling only 2–3 tods of wool may have received cash in hand. Others who worked for Johnson collecting included another cousin, Christopher Breten and a local merchant in Oundle, Richard Harrison.

Sabine his wife likewise took part in this operation. She sent her 'reconynge' to John in London in the summer of 1447 recording payments to local men for wool 'for my husband'.[77] Large suppliers were usually paid in installments, the long-standing custom of the trade. The terms of a typical contract for the purchase of a large amount of wool were recorded in Johnson's Journal for 1544. John and his close associate and his wife's cousin, Sir John Cope of Canons Ashby, had contracted to buy half each of a large parcel of wool from a Mr Hasilwood at Madewell. The consignment contained no refuse wool, but 'ii tod of cot or comber'. Johnson provided the canvas and the packthread for the wool to be packed for transit at Madewell. He made a note on 23 February 1544 that all the wool was not yet received so he had left a space in the obligations drawn up to pay for the wool; 'a place lefte for the sommes bycause we knew it not, which Mr Coope will set in when all the wull is waied then are signed and sealid and deyveryd byme'.

This took place as he also recorded on 22 March

The xxiijth daie of Marche, at Polbrok…
'Wulles owith for John Hasilwood of Maydwell, Esquyer. And is for the some of C
xxvii vjs mer st., by reason of the half of his wull at Maydwell and Traford, which

75 Winchester thesis, vol. 3, letter 337.

76 TNA SP46/5 ff.25–6.

77 TNA SP 46/5 f.

Mr. Coope bought of hym and receyved, being in all as the sayd Mr. Coope gevithe
me reconyng, some of, argent at vij li the sacke iic l li xjs mer st.the di. wherof I
must aunswer; bycause I have recyved the wull and covenentid with Mr Coope to
paie. at Our Lady Annunciacion next lxli st., apon an obligacion made dew in Mr.
Coope's name and myne cont – 83li 10s 8d mer st.,
and at Mydsomer apon a lyke obligacion xx li st.,
and at Mychelmes the di. of an obligacion cont. 83 li 10s 8d.
Some in all, dew for my parte of the same wull-125 1j 6s 0d.
John Hasylwood of Maydwell, Esquyer, owith for chest of redie monney.
And is for the some cf lxiij li xs mer st. the same daie sent to hym per Thomas
Holland my servant, in partie of an obligacion dew by Mr. John Coope and me at
th'Annunciacion of Our Lady next.
Some – 63 li 10s 0d'[78]

Generally the small parcels of wool collected from villagers was packed at Glapthorn,
a very important task since there were strict Staple regulations covering how this was
to be done. Sabine at times was responsible for seeing that all was done in the correct
way. John sent her instructions in 1545. The wool was to be handled with care and was
to be sorted into three sorts; 'one of th' end wull, which is thast is wond in the loke;
another of the fairest of the clyft wull; and the third of the darkyst colour of the clyft
wull'. The sarplers were also to be marked accordingly with 'pitche brandes' as well
as 'markes and nombers with reed stone'.[79] On this occasion Sabine was faced with a
threat from the wool-winders to walk off the job unless their pay was increased. In the
end the packing was finished in November; a total of 67 woolsacks and 10 tods were
packed. The 'reward' or bonus paid to the men was increased by Sabine from 10s to
11s, 'wherewith thay be content'.[80]

As well as trading on his own account and that of his partners, his brothers and
Antony Cave, John also bought wool as an agent principally for two wealthy widows,
Mrs Fayrey and Mrs Baynham of Calais. Mrs Fayrey contacted him in 1542 because she
suspected that her current agent was either incompetent or fraudulent. She wrote:
'as I perseve by his doing of my besynes that other he carythe not whether he doo
my byssenes or no or ells a wold kepe me as ignorant as he cane.'[81] The problem had
arisen over the exchange rate at which the agent sent money back from Calais. The
Johnsons acted for this lady till sometime in 1546 but found her a demanding client.
Otwell after a visit to her found her very loquacious but also precise in her demands;
if two sarplers of wool were bought for her, 'she wolld have then good Cottes and

78 The extract from John Johnson's Journal (TNA SP46/5 f.12r) is transcribed in full in the note
    to letter 48 Winchester thesis vol. 2, 89.
79 *Ibid.*, 2 letters 207, p. 394.
80 *Ibid.*, 2 letters 221, 260, pp. 429, 480.
81 *Ibid.*, 2 letter 9, p. 15.

good barkes withoute middell wull'. She also informed Otwell of a possible bargain she wanted to make requiring that John should tell her 'whether you will take any part of the bargain with her and also as nigh as may be to write unto her for what some of money should have of the foresaid two good sortes for she intendes to be doing with this straunger for all her fine wulles if she like his price.'[82]

Mrs Baynham with whom John often stayed when on business in Calais was a close friend as well as a client. She clearly trusted Johnson to do his best for her; on one occasion she reassured him that she understood the difficulty he had had in obtaining carriage for her wool to London for onward shipment to Calais 'knowing (as I do) howe diligently you have bene at all tymes in myne affaires and howe honestly and truly you have dealt with me hetherto'.[83] The wool normally travelled overland by carrier to London and was stored in the wool-house at Lime Street until it could be shipped to Calais or otherwise disposed of. Staplers were notionally bound by the rules of the Company not to sell wool, except refuse, other than at the Staple at Calais but there is ample evidence in the Johnson papers that they were actively selling wool of all grades in London from the 1540s. In a letter dated 18 November 1545 Otwell, at a time when wool prices had fallen sharply, advised his brother that he, 'could perchance sell all your Cottes wull good and middell (as I thinke) to straungers hier', (i.e. at London). He also complained that the wool house was almost completely full ('ther is skauntly room for the skaelles'), that clothiers would not buy wool at the price John wanted, since the cloth market had also collapsed, and finally John must accept that, 'truly men will not do butt as they may lyve'.[84] Wool that was to be sent to the Staple at Calais was divided into different parcels for shipping in different vessels. A fragmentary shipping account in the collection of papers gives the name of the ship, the master and the numbers of the pockets of Johnson wool on board. In this instance the ships used came from Calais itself, London, Hull and other mainly east coast ports.[85]

Otwell played an almost indispensable part in the business having oversight of the bargains made whether in England or Calais and attempting to control the flow of ready money and the many credit agreements and installment payments on which the success of the business depended. His plea to his brother to be more aware of their 'cash flow' in June 1547 makes clear how easy it was for their business to face considerable difficulties on this score.

> The moche occasion of this my vehemency hierin ryseth of the payements nowe in huande of 100 li ster to Mr John Coope and 60 li to Mr Breten etc besides your often writing to have money sent unto you this weke and that weke to Tycheford or to Glapthorne; and so in a manner weekly one great payement or other followith in eche

---

82 *Ibid.*, 2 letter 39, 69.
83 *Ibid.*, 2 letter 114, 229.
84 *Ibid.*, 2 letter 266, pp. 488–91.
85 SP46/5 ff.40–6.

other's necke so as I am no wise able to furnisshe money sufficient for all (so sodainly as you do appointe your payements) for my lyff th'exchaunge so much differing from your reconyng therof as indeed it doeth. Staye therfor (I pray you) for God's sake your haundes in tyme least all be tourned into dust and remember the Frensshe proverb, "qui trop embrace, peu reticent ou restraint."[86]

John's main responsibility was to buy wool in England. He also spent a considerable amount of time in Calais and the Netherlands, much as the Cely brothers had done over half a century earlier. He had to seek out buyers, conclude bargains keeping an eye on the Staple regulations, and arrange payment whether in ready money or in various credit instruments. He was always confronted with the complications of the various exchange rates being used in the marts of the Netherlands and in Calais. The 1540s were also a very troubled time in English relations both with France and the various counties of the Netherlands. The life of a merchant trying to conduct business in these circumstances was difficult and frustrating. Otwell in London meanwhile was in many ways in the position of the financial director of a modern limited company. The ledgers and the letter books relating to deals made by the Johnsons and their associates were in his charge and it is very likely that he was the only person who understood the complexities of the overall financial position and whether the family was trading profitably or not.

His task was made all the more difficult because, like Thomas Heritage and Peter Temple, the Johnsons did not rely solely on the wool trade for their income. John seems to have had the ambition of joining the ranks of the landed gentry by building up a substantial land holding. It has been claimed that this was the dream and ambition of every Tudor merchant.[87] He eventually leased from surrounding landowners over 200 acres (81 ha) mainly of pasture, the majority enclosed. He also had rights to run a flock on common land near his home at Glapthorn eventually owning around 1000 sheep. His lands also produced a surplus of grain for sale.

There seems little doubt that John, who suffered from recurrent bouts of ague, much preferred the relatively peaceful life of a grazier to the stresses inherent in the life of a merchant. Of greater potential profit to both John and Otwell, however, were probably their trading ventures outside the wool trade. These became quite complex and at times were undoubtedly profitable. Both brothers dealt in cloth as well as wool. John's Journal for 1543 details a series of transactions in cloth; one involved a parcel of 'Gentisshe (Ghentish) cloth' delivered to a customer in London worth a total of £68 5s 7d including insurance and carriage. Other bargains involved as much as 3575 ells of Holland cloth and also *frizadoes*, the cheap hard-wearing cloth made in Haarlem or Leyden for which there was a good market in England. In 1545 Otwell wrote to John requesting further shipments of frizadoes since these sold well.

---

86 Winchester thesis, vol. 3 letter 509, pp. 901–2. Mr Coope (Sir John Cope) and Mr Breten were wool suppliers Tycheford was Anthony Cave's house and Glapthorn, John's own home.

87 B. Winchester (1955), *Tudor Family Portrait,* London: Jonathan Cape, 90.

A case or ij of Harlam and also Lay frisados, if you do bargain for while you ar nowe at Andwarpe yourself, and provide that thay may be veray excellent, I trust I shal beable to dispatche away honnestly, for I am promised a chepeman shortely for them that I have hier alredy. I pray you therfor, cause spede to be made to have them sent hiether, when they may be made redy, and do what you can in the prices of them, for at 15s and l6s chascun lesvouldra.'[88]

Like the Cely brothers, the Johnsons also dabbled in the wine trade to Bordeaux. As early as the 1530s Otwell was part-owner of the *St George Bonaventure* which traded on this route. Later, around 1545–1546, the Johnsons had links with a Flemish wine trader, one Henry Gerbrand who was able to buy wine for the Johnsons in France at a time when English/French trade was embargoed because of the state of war existing between the two kingdoms. The brothers were known to be wine traders and were clearly open to taking orders, as it were, from business contacts.

A letter received around Christmas 1550 requested, 'you wyll be so good as to sen me a ton of wyn; you do me as moche plesur as ever dyd man and you shall have mony wythen vi days.'[89] Another letter of 1551 also shows the problems that could arise over the quality of wines. Otwell had received a shipment from Spain that was so poor that he would be glad to be 'rydd of for vli the butt and a year's payment rather than fayle... howbeit truly I was never maister of anny befor this that displeased me so moche.' A large consignment of Gascon wine was a much better prospect; he had sold 40 tuns at a good profit ('we shal be assured to be honest gaingers').[90] He expected as much as 144 tuns in all in '2 good Bretisshe shippes'. John Johnson also brought wine in through Lynn; this was the port, easily reached from Glapthorn by water along the Nene and the Ouse which he used for most of his grain and malt exports. General cargo of all kinds was imported from the Netherlands on the return voyage of the grain ships. Iron was always in demand and seems to have been stored at Glapthorn in some sort of warehouse so that local customers could easily be served. The clearest idea of the trading activities of both John and Otwell through the port of Lynn comes from the enrolled customs accounts for 1550–1552. Ships laden with corn and malt left Lynn for Calais and also ports in Sussex. Vessels chartered by the Johnsons laden with wine and other goods regularly entered the port; one ship in April 1551 carried 14 tons Gascon wine, 4 tons sack, 2 tons Rochelle wine, 2 tons iron and 3 lasts soap. A mixed cargo like that on board the *Nederyere de Andwarpe* included Colleyn pots (Cologne pots), paving tiles, hops, pitch grey paper and glass.[91]

Despite all this activity, however, it is clear from the tone of the letters exchanged between the three brothers, John, Otwell and Richard, that despite some profitable

---

88 Winchester thesis, vol. 2, letter 143, 282–3.
89 Winchester thesis, vol. 4, letter 635, 1122.
90 Winchester thesis, vol. 4, letter 637, 1125.
91 Winchester thesis, vol. 1, appendix xi.

ventures they were building up a burden of debt which it would have been hard to cover in the best of times. In 1551–1552 trading could hardly have been more difficult. The sales of both wool and cloth in the Low Countries had collapsed; the exchange market was in a turmoil which reached its peak on 12 June. It was the custom in the City of London for merchants engaged in foreign trade to meet in Lombard Street at around 12 noon to make bargains. On this day, 'at our Street tyme was publysshed th'enclosed proclamacion for the stay or rather abolysshing of the said exchaunge recchaunge etc wherby moost of merchantes ar brought into a vunderful perplexitie of thayer trade.'[92] This stop on the exchange was followed shortly by the 'calling down' or devaluation of sterling; a shilling would henceforth be worth 9d and later 6d and a 4d groat would fall from 3d and then 2d. The effect this had on buying and selling can well be imagined.

On 8 July Otwell wrote to John in Calais telling him of the uncertainty caused by the imminent devaluation; explain how he had advised the bailiff at Glapthorn, 'rather than to kepe any money laying annywhile by him ... to imploye his money in ernesting some good wull or fell bargains'. He also spoke of the need to pay their overseas creditors as much as possible as soon as possible. This was sage advice but before it could be acted on Otwell had fallen victim to the epidemic of the sweating sickness which was ravaging London. He had come back from the Street exchange session at 7 in the evening, taken to his bed and died early on the morning of 10 July. John and his remaining brother and their associates continued to trade for another eighteen months but, in March 1553, were declared bankrupt and their papers seized by the Privy Council. It seems there were at least 100 creditors eager to seize any goods they could lay their hands on; the most important 20 were owed no less than £8000. The cases in the High Court of Admiralty which were brought by some of these creditors concerned ships' cargoes but tellingly no wool was involved; Seville oil, wine and a whole range of goods from tapestries depicting biblical stories to bales of linen and pots and pans were fought over in court but no wool or fells the commodities in which John had traded in for many years.

What were the causes of the failure of the Johnson brothers' business? Were the problems unique to them, the sudden death of Otwell, or John's increasing desire to live in the Northampton countryside rather than promote the business whether in England or in Calais and elsewhere? What about the economic and political background? Was the origin of the disaster much more concerned with the decay of the export trade in English wool than the family troubles of the Johnsons? Did the parallel growth of English cloth-making have a role to play or competition from the wools of Spain on the markets in the Low Countries and elsewhere?

There is little argument about the decline in the amount of English raw wool going for export. This had been evident since the second half of the fifteenth century and by the middle years of the sixteenth century the average number of standard woolsacks

---

92 Winchester thesis, vol. 4, letter 679, 1197.

paying the export dues was 4576 in the years 1541–1545 and as low as just over 3005 in 1531–1535. At the same time the internal market for wool is estimated to have grown to around 43,879 sacks in the same five-year period. Cloth production had boomed and there may have been more than 15 million adult sheep in the country in the same period.[93] After the Black Death production did fall away but, it has been argued, rose 'dramatically from 1450 to the mid-sixteenth century'.[94]

Changes in agricultural practice especially the great increase in pastoral farming much of it on enclosed land had increased the size of flocks, many of them belonging to graziers like the Temple and Heritage families. Vocal complaints about the way this change was affecting rural life become increasingly frequent from the early decades of the sixteenth century. A ballad of c.1520 claimed that 'great men makithe now adayes a sheepcott in the churche'.[95] Legislation in 1533 attempted futilely to control the number of sheep which could be in the ownership of one man. 'Greedy and covetous people' motivated by 'the great profit that cometh of sheep' would be limited to 2400 animals.[96] The Staplers themselves bewailed the increase in the price of wool; in 1527 in a petition to Wolsey they claimed that the shortage of wool on the market was due to the amount, 'in the hands of rich grayziers, brogers and engrossers and by them enhaunced and lifted to such price that neither Stapler nor clothier is able to obtain his living theirupon.'[97]

The membership of the company had fallen probably by rather more than a half from its peak of around 400 in the middle of the fifteenth century. Evidence from the customs accounts suggests that 113 merchants shipped wool from London in 1517–1518 compared with only 40 in 1536.[98] The agreement made with the crown in the 1460s, the *Act of Retainer*, which made the company responsible for the financing of the garrison of Calais out of the sums paid in wool export duty had become relatively suddenly in the mid-1520s a millstone round their necks. Their petition to the crown in 1527 called it the 'ponderous acte of reteynour' and blamed the difficulties in which the company now found itself on 'continuall debate contention and warre' which was preventing their customers coming to Calais. It seems however, that the sudden deterioration in their financial position was caused as much by the sums of money that were being milked from the company by the crown as the state of trade. In 1528

---

93 J. Oldland (2014), 'Wool and cloth production in late medieval and early Tudor England,' *EcHR* 67, 25–47. The figures come from the table on p. 29.

94 *Ibid.*, 25. Earlier calculations by Eileen Power (1941) are to be found in *The Wool Trade in English Medieval History*, 37.

95 H. R. Tawney and E. Power (1924), *Tudor Economic Documents Illustrating the Economic and Social History of Tudor England*. London: University of London Historical Series, III, 19.

96 Act of 1533 quoted in D. Hurst (2005), *Sheep in the Cotswolds; the Medieval Wool Trade*, Tempus: Stroud, 163.

97 H. R. Tawney and E. Power (1924), *Tudor Economic Documents* II, 27.

98 D. Grummitt (2008), *The Calais Garrison; War and Military Service in England, 1436-1558*, Woodbridge: Boydell, 151.

the garrison's wages were in arrears and the company was forced to borrow money to cover them; by 1532 the staple owed the crown over £22,000. Finally in 1533–1535 the staple was suspended with the export of wool stopped; trade only resumed in 1535 under a new agreement with the crown.[99]

The company was relieved of a proportion of its debts while all its lands in Calais were taken back into the hands of the king with the sole exceptions of the prison and the hall in the market place. This latter had cost 20,000 marks to build and, as they said, they 'would be right sorry to sell if they were in like prosperity or wealth as their predecessors before time have been'.[100] Even the Place, the centre of their business and social lives in better times, would no longer be in their possession.

Johnson and other Staplers were able to make profits when trade picked up after the new agreement with the king. Our detailed knowledge of Johnson's activities all relates to the period after the changes made by Henry VIII in the relationship between the crown and the company. This was, however, to prove only a temporary improvement. It seems there were fundamental changes in both wool production, the way it was marketed and in the textile industry both at home and in Flanders which made it increasingly difficult for those whose main income came from the export of raw wool to trade profitably.

At home Staplers found that wool producers benefited from the increased demand from the cloth industry and were happy to sell to clothiers in relatively small parcels. This kind of trade did not involve observing any of the Staple regulations including those on the winding and packing of wool. Transport costs were also much lower. Thus broggers buying wool for the cloth trade could offer higher prices to producers since their overhead were lower. As the range of cloths of different weights and qualities made in England increased,[101] clothiers were also happy to buy lower quality wools. The Staplers, concentrating on the trade in high quality expensive wool which were still profitable despite the amount of duty it bore, were not much interested in these.

Perhaps perversely, it seems that sheep raised on enclosed pastures on a better diet produced wool with a longer staple. This was well suited to the cloth-making techniques of the so-called 'new draperies'; these were much less expensive than the thick heavy broadcloth which had dominated the market in earlier times. This could only be made of short staple wool. In the Low Countries the range of cloths made had also expanded; the range of wools used was similarly wider. In Diksmuide their *grooten claus* around 1523–1546 was made of a mixture of Spanish, English, Scottish, Rhenish and Flemish wools. The *small double say* made at Houndschoote in the 1570s required Flemish, Scottish, Friesian and Kempen wool.

---

99 *Ibid.*, 150–4.

100 *Letters and Papers, Foreign and Domestic of the reign of Henry VIII, 1509–1547*, ix, A18.

101 Straits, Welsh straits, kerseys, coloured kerseys, white kerseys and freize were all being exported in the fifteenth and early sixteenth centuries. J. Oldland (2010), 'The variety and quality of English woollen cloth exported in the late Middle Ages.' *Journal of European Economic History* 39, table 7, 211–51.

The Staplers had always had to compete with the coarse wool from the Borders and Scotland which was exported from Newcastle upon Tyne to the Low Countries without having to go through the Calais Staple but this was in effect aimed at a different market from the high quality wool they specialised in. The extent of the competition from Spanish wool, acknowledged as being of a quality comparable to that of much of the best English produce, was a relatively new factor and one of increasing importance. Until the 1550s or so, the very best wool from England was that required by the regulations of many guilds producing luxury cloth in the Low Countries. From the second half of the century cloth like Haubourdin *oultrefin* was two-thirds Spanish wool to one-third English while the Bruges *dobbel leeuven* was made entirely of Spanish merino wool at least from around 1530.[102] The simple market of the fourteenth century dominated by English produce was no more.

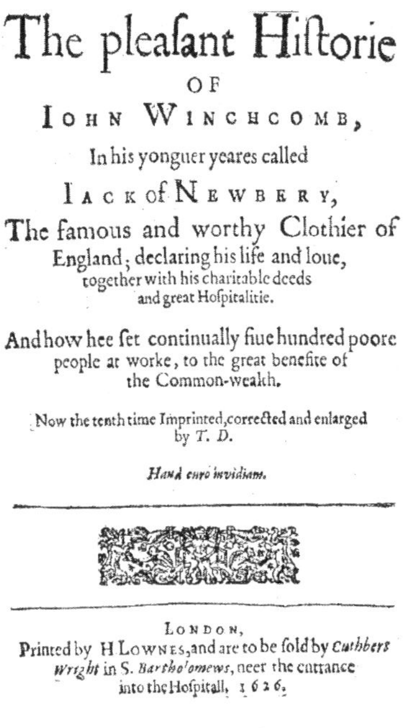

The pleasant Historie
OF
IOHN WINCHCOMB,
In his yonguer yeares called
IACK of NEWBERY,
The famous and worthy Clothier of England; declaring his life and loue, together with his charitable deeds and great Hospitalitie.

And how hee set continually fiue hundred poore people at worke, to the great benefite of the Common-wealth.

Now the tenth time Imprinted, corrected and enlarged by T. D.

Hand curo inuidiam.

LONDON,
Printed by H Lownes, and are to be sold by *Cuthbers Wright* in S. *Bartholomews*, neer the entrance into the Hospitall, 1 6 2 6.

Figure 27. Title page of Jack of Newbury alias John of Winchcomb *(see below)*

The wool trade in England was, by the middle of the sixteenth century, more reliant on the health of cloth manufacturing in England itself than the export trade in raw wool. External factors over which a wool merchant had little control, the political situation, the fluctuations in the exchange value of European currencies, competition from Spanish wools, rising wool prices whether real or inflationary, changes in fashion and in agricultural practices all influenced the ease with which a profit might be made. Some by lucky chance or skill managed to trade successfully. Others like Johnson failed in business and were forced into the difficult life of a bankrupt. It is not surprising that most of the folk heroes of the trade in English woollens in the sixteenth century were in fact clothiers, not wool merchants. Thomas Deloney's *The pleasant History of John Winchcombe in his younger yeares called Jack of Newbery,* first published in 1597 credited the character with many charitable acts andclaimed 'hee set five hundred poore people at worke to the great benefit of the common-wealth'.[103] The book went through no fewer than 16 editions by 1700. Nevertheless the belief in the superiority of English wool and the value and political importance of trade in this commodity

---

102 J. Munro (2003), 'Medieval woollens: textiles, textile technology, and industrial organisation c.800–1500', in D. Jenkins ed. *The Cambridge History of Western Textiles*, I, Cambridge: Cambridge University Press, 181–227, table 5.8 Composition of selected textiles.

103 Title page of Thomas Deloney, *The pleasant History of John Winchcombe in his younger yeares called Jack of Newbery,* consulted online 3/7/2016.

Figure 28. The Woolsack, the House of Lords; by tradition the seat of the Lord Chancellor (photo: Alex Ramsey, Alamy Stock Photo)

was deeply rooted. The author of *The Libelle of Englyshe Polycye* in the early fifteenth century had written:

> For Spayne and Flaundres is as yche othere brrothere
> And nethere may lyve wythowghten othere
> they may not lyven to mayntene there degrees
> Wythoughten oure Englysshe commodytees
> Wolle and tynne, for the wolle of Englonde
> Susteynth the comons Flemmynges I understonde.
> Thane, yf Englonde wolde hys wollw restreyne
> Frome Flaundres of nede muste wyth us have pease
> or ellis he is distroyde wythoughten lees.[104]

William Camden in his *Britannia* (published in 1607) still asserted that the 'Lemster Ore', wool from the Welsh marches, was acknowledged as the best in Europe.[105] The symbolism of the woolsack in the House of Lords remained powerful even as the export trade in wool continued its decline. The role played by politics in the heyday of the wool trade will be examined in the third part of this book with a final assessment of the benefits financial and otherwise brought to England by trade in this ubiquitous and useful commodity.

---

104 Sir George Warner ed. (1926), *The Libelle of Englyshe Polycye*, Oxford: Clarendon Press, lines 86–95.

105 William Camden (1607), *Britannia*, facsimile edition, 1970, Hildesheim and New York: Georg Olms, 472.

Part 3

The Crown and the Wool Trade

Chapter 7

The Crown's Attitude to Trade

In parts one and two we have looked at how wool was produced and traded in our period. In the view of many, both contemporaries and later writers, this trade was one of the glories of the kingdom. The Commons in the fourteenth century saw wool as England's treasure. John Lydgate, in the first half of the fifteenth century, called wool England's 'chief richesse'. In her Ford lectures in 1939 Eileen Power considering the development of the medieval economy as a whole stated that, 'in so far as there were elements of commercial and financial capitalism in medieval England they developed or failed to develop with the progress of the wool trade and the changes in its organisation.'[1] Derek Hurst in 2005 saw wool as 'a major economic asset and a particularly potent symbol of English power by the fourteenth century'.[2] Christopher Dyer in 2012, pointed out that 'the wool money funded every part of the commonwealth,' benefitting peasant producers, landlords, the church, merchants and industrialists.[3]

It is less easy to discover any clear statement of how the wool trade and its economic importance were regarded by the crown. Clear statements on any economic topic by a medieval monarch or his advisers are very rare. It is also difficult to deduce the existence of any kind of coherent attitude to the importance of trade from the actions of the crown or its advisers. It seems that, at least until the end of the fifteenth century, it was usually seen as a possible source of revenue. In addition at times the terms of trade might also be manipulated to put pressure on foreign rulers. Trade and the economy in general only become of greater concern in the mid-sixteenth century.

The authors of *Mirrors for Princes*, describing the ideal ruler, his character and his responsibilities, did not say much if anything about concerns of this kind.[4] Unusually,

---

1 E. Power (1941), *The Wool Trade in English Medieval History*, Oxford: Oxford University Press, 109.

2 D. Hurst (2005), *Sheep in the Cotswolds: the Medieval Wool Trade*, Stroud: Tempus, 15.

3 C. Dyer (2012), *A Country Merchant 1495–1520, Trading and Farming in the End of the Middle Ages*, Oxford: Oxford University Press, 223.

4 Giles of Rome whose *De Regimine principum* was the most influential of these manuals for rulers makes no mention of economic matters beyond the governance of the royal household. Walter Ullman's (1965) *Medieval Political Thought* (Harmondsworth: Penguin) also does not discuss this aspect of the theory of royal governance.

Sir John Fortescue, in his development of his idea of the way the governance of England was both 'political' (involving an element of consent by the people) and 'royal' (in the hands of a monarch), devotes some time to a ruler's need for adequate financial resources. In his view it is the bounden duty of a king to defend his realm against its enemies and also to dispense justice to his people. If he is poor a monarch will become entangled in borrowing and the payment of interest (he suggests he will lose 25 or 20% of his revenues in this way) and thus will become ever more indebted, forced to use assignments on future revenue to pay his creditors and finally compelled by sheer necessity into acts of tyranny.[5]

A monarch must have access to sufficient resources in order to perform his role both as defender of his realm and people and as the source of justice.

In Fortescue's analysis the king's expenses were divided into 'ordinary' and 'extraordinary' charges. The ordinary charges were mainly categorised as those of his Household and Wardrobe, that is, the everyday expenditure necessary to administer the kingdom and maintain his status. These charges also included the wages and fees of his servants and officers. Perhaps surprisingly to modern eyes, the costs of the king's building works, the expenses of the defence of the insecure border with Scotland and of the garrison of Calais were also included in this category. All could be estimated and allowed for on an annual basis and, therefore, should be met from the 'king's livelihood', that is the income produced by his lands and all the charges and fees he could collect by his royal prerogative. The 'extraordinary' charges were those which could not be adequately budgeted for in advance (though Fortescue hoped it should be possible to prevent them being 'excessively exorbitant'). These included the occasional need to send ambassadors to foreign courts, special rewards for good service, extra expenses with regard to new buildings and the like, but the heaviest expenditure of this type would be that pertaining to war. Fortescue argued that the people of England were obliged to support the monarch's need for resources to cover these expenses. He went on to argue that it was in the king's best interests that the commons, the people at large, should be rich; it was this which allowed them, through the medium of Parliament, to grant the king subsidies and taxes when these were needed for the defence of the realm. He contrasted this situation with that he claimed existed in France where the people were so impoverished that they would grant nothing to their king of their own free will.[6] He did not identify the source of the alleged wealth of England but the role of trade was mentioned in his assertion that the need to keep the sea was directly provided for by the proceeds of tunnage and poundage. The claim that a king should 'live of his own' in time of peace was not new.

---

5 S. Lockwood, ed. (1997), *Sir John Fortescue, On the Laws and Governance of England,* Cambridge: Cambridge University Press, 92–3.

6 *Ibid.* 85–7, 95–100, 110.

Edward IV had announced his intention to do the same in the parliament of 1467.[7] It was, however, unusual to state so clearly that while a monarch should be adequately funded, there was no benefit to him in reducing his people to penury.

The relevance of this argument to the taxation of the wool trade is clear. We need to examine the role the funds which were generated by the trade in wool (and the closely linked trade in woollen cloth) played in the finances of the English crown in this period. We need to have some understanding of how the English crown benefited from this source of wealth and also whether these trades were also actively encouraged or managed by the crown. The most direct way of raising money from these trades was by customs duties, which have already been discussed when looking at the operation of the trade itself. Was the ability to tap the wealth of merchants and graziers in this way of great importance to royal finances? Did access to this source of money allow England, a relatively small state much less populous than its closest neighbour France, to exert power and influence out of proportion to its size? Were its rulers as a consequence able to cut something of a dash on the European stage because of this source of wealth? In summary was the ability to tap the wealth generated by the wool trade crucial to the success of policies followed by the rulers of England in our period? Certainly by the beginning of the sixteenth century, in the view of Dyer, 'if there was a state policy on the economy it was closely associated with the need to protect and expand the crown's revenues.'[8]

---

7 Parliament Roll V in A. R. Myers, ed. (1969), *English Historical Documents 1327–1485,* London: Eyre and Spottiswoode, 525.

8 C. Dyer (2012), *A Country Merchant,* 13.

Chapter 8

The Wool Trade and Royal Finances

Customs duties and the crown. The rates of the customs and subsidies

By the reign of Henry V, Gerald Harriss was able to declare with confidence that customs duties and subsidies especially those on wool were 'far more lucrative then the hereditary crown revenues ... These were the bedrock of royal finance and upon their maintenance at a high level depended the prosecution of the war'.[1] The first successful money-raising endeavour on behalf of the crown based on the value of wool was the contribution to the ransom of Richard I of the wool clip of the leading religious houses engaged in wool production. This was followed by short-lived duties on both export and imports imposed by John between 1203 and c.1207–1210 and by Edward acting for his father Henry III in 1266.[2]

The national system, which lasted till the early seventeenth century, of a tax or duty on exports was set up by Edward I, not long after his accession to the throne in 1275. These duties have already been discussed in some detail, but the structure of the system of dues and the rates payable are repeated here in brief for convenience. The 'ancient custom' as it was eventually called was payable by all merchants whether denizen or alien and covered wool, woolfells and hides. The various changes and additions to the duties, and the added burden of so-called subsidies produced, by the end of the fourteenth century, a system which consisted of the ancient custom of 6s 8d per woolsack paid by all exporters, an additional 3s 4d paid only by aliens from 1303, together with extra sums by way of subsidy. This resulted in a total of around 40–45s per sack for denizens. Aliens paid more with their extra payments varying considerably from time to time. For this group the total of combined payments reached 110s per sack in 1450–1460 and the same level for a short period in the 1470s before settling at 76s 8d from 1471. Duties paid by alien merchants had totalled the more reasonable sum of around 60–65s from the 1340s to the end of the 1460s. For cloth exports, a new duty set at 1s 2d per cloth of assize (a standard measurement) without grain (a very expensive red dye) for denizens and 1s 9d for aliens was introduced in 1347. Aliens also paid the small duty of 1s per cloth introduced in 1303.

---

1 G. L. Harriss (1993), 'Financial policy' in G. L. Harriss ed., *Henry V: the Practice of Kingship*, Stroud: Alan Sutton, 172–3.

2 N. S. B. Gras (1918), *The Early English Customs System*, Cambridge, MA: Harvard University Press, 49–53.

Tunnage and poundage, as part of a separate system of *ad valorem* duties, imposed only occasionally until the later years of the reign of Richard II, were also paid on exports from 1340. Wool was included at first but, after 1371, this duty was applied only to general merchandise including cloth and wine. By the fifteenth century these duties had become permanent and were granted to the king at the beginning of his reign. The duty then consisted of a rate of 6d–1s in the pound on merchandise and 2–3s per tun for wine. The parliamentary grants of this duty always made mention of the fact that the money raised was intended to be used either to provide ships for the protection of trade or more generally for the 'keeping of the seas'.[3] It has been calculated that, with some rough estimate of the *ad valorem duties* where applicable, the combined duties and subsidies amounted to around 2–3% of the value of cloth exported for English merchants and around 4.5–6% for alien merchants. For wool exporters duties totalled about 4% for English merchants and 6% for aliens from 1303 till the later 1340s. After these changes, wool merchants were liable for duties of around 25% of the value of their exports with aliens' charges going as high as 33%.[4]

The value to the crown

The yield of these duties very quickly became a substantial proportion of royal revenues. One obvious advantage, of course was that while many of the fee farms and proceeds from the royal demesne and other elements in the king's customary revenue were fixed, the returns from the customs duties were elastic and closely related to the prosperity of the wool and other trades. A document from 1324 estimated royal income from the customary shire revenues, fee farms and the like at £11,742 12 s 3d. Receipts from Gascony (largely the duties on wine exported) totalled £13,000. The receipts from customs duties including some small sums from sources such as mines in Devonshire and fines and amercements in the law courts came to nearly £19,500.[5] Another document from 37 Edward III (1363) recording all the money received at the exchequer from 22 February till 16 May notes that the customs received from all the ports in England including an assignment for £723 0s 1½d from Berwick came to £6962 16s 8½d. This was very nearly one-third of the total of just over £21,000 which included some large payments of the outstanding ransoms of those captured at the battle of Poitiers.[6] An account for the whole of the same year put the revenues from the customs at 57,310 marks (£38,206 13s 4d) of which 10,400 marks (£6933 6s 8d) were assigned to the support of the queen. The total available to the king himself (46,910

3 W. M. Ormrod (2009), 'The origins of tunnage and poundage: Parliament and the estate of merchants in the 14th century', *Parliamentary History* 28.2, 209–27.

4 E. M. Carus-Wilson and O. Coleman (1963), *England's Export Trade 1275–1547*, Oxford: Clarendon Press, 22–3.

5 G. L. Harriss (1975), *King, Parliament and Public Finance in Medieval England to 1360*, Oxford: Oxford University Press, appendix B 523.

6 *Ibid.*, 527.

marks, £31,273, 6s 8d) was more than 80% of the total income from all sources except direct taxes of 53,294 marks (£35,529 17s 1d).[7] A detailed estimate of all sources of royal income made by Ralph, Lord Cromwell, the Treasurer of England in 1433, set out calculations that showed that the customs and subsidies on trade including tunnage and poundage had been worth an average of £30,722 5s 7d in the years 1430–1433, a decline from the amounts raised (not including tunnage and poundage) in 1363.

In the early 1430s these duties were, nevertheless, by far the largest single source of income for the crown which at the time faced a large deficit and many debts. It should also be remembered that the other major source of revenue, in addition to the king's so-called livelihood, direct taxation, had become ossified and somewhat ineffective as a way of raising money for the crown in emergencies. This impost was the tax on moveable property generally known as a 'fifteenth and tenth'. After 1332 no new assessments of an individual's chattels for this tax were carried out. All such subsidies collected for the remainder of the fourteenth and the whole fifteenth centuries were based on quotas set for each locality in 1334. These quotas took little account of the way the distribution of wealth in the country changed over the years. In 1334 when the first collections on the quota system were made it was expected that around £37,000 would be raised. In 1433 the amount anticipated was reduced by £4000 in order to relieve poverty-stricken towns of some of their burden; this deduction was increased to £6000 in 1446 by which time the tax was expected to raise only £31,000. A dramatic contrast with these figures is provided by some figures for the total revenue received by the exchequer from the taxation of overseas trade in the years 1351–1376. This came to £1,750,000; this exceeded the total from all direct taxation levied on both the laity and the clergy for the entire reign.[8] It is possible to interpret the efforts of monarchs in the fifteenth century to introduce new forms of subsidy, despite the hostility of parliaments to such innovations, as attempts to establish some new form of direct taxation which would be more productive from the crown's point of view and more closely related to the wealth of individuals.[9]

This became increasingly necessary as the revenue collected from the duties on wool continued to decline. A petition to parliament in early 1449 explained the situation. In the reign of Edward III it was claimed in respect of the total revenue raised from the customs that,

'it is of recorde in the kyngs eschequer ... in sum yere of his reigne lxviii m li. and more and so continued many yeres at whiche tyme grete riches come in to this reaume of Englond'.

---

7 A. R. Myers, ed. (1969), *English Historical Documents 1327–1485*, London: Eyre and Spottiswoode, 512–13.

8 W. M. Ormrod (2000), *The Reign of Edward III*, Stroud: Tempus, 169.

9 P. E. Soas (2006), 'Direct taxation in England: the experimental subsidies of the fifteenth century,' *Bulletin for International Taxation* 60.4, 157–76.

At the present time, however,

> 'the customes and subsidies of the merchandise repairing to the foresaid staple of Calais passe not yerely xii m li which is but litell in comparison to what they have be before tyme'.[10]

The petition was presented by the Company of the Staple, which had of course its own interests to protect and that of its members. The fall in the revenue from the wool customs was, however, real and presented many problems for the crown. The expedient of borrowing money was, of course, one route to take. Another was the whole system of the operation of the staple at Calais and its importance for royal finances in the fifteenth century which will be considered below.

The role of loans

Apart from the amount of money which could be raised directly from duties and taxes on trade (principally of course the export of wool), this source of fluid and elastic revenue had another notable benefit for the crown. It could be used to provide the collateral for loans which were essential to the financing of any military expeditions. Fortescue railed at this aspect of royal financial policy, as we have seen, but in many ways, the ability to raise loans and pay the resulting interest by assignment on future royal revenue was a necessary aspect of the rule of a successful monarch. It can be argued that trouble only loomed when loans increased too rapidly beyond the ability of the crown to service them easily, something which led to the rapid collapse of royal credit.

The first group to become, in effect, the bankers and financiers of the English Crown were Italian merchants who had the necessary capital themselves and also close connections with other banking and merchant houses which could provide access to extra funds when required, much in the way modern inter-bank loans are organised. The Riccardi of Lucca originally became involved with lending money to Edward I before his departure on crusade in 1271–1272 and his accession to the throne. Once Edward became king, after the establishment of the ancient custom in 1275, the relationship between the king and the Riccardi has been likened to a modern current account with a large overdraft facility.[11] In the whole period 1272–1294 this Italian banking house advanced over £500,000 to the king, an average of around £23,000 per

---

10 'Henry VI: February 1449', in *Parliament Rolls of Medieval England,* ed. Chris Given-Wilson, Paul Brand, Seymour Phillips, Mark Ormrod, Geoffrey Martin, Anne Curry and Rosemary Horrox (Woodbridge, 2005), British History Online http://www.british-history.ac.uk/no-series/parliament-rolls-medieval/february-1449 item 19 Staple of Calais [accessed 14 November 2017].

11 A. R. Bell, C. Brooks and T. K. Moore (2009), 'Interest in medieval accounts: examples from England 1272–1340, *History* 94, 416.

year. Most of the loans were repaid relatively quickly by way of the export of wool which could be sold easily and profitably in Italian cloth-making cities and which got round the great difficulties which would have attended acquiring and transporting the necessary amount of bullion. By 1294, however, the Riccardi were no longer able to cope simultaneously with demands for loans from Edward I who needed to finance military campaigns in Scotland and Gascony, and from the papacy, another major creditor. This merchant house was in fact bankrupted by these demands. The financial crisis of 1297 in England and the imposition of the infamous *maltolt* lay behind the failure of the Riccardi bank.[12] In this year Edward was faced with Wallace's rebellion in Scotland and the need to campaign in Flanders; the need for extra funds was acute. The extra duty on wool, despite the uproar it created, clearly seemed to his financial advisers to be the only way to relieve his difficulties.

The crown did not, however, abandon Italian merchant houses as the source of loans. Successive Italian companies took on the business, the Frescobaldi from 1299–1311 took over this business from the Riccardi, followed by the Bardi and Peruzzi from 1311 to 1341. All were from Florence with wealth ultimately derived from success in the manufacture and sale of woollen cloth. Their loans and the repayment of the same operated in very much the same way as that of the Riccardi in previous years. With the outbreak of the Hundred Years War the position of those lending money to the crown became more uncertain as the king's need for increased funds to finance his military ambitions in France and Flanders grew. English merchants, notably men like William de la Pole and Walter Cheriton, were drawn into the business of providing loans to the king as well as his long-established alien financiers. The mixture of direct royal intervention in the wool trade via such expedients as the operation of the so-called English Wool Company with repeated demands for subsidies in addition to the ancient and new customs, already discussed, were a testimony to the king's desperate need for money.

Throughout 1338, despite a royal ban on the export of wool by most merchants in place for much of the year, the agents of the Bardi and the Peruzzi were trying to ship wool from England to their Italian customers by sea if possible. At the same time the king's purveyors were seizing wool stocks on behalf of the king to settle other debts. The wool owned by the Bardi (which was the means by which loans already made were being repaid) was loaded in Spanish and Gascon ships, to conceal the fact that exports were continuing in the face of the royal ban. The plan was to transport the wool to Bordeaux and then to arrange onward transport by land but, even there, royal purveyors got their hands on it. Despite these and other similar problems both companies managed to deliver some wool to their customers and thus

12 A. R. Bell, C. Brooks and T. K. Moore (2011), 'Credit finance in thirteenth century England: the Riccardi of Lucca and Edward I 1272–94,' in J. Burton *et al.* eds *Thirteenth Century England XIII,* Woodbridge: Boydell, 101–16.

receive payment.[13] It was not enough. During 1341–1342 the major Italian merchant houses and bankers and other smaller companies which had also been drawn into the business of royal loans collapsed into bankruptcy. The credit of the English Crown had been almost extinguished by the various attempts to raise money from the wool trade whether by direct intervention in the market or by the imposition of extra subsidies and other expedients.

Although usury was outlawed both by the church as a sin and the state as a crime, various methods had been developed by the sophisticated bankers of the later medieval period to benefit from what amounted to interest payments on loans. Using the traces left by these methods in the records, it has been calculated that until the crisis of 1294, when the Riccardi were unable to satisfy Edward I's demand for loans for war expenses, this bank usually charged the king a rate of around 15%. When he could no longer rely on the Riccardi, Edward I probably had no choice but to pay an annualised rate of around 33% for a loan from another group of merchants from Asti in 1297. Even this rate was low compared to the enormous rate of 150% per annum paid for a loan from one Albisso Fifanti at much the same time.[14] The circumstances in which the *maltolt* was imposed and the urgency with which the assembly of merchants called at this time was pressed to agree to this imposition are made plain by this information. Looking in detail at loans to Edward III in 1328–1331 by the Bardi their overall profit has been calculated at around 26%. The annualised rate of interest would have been rather less.

In the difficult period of 1338–1340, discussed above, when Edward III was offering payments to his continental allies as well as facing the expenses of his own forces, one small loan of £6000 from a group of merchants from Malines in 1338 was repaid in 1341 by the payment of £12,000; thus the repayment appeared to be double that of the loan. If, however, this is treated as an annualised rate of interest it amounts to 41.4% per annum, still about three times the rate charged to Edward III before the outbreak of hostilities.[15] If this was how interest rates normally reacted to the need for emergency funds in a war situation it is no wonder that Fortescue saw royal indebtedness as leading straight to royal poverty. Assignments to debtors were in danger of eating up almost all royal revenue, especially that from a liquid source like the customs.

The failure of the Italian merchant houses' banking business in 1341 did not of course remove the royal need for loans particularly in time of war. Edward III and his successors had to turn to their own subjects rather than tap the resources of alien merchants for money for this purpose. The urgent need for funds also lay behind the many changes in the customs regime, particularly with regard to wool with the restrictions on trade and exports and the imposition of increased subsidies which we

---

13 T. H. Lloyd (1977), *The English Wool Trade in the Middle Ages,* Cambridge: Cambridge University Press, 185–9.

14 A. R. Bell, C. Brooks and T. K. Moore (2009), 'Interest in medieval accounts', 416–18, 426.

15 *Ibid.,* 418–19.

have already discussed. One consequence of these attempts to extract as much money as possible largely from the wool trade was the emergence of a group of the wealthiest merchants, mostly London-based, who had considerable influence with the king. To some extent they were able to manipulate royal policy to their own advantage, something which incurred the lasting hostility of the wider merchant community. This happened with the affair of the English Wool Company and the Dordrecht bonds. William de la Pole and his colleague Reginald Conduit did not suffer personally from the failure of this scheme which ruined other traders in wool. De la Pole regained royal favour in 1343 and two years later, with Thomas Melchbourn and others, had agreed to farm the wool customs for £50,000 per annum with any further profits available for loans to the king.[16] In fact from 1343 to 1351 various syndicates of the most prominent wool merchants loaned the king a total of £369,000.

The political turmoil in the last years of the reign of Edward III was at least in part due to the resentment of the apparent power of prominent merchants and the way this was perceived to work to the detriment of wool producers and traders outside the 'magic circle' of the monopolists. Nevertheless the wealth generated by the wool trade was an essential factor in the ability of the English Crown to wage war. It is very possible that English kings over-estimated the ease with which large sums could be wrung out of both producers and traders in this commodity. It is also the case that the willingness of the community to support royal wars and their costs declined swiftly if the wars ended in defeat or stalemate. Furthermore those who traded in raw wool bore a much heavier burden of taxes and suffered more from royal interference in the terms of trade than the relatively lightly taxed and much less closely regulated dealers in cloth.

Despite all the political and financial difficulties for the kings of the last part of the fourteenth century, it has been pointed out that in the hands of an intelligent, forceful and well-served monarch the fiscal system of England could successfully support a lengthy military campaign in France. Both Christopher Allmand and Mark Ormrod have shown how this was done in the reign of Henry V. Both pointed out the importance of the indirect taxation of the trade in wool in this process. Allmand explained how Henry was able to get the whole-hearted support of Parliament, especially in the atmosphere of euphoria existing in the months after his victory at Agincourt. The parliament of November 1415 granted the king the subsidies on the export trade for his life 'to dispose of the proceeds at his gracious will and discretion'.[17] Ormrod analysed the income stream accruing to the crown of both direct and indirect taxes in the whole of Henry's reign. In 1413–1420, while the war in France was at its height, the yield of direct taxes was larger than that of the indirect impositions. However while the total burden of direct taxes varied from £97,100 in 1416 to nothing in 1420 that of the indirect taxes remained remarkably steady throughout the reign

---

16 T. H. Lloyd (1977), *The English Wool Trade*, 197–9.
17 C. Allmand (1992), *Henry V*, London: Methuen, 391.

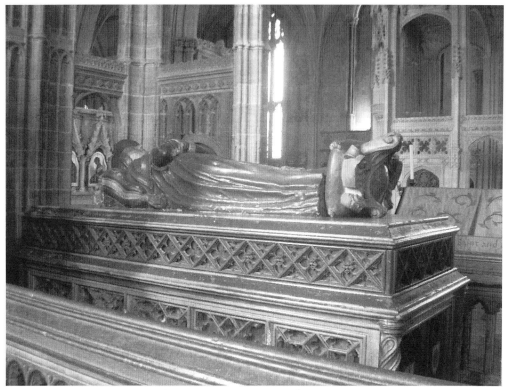

Figure 29. Tomb of Cardinal Beaufort, Winchester Cathedral (photo: P.J.P. O'Sullivan, Creative Commons CC BY-SA 3.0)

averaging around £50,000 a year. This was despite the inevitable disruption caused to trade by the wars, particularly in the staple town of Calais and the major wool market of the Netherlands.

There is little doubt that, just as Henry V and his advisors made strenuous efforts to collect the whole amount due in direct taxation, so a similar attitude was taken to the collection of the customs. The king ordered the provision of facilities for the packing and weighing of wool in all exporting ports, outlawing the practice of this occurring on a merchant's premises. Searchers in the ports were also appointed to seek out any uncustomed wool going for export. A memorandum presented to the Privy Council in May 1421 revealed the success of this policy. The duties on trade, of which the majority was raised from wool, brought in over £40,000 for the crown at a cost of only £547 in fees to officials.[18] The king also actively promoted the interests of wool merchants and their customers in his negotiations for the all-important alliance with Duke John the Fearless of Burgundy against Charles VI of France. Truces with

---

18 N. H. Nicolas ed., (1834–37), *Proceedings and Ordinances of the Privy Council 2*, London: Eyre and Spottiswode, 312–14.

Burgundy were carefully maintained in the period 1417–1419 while one purpose of the *Statute of Truces* of 1414 was to combat the number of English attacks on Flemish shipping in the Channel, much of it engaged in the wool and cloth trades. In particular the restitution of cargoes seized in these attacks was energetically enforced. Greater security for trading vessels in the Channel was a boon for both English and Flemish merchants and was further increased following successful naval actions against the Spanish and Genoese ships in the pay of France.

Henry could not, of course, entirely dispense with loans but his most notable creditor was not a merchant but his cousin, the enormously wealthy Cardinal Beaufort, Bishop of Winchester. It has been suggested that loans made before 1421 were intended to signal Beaufort's support of the Lancastrians and particularly the policy of allying with Burgundy. (Beaufort was concerned to push this policy as part of a feud in the royal council with Henry V's brother, Humphrey Duke of Gloucester.) His final loan to Henry V in 1421 of the enormous sum of £17,666 13s 4d also had a political element related to his need to recover the favour of the king. This had been forfeited when Beaufort had accepted the status of Cardinal from Pope Martin V against Henry's wishes.[19] Both this and the loan of £14,000 provided in June 1417 for the campaign which would lead to the conquest of Normandy were secured against all future customs in Southampton. Virtually all the wool exported by Italian merchants via the Straits of Morocco (that is, directly by sea to Italy not through the staple at Calais) went through this port. More than a third of the first loan was repaid within a year and the remainder in 1424–1425. Repayments of the second larger sum were extended to the customs of all ports in November 1422 and the loan was repaid in full in 1423–1424.[20]

After Henry V's death, however, the financial position of the crown worsened until by 1449 it was bankrupt. The generally weak and indecisive rule of Henry VI, and defeat in France against the re-invigorated forces of Charles VII, share some of the blame for this. Another important factor was that the revenue for the custom duties and subsidies which had provided the security for so many loans in the past began to fall steadily. By 1433, when the Treasurer Lord Cromwell produced his analysis of the resources and the expenses of the crown, the total received from all duties on trade was 20% less than it had been 10 years earlier. After 1425, Beaufort's frequent loans to the crown (there were no fewer than 18 between September 1429 and February 1436) were all to be repaid from direct taxation with, on occasion, items from the crown jewels pledged to him to provider added security for his loans. His last large loan of two tranches of £10,000 each in April and June 1443 was to be repaid from all the customs in Southampton and everything paid in London by Italian merchants.[21] On

---

19 C. Allmand (1992), *op. cit.*, 161, 341–3.

20 G. L. Harriss (1988), *Cardinal Beaufort: a Study of Lancastrian Ascendancy and Decline,* Oxford: Clarendon Press, appendix 1, 401–2.

21 *Ibid.,* 402–5.

this occasion, for added security, the collectors were bound by indentures to make the repayments in gold; no reliance could be placed on assignments to future revenues which might or might not materialise. The sources of the cardinal's wealth cannot be precisely identified. One suggestion made at the time (by the Duke of Gloucester, his rival for control of the King's Council) was that he was 'the chief merchant of wolles in youre lande'. This is hard to substantiate from the available evidence. He does not appear personally in the customs account as exporting large amounts of wool on his own account. It is possible that he used London merchants as his factors or some special arrangement with Italians resident in London. He also held at least four special licences to export wool from Southampton without going via the staple but his financial resources were far larger than the profits on deals of this kind.[22]

Apart from Cardinal Beaufort, the increasing need for loans to finance expeditions to France or to provide for the defence of the realm led to appeals to other possible sources of funds. The Company of the Staple, which, of course, had a direct interest in the defence of Calais and the payment of its garrison, was prepared to lend but on a much smaller scale than Beaufort. In 1436, when Burgundy directly threatened Calais and laid siege to the town, the Staplers lent £5393 and the city of London 5000 marks (£3333 6s 8d).[23] It had always been clear that the obligation on the subjects of the king to support the needs of the crown in an emergency was accepted but it was also evident that money was much easier to obtain if military success could be expected. The most important condition was perhaps that it should be fairly certain that the promises of repayment would be kept within a reasonable time frame. By the 1440s and 1450s neither military success nor rapid repayment were likely. By 1453 Calais and the Pale were the only places in former French territory still under English rule while in 1449 Parliament refused to authorise any further appeals for loans since the possibility of repayment could not be guaranteed.

In this situation it is easy to understand why Fortescue was so hostile to the whole system of loans to the crown. Wealthy individuals like Beaufort had wielded too much power. Assignments on the most reliable source of income particularly the customs revenue had run out of control. The merchants involved in overseas trade, particularly of course, that in wool, suffered in this situation whether or not they were personally involved in loans to the crown. It was self-evident that they needed the protection of the crown to trade successfully. The use of customs duties of all kinds as a major source of revenue together with other aspects of the regulation of the wool trade made the business of the merchant onerous and threatened the possibility of making a profit. The way these difficulties were handled by both crown and merchants can be seen in the development of the Company of the Staple, and its operation and responsibilities in the fifteenth century.

---

22 *Ibid.*, 412–3.
23 R. A. Griffiths (1998), *The Reign of King Henry VI,* Stroud: Sutton, 121, 390–4.

Chapter 9

The Crown and the Company of the Staple, 1399–1558

Once it became clear that the policy of establishing a staple town for the wool trade was unlikely to change in the foreseeable future many wool merchants must have been greatly relieved. The constant changes of the previous half century made for considerable difficulties when so many aspects of commerce depended on personal contacts and trust between trading partners. From the point of view of the crown, with the company established, most contacts and dealings with this important source of revenue would be concentrated either in Calais or in London with a relatively small group of merchants. Moreover, English law and practice would apply to both ends of the trade and even more importantly, since the value of Calais to the crown did not only consist in its value as a market but also in its value as a military base and a foothold in a strategic position between the lands of Burgundy and France, traders would, willy-nilly, have to fall in with crown policy with regard to their customers' home states, mainly of course the various counties of the Netherlands. A period of stability might be expected in which both the Staplers and the crown would prosper.

In many respects this happy outcome came to pass. Wool exports of which the great majority went through the staple were relatively stable from c.1399 to 1420, averaging around 13,000 to 15,500 sacks a year. There were, however, two factors which led inexorably to the Staplers becoming ever more entangled in the intricacies of royal finance. The first was the importance of the wool trade through Calais in the implementation of the crown's bullionist policies. A mint had existed in Calais since 1363 but its importance increased greatly when the staple permanently settled in the town. From the foundation of the mint its purpose had been to enforce the royal order that a merchant should deposit 2 marks-worth (26s 8d) of bullion at the mint for every woolsack he had sold. It was the firm belief of rulers that gold and silver, whether coined or not, constituted the wealth of a nation or of an individual. If bullion flowed out of a country it was made poorer; or to use the modern terms there was an adverse balance of payments. In the periods in the fourteenth century when wool was bought and sold at 'home' staples (those based in England itself) the 'bullion' obligation was not an issue since sales took place in English currency and, if cash was used, it was the responsibility of the foreign buyer to obtain English coins. When

Figure 30. Groat (8d piece) struck at the Calais Mint 1427-1430 (photo: Portable Antiquities Scheme/BM collection, Creative Commons CC 2.0 generic)

the staple was at Calais it was English merchants who might be paid in coins from many European mints but who had the obligation to surrender at least part of this money for re-coining into English gold nobles or silver groats. The Calais mint operated initially from 1363 till 1404; at first it was very busy minting more new English coins than the mint at the Tower of London in some years. When it closed, the prime reason seems to have been the severe shortage of bullion in western Europe, not any change in royal policy. Nearby mints in the Netherlands and France were also forced to cease operation at much the same time.[1]

The Calais mint re-opened in 1422, when more silver became available at least temporarily. The bullion requirement, however, became more onerous and disruptive to successful trading after 1429 when the *Bullion and Partition Ordinance* was passed by Parliament. The partition element in the ordinance related to the trading practices of the merchants of the staple. It laid down that all wool sent to the staple by any member of the Company would be graded and then pooled with all the wool of the same quality. A merchant would only be paid for his share when all the wool of that grade had been sold. The regulation disrupted trade and was gradually abandoned in the 1430s. The bullion clauses of the ordinance had a much more lasting effect. These required merchants to deposit one-third of the price of any wool sold at the mint for re-coining. The most important customers of the staplers, Flemish merchants, faced an equal reluctance on the part of their ruler, Philip the Good, Duke of Burgundy, to allow the export of bullion from his dominions. Traders faced the possibility of being searched and their money seized at Gravelines on the road to Calais while the English were also accused of seeking to impoverish the Netherlands. Tensions over this issue were in some measure responsible for the breakdown of the Anglo-Burgundian alliance in 1435–1436.[2] The question became somewhat academic by 1439 when the mint closed once more, again faced with an acute shortage of bullion in any form. It never re-opened, perhaps because more and more of the wool trade was conducted

---

1 P. Spufford (1979), 'Calais and its mint: part 1', in N. J. Mayhew, ed. *Coinage in the Low Countries (880–1500)*, Oxford: British Archaeological Report 54, 171–83.

2 T. H. Lloyd discusses the effect of the Bullion and Partition Ordinance in *The English Wool Trade in the Middle Ages* (1977), 257–68.

by credit instruments rather than specie after the 1470s. In any case, as the Cely Letters amply demonstrate, Staplers were very adept with dealing with all manner of currencies in their day-to-day calculations.[3] The belief, however, that the operation of credit instruments drained wealth out of England and that the way the Calais mint had operated was greatly to the benefit of the realm did not die. The writer of the *Treatise Concerning the Staple* in the 1530s lauded the advantages that customers paying ready money for the wool had brought the country, 'which was encrese of plenty of money to the holl welth of the reame.'[4]

The second and far more important factor which cemented the close relations between the company of the staple and the crown was the issue of how to pay for the garrison and defence of Calais itself. This was expensive and there was little chance of enough money being raised in the territory itself apart from through the wool trade. The total for the wages of the garrison alone around 1405 was £16,000 per year. This was at a time when the total income of the crown was around £52,000 per year. During the reign of Edward III, even before the Company of the Staple was finally located at Calais, a system had developed which ensured a degree of financial stability for the garrison. The greater part of the revenue from the subsidy on wool exports was reserved for this purpose. Wool merchants were permitted to pay these dues and the customs in Calais itself to the treasurer of the town, not to the collector of the customs in the port of export. This ensured that there was a good chance of there being sufficient coinage at hand in Calais itself to pay the garrison, an important consideration when a shortage of bullion was making itself felt.

Henry IV was somewhat profligate in his use of the resources of the crown probably because of the need to reward his supporters after his seizure of the crown from his cousin Richard II. Assignments on the all-important customs revenue were made with little thought of the consequences. In 1406 his indebtedness was rising so quickly that the decision was taken to put the repayment of debts, the redemption of 'bad' tallies and the costs of the royal household ahead of all other charges ignoring the reservation for the pay of the garrison of Calais. Faced with no pay, the garrison took direct action. The soldiers raided the Staplers' wool houses, took over all the stocks of wool and threatened to sell the lot for what they could get. Some of the most important merchants in the City of London, who were also members of the Company of the Staple, faced possible ruin; the king, according to one account, was reduced to panic. At a meeting with the merchants he screamed at them. '*Vos habetis aurum; et ego volo aurum; ubi est?*'[5] The soldiers had judged their action well; the wool merchants, led by Sir Richard Whittington, had little

---

3 See the transaction in TNA C47/15 f.11. S. Rose (2008), *Calais: an English Town in France 1347–1558*, Boydell: Woodbridge, 103.

4 R. H. Tawney and E. Power, eds (1924), *Tudor Economic Documents, Being Select Documents Illustrating the Economic and Social History of Tudor England*, London: University of London Historical Series, II, 90–1.

5 F. S. Haydon, ed. (1863), *Eulogium Historiarum Sive Temporis Chronicon,* London: Rolls Series, vol. iii, 411. You have gold; I want gold; where is it?

Figure 31. The Day Watch Tower at Calais (photo: author)

alternative but to grant a large loan to the crown with help from other leading men of the City including the Italian community: £16,000 was provided and the crisis resolved. The garrison's wages were paid and 'all youre soudiors that taken youre wages in youre towne of Caleys' were relieved of the 'outrage, pouverte and wrychdnes that we ben in'. The town, it was claimed in the same petition, was 'destitute and unpourveyd of stoffe and vitayle to the savegarde thereof'.[6] This petition to the crown, perhaps wisely, made no mention of the seizure of the merchants' wool.

After this incident the system of reservations from the wool subsidy was restored and worked well for the most part until the deteriorating military situation in France and the increasing chaos in the royal finances once more put pressure on the way the garrison of Calais was paid and its relationship with the wool trade. During the reign of Henry V most military activity was at some distance from the town while the crucial English alliance with the Duke of Burgundy did much to ensure its safety. Flanders and Brabant were not only Burgundian territories bordering the Pale of Calais but also the site of the vital markets for English wool in the cloth-making towns of this region. The gradual souring of the alliance in the late 1420s and early 1430s could only be bad news for the Company of the Staple. The large debts being built up by the regime of the young King Henry VI impacted directly on the town where the garrison once more mutinied in 1433. On this occasion the mutiny was forcefully put down by the Duke of Bedford.

The underlying problem of how to ensure that the garrison was adequately and timely paid without endangering the financial stability of the crown, and also ensuring the protection of the town and the all-important wool staple was, on this occasion, swept up into a tide of patriotic support in England for Calais as the Duke of Burgundy, now reconciled with the King of France, threatened to lay siege to the town.[7] The Staplers took advantage of the situation to petition the king, pointing out how they had kept to the letter of the Bullion and Partition Ordinances but others were slipping out wool from 'creeks and other secret places' without going through the staple; some bought licences to 'ship wool to Calais for their own advantage' avoiding the requirements of the ordinance. All this would lead to the destruction of the staple, the loss of the town and the damage and hindrance of the realm. Their plea was for the practice of issuing licences of this nature to be ended. The king's response was cautiously vague; he would modify the licences 'when it pleases him by the advice of his council'. A further plea that exports of wool should be confined to Calais on pain of forfeiture had a more clearly positive response.[8] Perhaps satisfied with this response loans for the defence of Calais from the Burgundians were forthcoming. Cardinal Beaufort loaned the crown nearly £20,000 between February and August 1436, to

---

6 F. C. Hingeston, ed. (1860–65), *Royal and Historical Letters During the Reign of Henry IV King of England and of France*, vol. 2, London: Rolls Series, 145–7. The original petition is Cotton MSS Caligula D iv fol. 105 badly damaged in the Cotton Library fire.

7 Details of the collapse of the alliance with Burgundy, the siege and the successful defence of the town can be found in S. Rose (2008), *Calais*, 62–71.

8 'Henry VI: Parliament of October 1435', in *Parliament Rolls of Medieval England*, Items 19 and 22.

be repaid out of the subsidy granted by parliament and the customs of London and Southampton. The Staplers and other individuals also lent a total of £4277 in 4 weeks between mid-April and mid-May 1436. Much to their relief and that of the crown the siege of Calais collapsed and the Burgundian forces retreated in July 1436.

These loans, of course, provided no long-term answer to the problem. The fact that in many cases re-payment was secured on the customs revenue brought little comfort to the lenders, since the Duke of Burgundy had closed the borders of his realms to the import of English wool or English cloth as part of his campaign against his former allies. This ban reduced the average annual export of wool to just over 5000 sacks between 1436 and 1440, just over half of the average in the previous five years. The wool trade recovered somewhat after 1439 when sales to Flemish merchants resumed but it never regained all the ground lost.[9]

A fresh crisis arose in 1449. The royal government faced defeat in both Normandy and the remaining lands of the Duchy of Aquitaine. The need for extra money was acute with Calais only one among all the urgent demands on the royal purse. The Staplers once more tried to turn this state of affairs to their advantage. Their complaint about the number of licences issued by the crown to export wool avoiding the staple or with freedom from the customs and subsidies was reiterated more forcefully. In the days of Edward III as much as £68,000 per year or more had been raised by the duties on wool. The merchants of the staple were numerous and rich while Calais and its fortifications were in good repair and the garrison paid. Now the issue of licences to avoid the staple, sometimes by those who sold wool in Brabant instead of taking it by land to Italy, and the actions of those who paid no customs having suborned the officials, had led to the customs revenue falling to £12,000 per year. As a result the nation was impoverished and the defences of Calais were in great need of repair. The issue of licences must cease and those already issued must be revoked with heavy penalties for infringement. The king accepted this petition with few exemptions. No licence would be issued from 24 June 1449 for the ensuing five years.[10]

This looked like a triumph for the Staplers who were well represented among the Commons. There was, however, as might be expected a quid pro quo for this concession by the crown. The Staplers who had continued to lend money to the crown after 1436, were expected to support further loans. A sum of around £10,700 was lent in various tranches in 1450–1451. The loans seem to have been provided in the name of the company with groups of merchants taking up shares in the total amount. These were organised on a regional basis with groups in London (headed by William Cantelowe, an alderman and mercer, knighted in 1461), Boston, Hull and Ipswich. Much of this money was repaid, if slowly and irregularly, with the crown refusing to extend the

---

9 The figures of total wool exports in these years can be found in J. H. Munro (2003), 'Medieval European woollen industries and their struggles for international markets, *c.*1000–1500', in D. Jenkins, ed. *The Cambridge History of Western Textiles*, vol. 1. Cambridge: Cambridge University Press, 301–5.

10 'Henry VI: Parliament of February 1449', in *Parliament Rolls of Medieval England*, item 19.

ban on licences beyond the end date of 1454. The situation was thrown once more into confusion by the mutiny of the garrison in the winter of 1454. As recalled by the Company of the Staple in their petition to the crown in 1527, the garrison of Calais,

> 'in a great rage and fury for want of money fell upon the stapull and closed them in a house and would not suffer them to be at large unto such tyme as they had promised to content and pay them all their said wages beign behinde and unpaide so that at length they did so to their greate damage hurt and dekay of many of the said stapulle for the tyme'.

The garrison had taken possession of the wool stored in the town and would not release the Staplers until they had agreed to sell this and use the proceeds to pay the garrison.[11] However much money had been loaned or otherwise provided in the immediate past for the soldiers' pay it had been insufficient. The wool seized seems to have been sold for over £17,000; this was an enormous sum for the Staplers to provide for what was eventually treated as yet another loan. It is no surprise that it was bitterly remembered in 1527.

These continual financial demands were not the only problems concerning their relations with the rulers of England which confronted the Company of the Staple in the 1450s. Because of the strategic position of Calais and the fact that its garrison was the only considerable body of trained and armed professional soldiers available in England, the town was perhaps inevitably drawn into the web of intrigue and rivalry that marked the outbreak of the civil wars between the Lancastrians and the Yorkists. The rivalry over the position of captain of Calais which developed between the Lancastrian Edmund Beaufort, Duke of Somerset and the Yorkist, Richard Neville, Earl of Warwick in the 1450s inevitably impinged both on the Staplers themselves and their trade. In the 10 years 1455–65 the number of woolsacks exported fell to a yearly average below 6500 including the wool exported legally by sea (via the Straits of Marrok) to Italy. Despite the changing fortunes of the parties involved in the civil war in England, Warwick managed to hang on to his position in Calais throughout 1458–60. Had the Staplers, in fact, become fervent Yorkists? It seems that most calculated that the Yorkists were more likely in the end to repay the money the company had been virtually compelled to provide for the garrison after the 1454 mutiny, since the biggest loans had been provided during the period of Yorkist ascendancy when Warwick became Captain. Many members also had strong links with the southern counties of England which supported the earl. The Staplers also approved of his adventures against corsairs in the Channel and his favouring of Burgundy, the market for both wool and cloth as an ally, rather than France. The crushing victory of the Yorkists at Towton in March 1461 over

---

11 W. I. Haward (1933), 'The financial transactions between the Lancastrian government and the merchants of the staple from 1449–1461.' In E. Power and M. M. Postan, eds. *Studies in English Trade in the Fifteenth Century,* London: Routledge, 293–320.

Henry VI and the Lancastrians ensured that in their support for the Earl of Warwick and Edward IV the Staplers had backed the winning side.[12]

Despite the victory of Edward IV the underlying problem remained of how, simultaneously, to support the wool trade and ensure a flow of welcome cash to the crown and pay for the garrison. In 1463 parliament turned once more to considering the plaints of the woolmen. A new element in the arguments put forward, however, was that the problems facing English clothiers were also articulated at the same time; the two branches of the wool trade, the export of raw wool and the export of cloth at times had common interests. The Commons petitioned for the better treatment of workers in the cloth industry and for its protection from foreign imports of cloth. As far as raw wool was concerned the Commons for the first time pointed out forcefully that exports of raw wool must not be so large as to deprive the clothiers of the wool they needed to maintain their business and the prosperity of the towns in which it was located. The monopoly of the staple at Calais was to be observed and enforced except for the poor quality northern wools exported through Newcastle.

The definitive step was taken in 1466. By this time the Staplers had lent a total of around £55,000 to Edward IV of which nearly £33,000 was outstanding. It was claimed that the king had been unable to campaign successfully in Scotland in 1464 because most of the available money had already been spent largely on the defence of Calais. A wholly new system for the way the garrison of Calais was paid and the fortifications maintained, was devised. This would, it was hoped, break the cycle of royal debts, mutinies by the garrison when unpaid and loans from the Staplers. The plan originally took the form of an indenture between the Company of the Staple and the king; this was confirmed in an agreement recorded on the Parliament Roll in 1473. The deal agreed between the two was that the company would take responsibility for the support of the garrison and the defence of the town. The annual sum for the pay of the garrison of the town, the upkeep of the Tower on the Rysbank at the entry to the harbour, and the castles of Guines and Hammes would be £10,022 4s 8d per year (two-thirds in cash and the rest in victuals). The company would also pay some fees and expenses including 1000 marks (£666 6s 8d) for judges' salaries and the costs of the two wool fleets per year. The maintenance of the fortifications and the artillery would also be their responsibility. To cover these costs, they would have the right to reimbursement from the customs and subsidies on wool going through the staple. The company would receive £3000 per year in addition from the customs revenue to reimburse them for their outstanding loans to the crown. If the revenue from the customs exceeded £15,022 4s 8d, the estimated total of all these expenses plus the debt repayment, any surplus would go to the Exchequer. With the Mayor of the staple also holding the appointments of Treasurer and Surveyor of the Works of Calais and his lieutenant being the Victualler of the town, the staple had become fully responsible for the finances of the garrison.

---

12 S. Rose (2008), *Calais*, 76–86. See also G. L. Harriss (1960), 'The struggle for Calais; an aspect of the rivalry between Lancaster and York.' *EHR* 75, 30–53.

In many ways the scheme worked well. It has been pointed out that 'the arrangement transformed the management of the Pale's finances … far from being a burden by the late fifteenth century Calais was actually returning a sizeable annual profit to the crown'.[13] The loans from the Staplers had also been repaid by around 1473; this scheme, what modern politicians might see as a form of privatisation, apparently worked to the benefit of all parties to the agreement. This is perhaps an unduly sanguine view of the way the scheme operated in practice. It is clear from the Cely correspondence that the way the soldiers were to be paid continued to be a matter of strenuous negotiation between the company, the garrison and the crown. This was largely over where the money was to be provided; London suited the company since that was where business deals with their customers in Flanders were largely concluded while not surprisingly the garrison needed ready money in Calais. In 1482, for example, it was decided between Lord Hastings the captain of Calais, the royal council and the mayor of the staple that half would be paid in London by the end of July while the remainder would be paid in Calais by midsummer.[14]

This deal also pointed to another problem; much of the specie available in Calais was a mixture of gold and silver coins of different values from different mints in different jurisdictions; how were they to be valued for exchange to sterling? The 1482 agreement was for Flemish money to be valued at 26s 8d the pound sterling. The rate of exchange was of crucial importance to the Staplers not only in their own dealing in wool but in the matter of the garrison's pay. The rates changed frequently and not always to the merchants' advantage as the Cely letters make clear. The scheme also had the effect that the crown could and did try to interfere in the Staplers' business. If the king wished to increase his 'surplusage', as certainly happened in 1482, pressure was put on the Mayor of the Staple to force the members to advance their exports of wool so that half of the amount needed could be handed over before 6 October in that year. This was all set out in a letter from William Cely in Calais to Richard and George Cely in London. Sir William Stocker, the mayor of the staple had written a letter read to the court of the Company of the Staple in Calais in August. The

'Kynge wull hawe iiM pownd for his syrplyssage off all soyche wullys and ffellys that hath ben schyppyd from the vi day of Apryll last past tyll the vi day of October nexte'.

William Cely also reported to his employers about a week later that

'hytt was agreydd here be the court that euery man that had any goode comyn from London or Ypswyche wyth thys last fflete schall bring yn hys bylls off costum and subside off the sayd goodys be that day senyght'.[15]

---

13 D. Grummitt (2008), *The Calais Garrison: War and Military Service in England, 1436-1558*, Woodbridge: Boydell, 149.

14 A. Hanham (1985), *The Celys and their World*, 232-3.

15 A. Hanham (1975), *The Cely Letters 1472-1488*, Oxford; Oxford University Press for the Early English Text Society, letter 185 and letter 187.

A proportion of the customs paid would have to be used to satisfy the king's demands. The letter finished with a list of the new values to be set on various coins which also would have to be used to satisfy the king's demands.

The system as set out on the Parliament Roll continued in use almost to end of the fifteenth century. Around 1495, however, Henry VII became more concerned about the money accruing to his coffers as surplusage than the prompt payment of the garrison. More money seems to have been delivered to the Chamber (Henry's preferred financial office) and less handed over to the garrison for their wages. The export of raw wool, however, was gently declining in this period; less was going through the staple and of course, while individual merchants could still trade profitably, the revenue produced by the duties on wool was also falling. Both Henry VII and his successor Henry VIII seem to have either ignored or perhaps were not fully aware of this trend. Both acted as if the company was enormously wealthy and well able to meet the demands made on it by the *Act of Retainer*. The agreement with the staple was renewed in 1504 and again in 1515 for a further period of 20 years from April 1516. It was the case that 'the king now saw the merchants of the staple and the act as an easy way of collecting the wool customs and providing a regular supply of foreign specie which he could hoard or assign as the need dictated.'[16]

The financial dilemma this caused for the company became evident in 1523–1524; this was a time when Henry's move to ally with the Emperor Charles V had led to bad relations with France and increased military expenditure. In this year the money demanded by the crown and that needed to pay the garrison exceeded the customs revenue by £2150. The company had no alternative but to seek loans from its members and in the succeeding years became more and more indebted to the crown. In 1527 the company pleaded for some relaxation of their responsibilities, claiming that only 40 merchants now regularly shipped wool to the staple. Certainly exports were falling rapidly; those from London declined from 4345 sacks in 1526 to 1863 in 1528. The garrison of Calais found its pay in arrears with no actual money apparently available, only indentures without any certain date of redemption. The company's debts to the crown stood at £22,163 9s 10d. The final blow came the following year. The king suspended the staple in March and all trade with the Low Countries in wool was prohibited.

This did not go down well with the clothiers in Flanders and Brabant as might be expected. Chapuys, Charles V's ambassador to Henry VIII, included a long report of a meeting with the king discussing the matter in a letter sent to his master in August 1528. Chapuys had requested that the prohibition be lifted only to be told that this was due to a dispute between the king and his subjects and nothing to do with him. Chapuys pointed out that the clothiers in the Low Countries could easily use Spanish wool rather than English. The discussion was then cut short but significantly Chapuys added that his colleague later received a gold cup from Thomas Cromwell and an assurance that 'he hoped in two or three days the king's dispute with the Staple would

---

16 D. Grummitt (2008), *The Calais Garrison*, 151.

be settled and the wool trade return to its usual course.'[17] The negotiations between the king and the staple in fact lasted much longer than this optimistic assumption. The trade was resumed by November 1533 but a new agreement took much longer. Cromwell had the matter, the final order concerning the staple of Calais, prominently listed in his 'to do' list or remembrance of January 1535.[18]

A great deal of information gathering had gone on in the intervening period with Cromwell seeking lists of the value of the company's rents in Calais and the dues from any lands held by it; he also wanted to know where wool was produced in England and the prices charged for the different qualities, with this varying, according to the reports he received, from £13 10s for the best 'Lemster' (March) wool to £5 4s for the poor 'clifte' wool. Finally he also commissioned a paper showing the profits apparently made by the individual Staplers.[19] The company was in no position to resist royal demands. An agreement, which was scheduled to last for five years, was finalised in October 1535; while the company was acquitted of £15,000 of its debts to the crown, the Staplers would receive no repayment for the £10,000 lent to the crown by the company in earlier periods. All the company's lands and possessions in the Pale would be taken into royal hands with the exception of their hall in the market place and the Staple prison. As the Staplers sadly said, 'they would be right sorry to sell it if they were in like prosperity or wealth as their predecessors before time have been'. They also agreed to pay their remaining debts of £10,000 to the crown in one instalment of £6000 and further instalments of £1000 per half year.[20]

The agreement did not prevent the Staplers, on an individual basis, being expected to continue to make large contributions to the support of the garrison and the defence of the Pale. These loans came to as much as around £5500 a year in the mid-1540s when Henry was at war with France. Payments of this kind continued in the reigns of Edward VI and Mary but the company was no longer the major source of finance for the Pale and the garrison as it had been in the past. There is evidence that stricter control was exercised over the garrison's finances by the crown while the resources of the Pale itself were developed to produce a greatly increased income. Some of the money flooding into the Treasury from the dissolution of the monasteries via the Court of Augmentations also found its way to Calais. The garrison thus survived the decline of the wool trade largely because the crown had 'consolidated and expanded its fiscal resources in the late fifteenth century'.[21] The two were no longer inextricably linked together after 1531 as they had been since the establishment of the Company of the Staple at Calais.

---

17 Item 1018 August 1533 21–31, in J. Gairdner, ed. (1885), *Letters and Papers, Foreign and Domestic, Henry VIII, vol. 6*, 32–53. *British History Online* http://www.british-history.ac.uk/letters-papers-hen8/vol8/pp32–53 [accessed 5 December 2016].

18 'Henry VIII January 1535, 26–31', in J. Gairdner, ed. (1885), *Letters and Papers*, 32–53.

19 Item 18, in J. Gairdner, ed. (1885), *Letters and Papers*, 32–53.

20 'Henry VIII: January 1535, 26–31', item 716 in *ibid.*

21 D. Grummitt (2008), *The Calais Garrison*, 156–7.

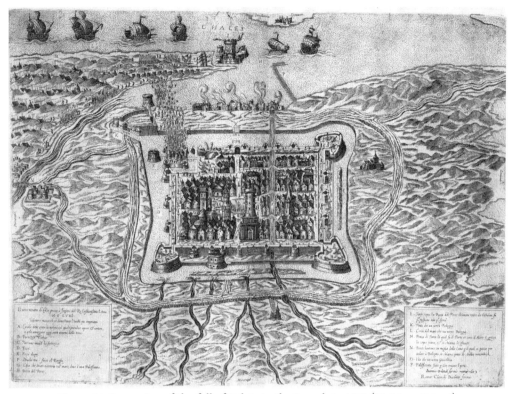

Figure 32. Engraving of the fall of Calais to the French in 1558 (BL Maps C 7.e.4)

The successful capture of the town and the Pale in January 1558 by the forces of the Duke de Guise was not due to lack of financial support for the town but to 'the precise planning and energetic efforts of Guise' and the lackadaisical and ineffective response of Mary's government to the growing threat from France. The accusations of treason thrown around in England, with little justification when the news of the fall of the town reached the court, provided a most convenient excuse for the disaster and could also absolve the accusers of blame. Many historians have also tended to see this defeat as ultimately to the benefit of the realm, turning English ambitions away from adventures on the continent to fresh fields across the seas.[22] The loss of the town was, however, calamitous for the Company of the Staple and the whole system of managing the export trade in wool with which they were identified. The company lost all its archives, which had been kept in Calais rather than London; all were abandoned with its property including the Staple Hall. Its legal position was also uncertain since the basis of the Staplers' trade was the legal requirement that exports of wool must for the most part go via the staple at Calais. In the early months of 1558 the prospects for any profitable trade in wool must have looked very unlikely to a depleted and disheartened group already suffering badly from the economic turmoil of the mid-sixteenth century.

---

22 *Ibid.*, 165–77.

Chapter 10

The Wool Trade's Increasing Difficulties

The most immediate problem for the Staplers was the Act of Parliament passed in 1552,[1] with their support it must be said, which made it illegal for any save merchants of the staple and clothiers to buy raw wool between the time of shearing in the summer and following spring, with the added proviso that all purchases made by Staplers must be exported via Calais. What had been intended to drive the broggers or middlemen out of business and reduce the price of wool, for the mutual benefit of clothiers and Staplers, would, in the situation after the fall of Calais, make it impossible for the Staplers to trade legally. As the Staplers lamented to the crown the loss of Calais had done them great harm; 'ffor we did not only lese there presently such a masse of goodes as no other subjects did but also synce that tyme our hole trade to lyve is cut away from us our lawes established for that only place beinge more by the losse thereof quite disannulled and made of non effects.'[2] The Staplers' only available course of action was to obtain licences to export outside the provisions of the Act. These were forthcoming but at a price; the crown insisted on raising the customs on a sack of wool by 1 mark (13s 4d); in 1560 this was increased to 2 marks (26s 8d). The size of the problem is indicated by some 188 merchants being forced to sue for pardons having exported wool from London, Hull or Boston in 1559, to Bruges for the most part, without obtaining licences.

At the same time negotiations went on with the government of Elizabeth for a new charter for the company which would deal with the difficulties caused by the loss of Calais. The old idea of home staples was resuscitated by William Cecil but found little support. A committee was set up by the Queen's Council to decide what should be done; this consisted of leading councillors including the Marquis of Northampton, the Earl of Pembroke, Sir William Cecil and Sir William Peter. A new charter was finally negotiated and granted in 1561. This allowed for a new staple to be established in the Low Countries in either Bruges, Middelburg or Bergen but even more new additions to the wool duties were mandated at an even higher level; on exports up to 3000 sacks per year the new charge would be £3 per sack; after that level the charge would be 53s

---

1 *Statutes of the Realm* 5&6 Edward VI cap. 7.

2 E. E. Rich (1937), *The Ordinance Book of the Merchants of the Staple,* Cambridge: Cambridge University Press, quoting *State Papers Elizabeth vol. 15*, 50.

4d.[3] These duties took little account of the rapidly changing fortunes of the wool trade. A Staple was set up at Bruges but there was little hope of any restoration of the trade to the level existing before the loss of Calais. Merchants were faced with continuing political problems between England and continental rulers. The competition from Spanish wools on the markets in the Low Countries did not lessen while the demands of cloth manufacturers in England for wool, their essential raw material, increased. The Company of the Staple continued to exist and even trade a little but was soon manifestly without economic significance or political influence.[4]

The root of the problems for the wool trade

The company's relatively swift final decline from its position as the pre-eminent trading body in England in the fifteenth century to virtual oblivion in the second half of the sixteenth century did not have one obvious cause. The Staplers themselves in 1527 in a petition to the crown bewailed their 'poore and lowe estate' looking back to when they had been 'in tymes past reputed and taken the most worshipfull company of merchantis subiectis to a king that any prince christened hath had.' They saw the causes of their fall as, first, the 'continuall debate contention and warre' with both France and the Empire which had made it impossible for them to trade at a profit. A second cause was the competition in the market of Spanish wool. This had increased in 'fynes as well as in quantitie'. A serious epidemic of 'morins' in sheep in England with a high death rate was finally cited, along with the assertion that the English clothiers had first call on what wool there was on the market. The staplers had, in effect, been almost entirely squeezed out of the market for raw wool in England by the ever increasing demands of the cloth industry for its basic raw material.[5]

There is some degree of truth in these assertions. With regard to royal intervention and the effect of royal policies on the trade in wool, it is evident that, at times, merchants had carried a heavy burden. Not only were the export dues on wool regarded as an essential element in the revenue of the crown but direct state interference in the trade in wool became more common in the later fifteenth century. Henry VII's tense relationship with the Emperor Maximilian, also the ruler of the Burgundian territories in the Low Countries, impacted seriously on merchants trading in both cloth and wool in these vitally important markets. Henry's policy was largely motivated by his fury at Maximilian's support for Perkin Warbeck, the pretender, as the supposed Duke

---

3 *Ibid.*, 115–117.

4 The Company of Merchants of the Staple of England (as it is now styled) ceased to export wool in 1614 when this was banned by the crown. Since that date the company has continued to exist, at first trading locally and finally becoming a charitable and educational body promoting the use of wool.

5 R. H. Tawney and E. Power, eds (1924), *Tudor Economic Documents: Being Select Documents Illustrating the Economic and Social History of Tudor England*, London: University of London Historical Series vol. 2, 24–8.

of York, to Henry's throne, a continuation of the policy of Margaret of Burgundy, formerly Margaret of York and sister of Edward IV.

Margaret acted as protector of the Low Countries for her stepdaughter Mary of Burgundy until Mary's marriage to Maximillian; he saw no reason to abandon this policy, at least initially. Despite the political ramifications the real effects of the bad relations between the Low Countries and England were economic and commercial. The cloth manufacturing towns of Flanders and Brabant were the prime market for English wool and essential to the operation of the staple at Calais and the financial system of the Staplers. The same area was also important to the Merchant Adventurers exporting increasing quantities of English-made cloth and thus in competition with local clothiers. Maximilian, as guardian for his son Philip, Duke of Burgundy, had poor relations with the independent-minded Flemish cities, especially Ghent and Bruges the trading partners of the Staplers, promoting instead Antwerp, a town firmly under his control, as a rival trading centre.

Henry VII raised the temperature in this rumbling dispute in late 1493. He banned all direct trade between England, Antwerp and the Low Countries. The notion that the trade in raw wool could continue via Calais was soon shown to be a vain hope when Maximilian imposed a counter embargo on all trade between the Low Countries and Calais in May 1494.[6] The impasse, which probably caused economic damage to both parties, was resolved by a treaty negotiated in 1496 usually known as the *Magnus Intercursus*. There are significantly large gaps in the surviving figures for cloth exports in these years.[7] The treaty itself laid down that, 'neither of the allies [Henry VII and Philip] shall promote the rebels of the other ally to stay in his dominions or shall in any way help them but shall expel them within fifteen days'. It also provided that 'the merchants of both allies are free to come and go and to buy and sell in the dominions of the other ally in towns and ports where there are customs officials established to supervise traffic.'[8]

The treaty provided a useful benchmark for the way trade between these two states should be conducted. It did not prevent other quarrels over trading rights and newly imposed taxes causing difficulties in the succeeding years. The interdependence of the economies of England and the Low Countries, especially since the latter were firmly in the orbit of the Empire, provided tempting opportunities for the rulers of either side to influence policy and the relationship between England and the Empire by interfering with the freedom to trade. War or the threat of war between England and France, in the same way had almost immediate adverse repercussions on the prosperity of trade across the Channel.

Competition between traders in raw wool and cloth manufacturers was no new thing in 1527. According to one calculation based on the customs records, the total number

---

6 S. B. Chrimes (1977), *Henry VII*, London: Eyre, Methuen, 232–6.

7 E. M. Carus-Wilson and O. Coleman (1963), *England's Export Trade, 1275-1547*, 111; T. H. Lloyd (1977), *The English Wool Trade in the Middle Ages*, Cambridge, Cambridge University Press, 283.

8 R. H. Tawney and E. Power, eds (1924), *op. cit.*, 11–15.

of broadcloths exported exceeded the total number of wool sacks exported as early as 1381–1385. From that date the export of raw wool declined relatively slowly while that of woollen cloth rose rapidly. In the five-year period including 1527, the date of the Staplers' petition, wool exports totalled 4834 sacks while 93,534 broadcloths paid the duty on exported cloth.[9] It has been claimed that the fact that raw wool, destined for the looms of the cloth manufacturing industries of the Low Countries and of Italy, bore a much heavier burden of taxation than woollen cloth made in England created a high degree of protection for English clothiers. Their essential raw material was much cheaper than that of their competitors overseas, even if the English producers were not as skilled as their rivals. It was not the case, however, that English clothiers were able to dominate the market completely from as early as the late fourteenth century. Wool merchants do not seem to have complained about competition from clothiers or their agents buying up wool supplies or causing the price to rise before the mid to late fifteenth century. The writer of the *Libelle of Englysshe Polycye* in around 1436 was convinced that Flanders was dependent on trade with England, 'for the wolle of Englonde/Susteyneth the comons Flemmynges I understonde.'[10]

It has been argued persuasively that trading in raw wool only became much more problematic when other factors came into play as well as the differential in the tax rates on raw wool and English cloth. One was a change in the market for wool in the main cloth making areas. The most profitable sector of the wool trade for Staplers was that devoted to the finest wool; the 'Lemster Ore' of the price lists, from the Marches of Wales, closely followed by that from the Cotswolds. This was short-stapled and curly and very suitable for heavy, quality broadcloth which gave years of wear and warmth.

It was not only made from the best quality wool but needed extensive skilled treatment from the clothiers beginning with the preparation of the fleece. This was oiled or greased to replace the lanolin lost when a fleece was scoured to remove things like thorns, twigs or dirt trapped in the wool. The wool was then combed or carded to align the fibres before being spun and woven. The processing of wool to make cloth of different grades is explained in John H. Munro (2005) 'Spanish Merino wools and the *Nouvelles Draperies*,' EcHR 58, 431–4. The next process was fulling; the cloth was soaked in a trough of warm water and a mixture of fuller's earth and urine; it was then hammered in a water-driven fulling mill (often found in England) or trodden by workers in troughs (more usual in the Low Countries). During this process the cloth shrank considerably and the fibres interlocked. The piece was then stretched to an even shape on a tenter frame fastened with hooks. Finally, the nap was raised

---

9 These figures come from J. H. Munro (2003), 'Medieval woollens: The western European woollen industries and their struggles for international markets, *c*.1000–1500', in D. Jenkins, ed. *The Cambridge History of Western Textiles*, Cambridge: Cambridge University Press, vol. 1, 304–5.

10 G. Warner, ed. (1926), *The Libelle of Englyshe Polycye: a Poem on the Use of Sea-power 1436*, Oxford: Clarendon Press, 6–7.

(sometimes by teasels) and shorn to an even length. All this completely obliterated the weave and produced a very soft texture almost like silk. Coarser longer-stapled wool was suited for the worsted type of cloth or the so-called 'dry' draperies. There was no scouring or greasing and the cloth was finished once the wool had been spun and woven often from carded fibres. Patterns in the weave were visible and could be a feature of the cloth.

English wool with its varying qualities was suited for both processes and thus could all be sold abroad. Much of the cheaper worsted style cloths made of the lower grades of English wool in the Low Countries found a ready market in southern Europe until around the first half of the fourteenth century. In England the London burellers' guild also produced this kind of cloth both for export and the home market. Munro, however, has pointed out that the fourteenth century was marked by almost continuous warfare in much of southern Europe; transport costs also rose so that selling relatively cheap cloth into this market became increasingly difficult and unprofitable. These cloths almost entirely disappeared from their former manufacturing centres where they had constituted a majority of the cloth made. Both in England and Flanders the high-priced luxury 'greased' woollens became much more desirable and profitable both for merchants and manufacturers. The price of the best wool rose accordingly and the trade could thus bear the burden of high taxation. Wool merchants made a good living despite the uncertainties of the political climate of the late fourteenth and early fifteenth centuries in northern Europe. Guild regulations in Bruges and Ghent specified that the very best of the luxury woollen cloths could only be made of the best English wool. In 1456 Ghent was even more specific issuing a regulation that stated that 'its fine cloths called *dickedinnen* and other cloths that are woven and made within the city of Ghent should contain only Fine march, Middle march wools, fine Cotswolds and Cotswolds-Berkshire wools and no others'.[11]

Spanish wool and the European market

These circumstances changed for the worse from the point of view of English wool merchants in the final decade of the fifteenth century and the early years of the sixteenth century when a realistic alternative to good quality but expensive English wool became easily available in the Low Countries. Poor quality Spanish wool was obtainable in the Low Countries at least from the early years of the fifteenth century, used mainly for the making of coarse cloths or items like hats and caps. What alarmed English wool merchants was the direct competition to all but the most expensive fine English wools presented by Spanish *merino* wool. The origins of this distinctive breed of sheep are not entirely clear. The most likely explanation is that cross-breeding

---

11 John H. Munro, (2002), 'The Western European Woollen Industries and their struggle for International Markets *c.*1000–1500.' In David Jenkins, *op.cit.*, 228–324.

between the indigenous sheep of Castille and sheep from the high lands of North Africa occurred on a large scale sometime after the Merinid dynasty took control of the Moslem emirates of southern Spain in the late thirteenth century. The uneasy frontier between Moslem and Christian Spain at this time presented plentiful opportunities for the rustling of livestock and the gradual mingling of the blood lines of the local and the newly introduced flocks to produce a new breed of sheep capable of producing the finest wool.

To some extent political developments from second half of the fifteenth into the sixteenth century favoured the entry of Spanish wool onto the European market. After the death of Charles the Bold, Duke of Burgundy, in 1477 at the battle of Nancy, his heir was his daughter Mary who was almost immediately betrothed to Maximilian of Habsburg, the future emperor. In 1482 she died in a riding accident leaving a young son, Philip. The dynastic planning of his father resulted in the marriage of this young prince to Juana the daughter of Ferdinand and Isabella of Aragon and Castile in 1495. Maximilian could not have planned that Philip died early in 1506 nor that his son would become King of Spain as Charles V but these links ensured that Spanish influence in the Burgundian court and thus in the Low Countries was strong. Similarly as the economic dominance of the Flemish towns including Ghent and Bruges waned, that of Antwerp grew also to the advantage of merchants from Spain.

A change in the popularity of different types of woollen cloth among buyers may also have been to the advantage of Spanish wool. The heavy fulled broadcloths made from short-stapled wool, regarded with such favour in the fourteenth century, no longer dominated the market. The lighter worsted weaves made from wool with a longer staple were increasing in popularity and this kind of textile used Spanish wool extensively. The way in which Spanish wool was produced also seems to have made it possible for a rapid increase in the quality as well as the quantity of the wool exported from Spain. The basis of Spanish wool production was the organisation formally set up in the late thirteenth century known as *El Honorado Consejo de la Mesta de los Pastores de Castilla* or simply the *Mesta*. This body controlled and set the rules for the regular pattern of migration of the very extensive flocks of sheep from winter pastures in the south of Castile to those in the uplands of the north in the summer. From 1454 all private investors in these flocks were absorbed into the *Cabaña Real* under royal protection and royal law. The overall head of the *Cabaña* was a member of the royal council and a person of great importance. The routes followed by the flocks on their annual migrations were protected; stopping places on the way, the timing of lambing and shearing and other matters of sheep management were all laid down in the rules of the *Mesta*.

Each flock of around 10,000 sheep travelled as a unit led by bell wethers in charge of around 50 shepherds and the same number of dogs. Shearing took place in late April or May before the flock had reached the summer pastures. Once there the rams were put to the ewes in late June or July so that lambing would take place in early winter in the south. Because the flocks were managed in this way, it was much easier

Figure 33. Modern Spanish Mesta *flock enforcing its rights in Madrid led by a bell wether (Creative Commons CC BY-SA 3.0)*

to select rams to improve the quality of the flock and the fleeces produced. By around 1530 an average weight per fleece of 5 lb (2.27 kg) could be expected, much more than that produced by the sheep on the Marches of Wales and in the Cotswolds. It was true that Spanish wool faced a journey by sea from Spain to the markets in the Low Countries but the burden of tax was lower than on English produce.[12] The quality of the best Spanish wool was also comparable to that of the best Cotswold produce if not quite as fine as 'Lemster ore'. There was no doubt that it was a formidable competitor to English wools, something which was widely recognised by clothiers in the Low Countries.

The crown had profited greatly from the wool trade in the past. By the third decade of the sixteenth century, however, it is fair to say that royal policy seemed almost unaware of its decline and certainly did little or nothing to arrest it. The attitude of Henry VIII to the Company of the Staple was more concerned with ensuring that debts to the crown were paid than the wool trade was offered support or encouragement. The manipulation of the currency by the debasement of silver coins in the 1540s made

---

12 C. Rahn Phillips and W. D. Phillips (1997), *Spain's Golden Fleece: Wool Production and the Wool Trade from the Middle Ages to the Nineteenth Century*, Baltimore; Johns Hopkins University Press, 97–166.

export trade difficult and risky since the exchange value fluctuated greatly generally to the disadvantage of English merchants. The 'calling down of the currency' in 1552 caused even greater difficulties for traders. Gresham claimed to Elizabeth in 1558 that by doing this he had brought, 'the Kinges majestie your brother outt of deptt ... but savid his tresore within the realme'.[13] He had certainly also caused the failure of some wool traders. The gradual decline of the export trade in raw wool was, however, due to factors beyond the control of any individual ruler or his advisers. This did not prevent more discussion in England of the fortunes of the wool trade and its close associate the trade in woollen cloth as they declined than had ever occurred in the days of their outstanding success. Some of this discussion will be examined in Part Four.

---

13 R. H. Tawney and E. Power, eds. (1924), *Tudor Economic Documents*, vol. III, item 8 146–9. Sir
    Thomas Gresham to Queen Elizabeth I.

Part 4

Decline

Chapter 11

Excessive Numbers of Sheep?

During the period from around 1280–1390, when the wool trade was most flourishing with well over 20,000 woolsacks leaving English ports every year, no-one complained that there were too many sheep in the land. Direct comments on the trade were few but those that were made boasted of its profitability, lauded the quality of the wool produced and extolled its fineness said to be without rival. The best known comment is probably the wry and pithy words engraved by a wool merchant in Nottinghamshire on a window in his hall in the fifteenth century, 'I praise God and ever shall/It is the sheep hath paid for all.'

It is hard to calculate the total size of the flocks which produced this wondrous product since this depends on estimates of the wool used within the country itself as well as that exported and also on estimates of fleece weights. It is safe to say that there were many more sheep than people in England throughout our period. The public view of sheep numbers began to change, however, in the final decades of the fifteenth century. Writers begin to take a much harsher view of sheep farming with some focusing particularly on the supposed adverse effects of the apparently soaring numbers of sheep. Why did these opinions become sufficiently widespread to be expressed, for example in parliament, influencing legislation, when the number of sheep was probably slightly smaller than it had been a century earlier? Why was there opposition to the wool trade when the export of raw wool was a fraction of what it had been in earlier times and exports of woollen cloth, though rising, did not make up for this decline? Why was there such hostility to raising sheep for wool when this was perceived by some at least as the basis of the nation's wealth?

The issue was seen both amongst the people most directly affected and by commentators as very closely connected with the upheaval caused in certain parts of the country by the spread of enclosures, virtually always said to have taken place to enable the conversion of plough-lands to pasture. As set out in an *Act Against Pulling Down Towns* passed in the Parliament of January 1489, 'great troubles increase daily because of the ruin, pulling down and wilful abandonment of houses and towns within this realm.' This was caused by 'putting lands to pasture which customarily had been used for tillage whereby idleness, the foundation and beginning of all misfortunes, increases daily'.[1] The high and rising price of wool at this period compared with the

---

1 *Parliament Rolls of Medieval England*, Henry VII; Parliament of January 1489 item 48.

relatively low and stable price of grain provided an economic argument for increasing pasture at the expense of plough-lands.

The consolidation of land holdings with the consequent erection of fences and planting of hedges was clearly evident in some parts of the Midlands and the southeast. This process was associated with the abandonment of the old system of open field agriculture with holdings scattered in strips and was, of course, an aspect of social and economic change in the countryside which had more complex origins than simply the lure of high wool prices. The changes could be associated with the shift away from the old 'feudal' forms of lordship based on the manor on which tenants held land of the lord and were subject to the rulings of the manorial court. The rulings of these courts covered the way agriculture was organised in a communal way. The system itself involved matters relating to personal status and the organisation of village life, much of which had been falling gradually out of use for some time. In the last decades of the fifteenth century, more entrepreneurial yeomen, often originally tenants of landlords under the old system, began to build up their holdings by leasing demesne lands. These could be readily enclosed and thus could also be individually managed.

Lease holders were also increasingly accused of extending their leased lands onto the common pastures which had been shared by all, to the detriment of the tenants of small 'traditional' holdings. One way of doing this was by the lessees ignoring the stints or numbers of beasts determined by the manorial court, which could be pastured on common land. These stints were assigned to each landholder and by ignoring these arrangements lessees swamped the available grazing with their over-large flocks.[2] One example from Cambridge in a presentment alleged that 'Mr Hynde unlawfully doth bringe into Cambridge felde a flock of shepe to the number of vi or viic to the undoing of fermours and great hyndraunce of all the inhabitants of Cambrydge'. Moreover the same Mr Hynde did the same after harvest bringing 'his cattall in great nombre' so that they 'eateth uppe the common to like hyndraunce'.[3] The Heritage and Temple families are examples of this 'new' kind of landholder and, as we have seen, in their case it is clear that they were closely involved in the raising of sheep and trading in wool.

The advantages of changes in agricultural practices like these were clear. Establishing large pastures under the control of a single ownership made for better flock management, especially with regard to the prevention and treatment of sickness and the possibility of more selective breeding. The yield could be improved while merchants could also benefit from being able to buy wool in larger quantities. Some of the same advantages in ease of management and possible improvements in yield, however, could also accrue to a landholder enclosing in order to grow grain. Moreover

---

2 C. Dyer (2012), *A Country Merchant: Trading and Farming at the End of the Middle Ages*, Oxford: Oxford University Press, 9–12.

3 R. H. Tawney and E. Power, eds (1924), *Tudor Economic Documents Being Documents Illustrating the Economic and Social History of Tudor England*, London: University of London Historical Series I, 44–6.

enclosures at this period were patchy with profitable sheep farming occurring in areas where the older systems still prevailed.

Issues of local climate and the fertility of the soil also had a bearing on the spread of enclosures and the incidence of deserted villages. For example the chilly bleak uplands of the Cotswolds seem to have suffered more from the abandonment of settlements at around this time than the more sheltered Severn Valley.[4] The foldcourse system widely used in East Anglia also did not favour enclosure. In this, landlords had the right to pasture and fold their flocks at night time on the open fields after harvest, since the sheeps' dung fertilised the light soils used for tillage to the general benefit. The most obvious adverse effects of enclosure at this period were mainly felt in the Midland counties where the soil and climate was suitable for both pastoral and arable farming.

It is clear, however, that it was the common belief in a majority of the country that many poor families had been virtually forced to abandon their villages causing the collapse of these communities. The reason always cited for this was that land used for tillage for centuries had been converted into sheep walks. In the words of a well-known ballad from the early sixteenth century:

> Commons to close and kepe;
> Poor folk for bred to cry and wepe
> Towns pulled downe to pastur shepe
> This ys the new gyse.

The final horror was that:

> The townes go down the land decayes
> Of cornefeldes, playnelayes
> Gret men makithe now a dayes
> A sheepfold in the churche[5]

The widespread influence of this image of heartless sheep-farming landowners is demonstrated by the way it also appears in Thomas More's *Utopia* first published in 1516. More's introduction to the description of the ideal society of Utopia contains an imaginary conversation between one Raphael who has visited Utopia and the Archbishop of Canterbury; they discuss the problems of their own society including what drives men to steal. Raphael explains to the Archbishop that in England there is a particular problem – sheep. He explains:

> These placid creatures which used to require so little food have now apparently developed a raging appetite and turned into man-eaters. Fields, houses towns everything goes down their throats.[6]

---

4 D. Hurst (2005), *Sheep in the Cotswolds: the Medieval Wool Trade*, Stroud: Tempus, 163–4.

5 R. H. Tawney and E. Power, eds (1924), *Tudor Economic Documents*, III, 18–20.

6 Thomas More, trans. Paul Turner, (1972), *Utopia*, London: The Folio Society, 46.

He goes on to accuse landowners of actively harming society, 'by enclosing all the land they can for pasture and leaving none for cultivation'; churches are preserved only as sheepfolds. The people are driven off the land to beg and to make matters worse the price of wool is so high that clothiers cannot afford it which means even more men thrown out of work. The wool market is in the hands of a few rich men who control the prices. The only solution is legislation against enclosures and the establishing of monopolies by the rich.[7] The harm allegedly caused by the wool trade was a familiar idea not only to displaced villagers but to the elite readers of More's social satire.

Depopulation also worried the authorities, as did the spread of 'idleness'; Henry VII's Act of 1489 painted a dramatic picture of 'churches destroyed, the service of God withdrawn, the bodies buried there not prayed for, the patron and curates wronged and the defence of this land against our external enemies enfeebled'. The remedy was to demand that any house let to farm with at least 20 acres (8.1 ha) lying in tillage or husbandry within the last three years must not change the way the land was used. The sanction against any change away from tillage was that half of any proceeds would be forfeit to the landlord.[8] There is little evidence that this Act was energetically enforced but it was a powerful and public statement of what were felt to be the effects of the boom in sheep-farming.

The idea that it was the sheer number of sheep which caused the problems did not go away. A further Act of Parliament in 1533 attempted to limit the number of sheep one person might possess. The preamble of the *Act* almost reads as if written by More; all sorts of evils are ascribed to the conversion of tillage to pasture including 'theft robbery and other inconveniences'. The root problem is, however, stated to be 'the great profit that cometh of sheep' with some people having flocks, it is claimed, of 24,000 animals. The conclusion was that, 'if remedy is not found it may turn to the utter destruction and desolation of this realm which God defend'.[9] This is inflammatory language and perhaps hardly justifiable by the figures for exports in the five-year period 1531–1535. In that time span an average of 3951.4 woolsacks were exported and 109,278 broadcloths, less than in the previous five-year period. Certainly the price of wool was rising but even so it seems unlikely that all the ills of society could be laid at the door of this one cause.

The *Act* set out various provisions to reduce the size of flocks but with so many exemptions that it is probable that it would always have been ineffective. For example inherited sheep were not counted in the overall total of a flock. Moreover it would be lawful 'for every person or persons keeping a houshold' to have as many sheep 'as shall be necessary for the only expences of his household; to be provided kept and fed in and upon his own lands'. Finally it laid down that 'all Spiritual persons and every of them to keep such and as many Sheep upon their own lands', despite the provisions of

---

7 P. Turner, ed. (1965), Thomas More, *Utopia,* London: Folio Society, 46–8.

8 *Parliament Rolls of Medieval England*; Henry VII, Parliament of January 1489 item 48.

9 Statute 25 Henry VIII cap.13.

the *Act*, as they had done in the past.[10] Nevertheless the *Act* did express a widely held view of the disastrous social consequences of the feared rise in the number of sheep and the obvious rise in the price of wool.

There are good reasons for linking this view with members of the household of Thomas Cromwell, then at the height of his influence in the King's Council (Cromwell was appointed Principal Secretary to Henry VIII in April 1534). One of Cromwell's respected agents was John Rastell, a recent convert to Reformed ideas in religion despite the fact that he was married to Thomas More's sister, who worked for Cromwell on various legal matters in 1533–1534. He was also involved in a printing business and had earlier, in 1520, been one of the many employed in the decoration of the pavilions erected near Calais to provide a suitable setting for the meeting of Henry VIII and Francis I of France, the *Field of the Cloth of Gold*. It was probably here that Rastell met and became friendly with one Clement Armstrong, a Londoner of merchant stock.[11]

By 1534 Armstrong probably also held similar religious views to his friend. He had certainly become deeply concerned about what he called 'the comonweale' of England. Probably using Rastell's valuable contacts with Cromwell as his opportunity to get his views into the hands of a powerful man, Armstrong sent to Cromwell, in early 1535, at least two long pamphlets on this topic of the 'comonweale' which were found among Cromwell's State Papers. We cannot know what Cromwell thought of them but the one usually called *A Treatise concerning the Staple and the Commodities of this Land* reveals ideas which have much in common with those expressed in the 1533 *Act*. Armstrong's father was very probably a Stapler and his paper first of all attacks what he sees as the unfair and damaging trading practices of this group.

The fact that the wool trade was (or so he claimed) largely conducted on a credit basis using bills of exchange and the like roused his ire. At the root of his attack was the idea that there was a God-given balance to the benefit of all between producing wool and producing food which the Staplers had distorted by encouraging so mightily the export of wool. He also attacked cloth merchants as part of the same evil and

> 'fermoursyhe and gentilman began to putt ther erthe to idulness making pasture to fede more shepe to increase the more staple wuolle in as much they begane to serche and stody ther wisdom to account the gret profite that they might wynne therby'.

He berated all who meddled in the wool trade in any way calling them, 'What wretchis are thos, that for theyr own syngler weale werkith ageynst Goddes wille and ordinaunce to destroy ther common weal of the hollrealme'. In many ways it is easy to see the whole pamphlet as a somewhat incoherent rant against the way England traded with the Low Countries and against the import of what he called 'straunge merchaundise' as well as the Staplers and the Merchant Adventurers, the merchants most prominent

---

10 Statute 25 Henry VIII cap.13, clauses 3, 9, 16.

11 ODNB John Rastell, *c*.1475–1536 lawyer and printer.

in the export of cloth, perhaps reflecting the bitterness of an individual who had failed in business. There is also little evidence that this particular paper had any influence on Cromwell himself or his policies. Yet elements of his arguments relate to views that were more widespread than those of just one Londoner.

Another member of Cromwell's legal staff was John Hales. Hales survived Cromwell's fall to become an MP in 1547 during the ascendancy of Protector Somerset. He unsuccessfully introduced at least three bills into the Commons to deal with the problems of the conversion of tillage. Probably as a result of his clear interest in the matter he was appointed to the 1548 Commission to inquire into the extent of enclosures in the Midland counties.

Among the queries to which the commissioners had to find answers was,

> 'if any persone hath or doth kepe above the number of two thousande shepe, besides lambes of one yeres age either in his awne right or in the name of his wife child, kinsman, or any other persone and whether he hath kept the same upon his awne landes or upon his ferme (leased) landes or otherwise by couon or fraude and how long he hath kept them'.

Another was, 'hoe many Shepe ye thunke haue been necessary for the onely expences of such persones household for one yere'. A question also dealt with the issue of whether land had been taken from commons so that husbandmen were impeded from breeding animals as they had done in the past.[12] There was a widespread suspicion that the work of the Commission encouraged the unrest among many country people on the subject of enclosures which played some part in Kett's rebellion in eastern England in the summer of 1549. The first demand of the rebels mentions enclosures in a somewhat ambiguous manner and another demands that the price of 'medowe ground may be at such price as they were in the first yere of Kyng henry the vii'.[13]

More directly related to the debate about the problems caused by sheep farming agitating the minds of the so-called 'common weal' men was the *Act* passed by the Commons in March 1549.[14] Although this was presented as a straightforward revenue-raising measure, it was clearly based on the ideas behind previous attempts to control the number of sheep in the kingdom and thus promote tillage over pasture. It set up a poll tax on sheep and as a contemporary put it, 'ther coulde have byne no redier waye to cause a great quantity of the said Ship pastures to be converted into erable then this Subsidie upon Shippe'.

The *Act* was repealed within a year but it was no hastily cobbled together measure. Trouble had been taken to try and estimate the number of sheep which might be covered by such a tax and what might be its effect. John Hales wrote a paper on

---

12 *Tudor Economic Documents* I, 39

13 BL Harleian MS 304 f.75.

14 2 & 3 Edward VI cap.36 Statutes of the Realm, iv, 78.

the proposal called *The Causes of Dearth* which can be found in the State Papers. He calculated that there were 'thirty hundred thousand sheepe' (3,000,000) in the land of which half were pastured on the common lands and the remainder on other pasture (that is enclosed). He suggested that sheep on common land should be rated at one penny each; on enclosed pastures ewes with lambs should be rated at 2d each and wethers 1½d each.[15] There is no way of knowing if Hales' sheep estimates were accurate; an earlier paper had come up with a total of nearly 8½ million animals. This total was reached as follows:

> After the rate of xv sheepe to the todde [of wool] clxxxxv to the sacke and xlv to a clothe [of assize] it appereth by the woll wolfelles and clothe carried out of the realme in the xxxviii yere of the reigne of Kyng Henry the eight as appereth before that ther maye be saied justly that ther wer in the Realme the same yere 8407819 sheepe[16]

The bill in fact enacted put forward a much more complicated scheme than that proposed by Hales; the tax payable on sheep would be set off against a subsidy imposed at the same time payable on goods; only if the sheep poll tax exceeded that on goods would anything be due under this head. The different rates on ewes and wethers on enclosed grounds and all sheep on common pastures, which Hales had suggested were implemented at the rates of 3d, 2d and1½d. Perhaps not surprisingly, although some counties set about the process of implementing this legislation, it was rapidly repealed coming off the statute book in in November. A new *Act* passed the following January made the reason why clear. The preamble pointed that

> 'the relief (tax) of sheepe is to your poor Commons having but fewe sheepe in number a great charge and also so cumberouse for all your Commissioners and officers ... that they cannot in manner tell how to serve your Highness therein according to their duties'.[17]

Many groups were still very hostile to the idea of enclosures and blamed the profitability of sheep farming for their spread and the ensuing distress and poverty in some rural areas. It is somewhat ironic that the collapse in the export market for raw wool in the 1550s, and the increasing difficulties suffered by the export trade in cloth a little later, changed the balance of profitability in agriculture so that once more the growing of grain was a better prospect than a sheep walk. As M. W. Beresford wrote, 'never again would the wolf-like sheep be an increasing menace to corn-growing husbandmen'.[18] Nevertheless Hales' views were sufficiently influential for him to have

---

15   State papers domestic Edward VI, v, 20.

16   R. H. Tawney and E. Power, eds. (1924), *Tudor Economic Documents,* III, item 5, 180.

17   3 & 4 Edward VI cap.23.

18   M. W. Beresford (1954), 'The poll tax and census of sheep, 1549', *Agricultural History Review* 2, 15–29.

been put forward at one time as the author of *A Discourse of the Commonwealth of this Realm of England*. This was written by the very distinguished academic and courtier Sir Thomas Smith in 1549 and first published in 1581. This work was a sophisticated analysis of the economic woes of England in the 1540s and displayed something of a bias in favour of an agrarian economy where mixed agriculture was supported in order to provide work and a living for all the people. Trade should also be in balance with 'no more bought of strangers than we do sell them'; an idea that Clement Armstrong also tried to express in his earlier paper. The hostility of the 'common weal' party to a booming export trade in wool and cloth lasted for much of the sixteenth century. It is probably the case that the sound and fury generated had little effect on the fortunes of either the wool or the cloth trade.

Chapter 12

The Activities of Broggers and a 'Disorderly' Market in Wool

Another perhaps more pragmatic approach to the decline in the wool trade was also very influential on government servants, the crown and parliament throughout much of the sixteenth century. We have already looked at some of the problems that afflicted the Company of the Staple in the 1520s. Most of their petition to the king in 1527 was concerned with issues of royal policy on taxation and customs dues but the Staplers also raised the issue of the effect on wool prices of the entry of 'rich grayziers, broggers and engrossers' into the home market for wool. The activities of these groups, in the eyes of the Staplers, led to the price of wool becoming so high that the Staplers were almost squeezed out of the market. The same document accepted that clothiers 'as standeth with reason and with the comen wealth must first be served'.

This belief that if only middlemen could somehow be eliminated from the market in wool at home and the rivalry between Staplers, clothiers and merchant adventurers could somehow be amicably resolved, all would be well, was widely held. Restrictive legislation against broggers was passed in the later fifteenth century and also in 1531. By 1551 in the economic chaos caused by the 'calling down' of the currency the Staplers were arguing that if the manufacture of cloth continued to expand as fast as it had done in the recent past the supply of wool would fail to satisfy their demands and would allow no export of raw wool at all.[1] One consequence of this somewhat exaggerated claim was the *Act lymittinge the tymes of buying and selling of woolles* of 1552.[2]

This act laid down that because of the 'gredye and covetous myndes as well as of such as have the great plenty and habundaunce of sheepe and woolles as also by the corrupt practices of diverse broggers ingrossers woolgatherers and regrators and sondire other persons' the price of wool has risen excessively. The *Act* therefore allowed only denizen Staplers and manufacturers of all kinds of woollen garments and cloth to buy wool; alien merchants could only do so after the feast of the Purification (Candlemas, 2 February), well after the sheep shearing season in June and July. There was an exemption for northern wools of poor quality and similarly before the loss of

---

1 'Calendar of State Papers Domestic: Edward VI, Mary and Elizabeth,' 1547–80, Edward VI – vol. 13 August 1551, 34.

2 Statute 5 & 6 Edward VI cap.vii.

the town in 1558 Staplers could sell poor quality waste originally packed with better wools in England, rather than at Calais.[3]

Not surprisingly the main provisions of the *Act* were circumvented by the issuing of licences which gave many opportunities for corruption. The Earl of Leicester, for example, was granted a licence to export the very large quantity of 1000 sarplers of wool in April 1560. This ended up in the hands of a group of alien merchants, no doubt to the profit of the Earl.[4] The licence system was very unpopular with those the *Act* was intended to benefit, especially the remaining Staplers, since exports under licence were not obliged to go via the Staple. The broggers were also in the main still able to operate with impunity. It was very difficult to get reliable evidence of breaches of the *Act* in the case of those trading in large amounts of wool. Where small traders were concerned, enforcement depended on informers who had little interest in pursuing those making bargains in small amounts of wool. A proclamation in 1576 placed further restrictions on the purchase of wool again in an attempt to drive down the price. This was both very unpopular and ineffective. A government inquiry was instituted in 1577 which elicited a heartfelt and also soundly based plea from wool growers producing coarse wools in the North of England. As they pointed out:

> The trade thereof [in wool] wyll be driven into a fewe ryche mans hands soe that the poore shall not be paide for their worke but as it pleaseth the ryche, and the cloth shall reste in their hands to sell at their pleasure.[5]

The government of Elizabeth, however, was reluctant to abandon this policy in its entirety. Even as late as 1602, a proclamation was issued referring to the lack of wool at 'convenient and reasonable prices' despite the 1552 *Act*. Once again the corrupt practices of 'broggers, ingrossers woolgatherers and regrators of wools' were blamed for this state of affairs. It was claimed that they had grown to an excessive multitude and must be brought before the Justices and bound over to 'desist from such their dealings and conforme themselves to her Maiesties Lawes'.[6] By this time the wool trade was a shadow of its former self and there is little reason to suppose that the proclamation had any effect. The assumption often seems to be made by those attacking broggers and the like that their activities were a relatively new phenomenon. It was of course the case that some sort of middlemen had been active in the wool trade from its earliest days as has been shown above. It is doubtful if the trade could have flourished as it did without their involvement.

Clearly royal governments in the second half of the sixteenth century were at something of a loss when it came to devising or implementing policies which might

---

3 *Ibid.*

4 P. J. Bowden (1962), *The Wool Trade in Tudor and Stuart England,* London: Macmillan, 127–9.

5 SP/12/117/38 October 1577.

6 Text from EEBO; proclamation of 1602.

have helped the wool trade recover some of its former success. There was, however, one individual who put a great deal of energy into devising schemes which he claimed would produce this desirable result. This was John Johnson, the grazier and Stapler whose business had failed leading to his own bankruptcy in the commercial turmoil following the 'calling down' of the currency in 1551. Johnson's bankruptcy led to litigation and his confinement in a debtors' prison. When he was finally released in 1557 he turned to his family contacts for support; these included William Cecil whose influence probably helped him get some sort of position as secretary to Lord Paget. He later claimed that because he held this position he was able to be instrumental in proposing the increased export duties on cloths imposed in the first half of 1558, duties which greatly benefited the royal finances.[7] As he wrote at the end of 1576:

> I remembred the greate benifite of five hundredth towsande poundes and more comme to passe unto her Quene's majestie syns the begynnyng of her Highnes raigne proceding of a device of myne decelared unto the late and oldest Lord paget then my singular good Lord and master'.[8]

We have no way of knowing if his claim to have originated this new imposition is correct, but it is the case that if so, it was the only one of his many schemes to be successfully implemented.

His other schemes or projects were in the great part focused on the wool trade or that in cloth. His first attempt to be taken seriously by Elizabeth's leading councillors, and (it must be said) to find himself a post that would restore his battered finances and his reputation, was to lobby Cecil to support a scheme for the queen to have complete control over a new Staple for wool to be located in England. This was in 1560 as the Staplers campaigned energetically for a new charter. His scheme was based on a careful analysis of wool prices at the time of the *Magnus Intercursus* of Henry VII and, he was careful to add, would not be to the disadvantage of the remaining Staplers. They did not agree, furiously attacking the scheme and suggesting it was more to Johnson's own advantage than that of the queen. Though no contemporary made this comparison, the scheme has echoes of Edward III's disastrous attempts to manipulate the wool market in 1337. Despite the number of documents sent to Cecil by Johnson the scheme came to nothing when the Company of the Staple was granted a new charter in 1561.[9]

Johnson was not apparently deterred by this rejection of his ideas from working on a further and much more elaborate and detailed scheme. The inspiration for this work was twofold; Antwerp had become the prime centre of trade of all kinds in northern Europe. Much of the trade in the exotic goods from the Spanish empire in the New

---

7 The new duty is discussed in N. S. B. Gras (1918), *The Early English Customs System,* Cambridge MA: Harvard University Press, 91–2.

8 Addition to the Book of Marts SP12/109/36.

9 The scheme is discussed at some length in B. Winchester (1953), 'The Johnson Letters 542–1552', unpublished PhD thesis, University of London: vol. 1, 479–85.

World went through the city. It was also a successful and flourishing centre of banking expertise. The pre-eminence of Antwerp as a mart was no secret to English merchants at the time but was also described in glowing terms in a book by the Italian Ludovico Guicciardini published in 1567. Johnson acquired a copy of this book and was clearly much struck by its description of Antwerp and the basis of its commercial prosperity.

The other driver of Johnson's scheme was that relations between the England of Elizabeth and the Low Countries, part of the empire of Philip II of Spain, were tense and difficult, making trading through Antwerp difficult or even dangerous for English merchants. The principal group affected by these insecurities were the Merchant Adventurers trading in cloth. Johnson got together with a young merchant from Ipswich, Christopher Goodwyn, to produce a plan for establishing a mart to rival Antwerp on English soil, in fact at Ipswich. The scheme was called *Antwerp in England* and was worked out in ever increasing detail between 1571 and 1580. Ipswich was Goodwyn's home and Johnson had occasionally used the port as a trader in the 1540s when his wool business was solvent and successful.

The scheme needed, as a first priority, the support of the Merchant Adventurers; this was not forthcoming, since most found it impractical. The obvious flaw in the plan was that it ignored the dominant position held by London and Londoners in England's trade. Johnson and Goodwyn were not, however, entirely without support for the scheme. Sir Thomas Smith had cautiously stated, 'if the trade [that in cloth] could be removed from Antwerp and settled in England it could be the foremost diamond in the Queen's Crown'. They also attempted to woo the Merchant Adventurers by suggesting that the company would have many trading privileges in the proposed new mart; they would also benefit from much shorter and easier journeys than the crossing to Antwerp. Foreign merchants would be lured to Ipswich in the opinion of the pair by the advantages of trading in England. This they described as:

> a land of pleasure, lyberty and freedome as well of their conscience in religion surety of their bodyes and goods (for which cause very many have abandoned Antwerpe and the Lowe Countreys at this day) and also to be free from the greate and manifold exactions of excises.[10]

The queen meanwhile would benefit enormously from an inflow of bullion and higher customs receipts. This scheme was nevertheless rejected by Cecil (now Lord Burghley) after six months delay. Johnson was not minded to give up on his plan at this first setback. He promoted it energetically with some new material, the *Addendum to the Book of Marts,* in 1576 and when that got nowhere presented it again and again in 1578, 1580 and 1582. The Merchant Adventurers never supported it; in fact to imagine that Ipswich could ever come to rival London as a centre for trade was a fantasy that Johnson was unable to let go. There are several long documents written by him on

---

10 SP 12/88/39 and 40. There are several copies in other archives so the scheme was circulated to some extent.

this topic in the papers of Lord Burghley which are in the archives at Hatfield House; Burghley's heart must have sunk when presented with yet another presentation of a device which, as a contemporary said, 'will never be executed'.

Johnson had, in fact, been Clerk of the Company of the Staple since 1572, a position for which he was in some ways very well suited.[11] He was, perhaps, unlucky that another of his schemes was also not taken up by the crown. This was sent not to Burghley but to Walsingham in November 1576 and was intended to remedy what Johnson called 'the disorder in the buying and selling of wool' despite the 1552 *Act* and subsequent royal proclamations including one issued just before Johnson wrote to Walsingham. He pointed out that:

> the buying of wulles disorderly and contrary to the lawes is so common a thing,that a nombre of glovers and others called chapmen dwelling in market townes and diverse other places are entred into soche a trade of buying and selling of wulles that it is not possible by anny lawe made or to be made to remedy the same disorder for how can informacions be geaven against so many persones seeing that fewe or none in the country occupying buying and selling but they dayly offend therein.[12]

His remedy for this state of affairs was to suggest to Walsingham that a registry of all licences to buy and sell wool should be established in the Exchequer. This might be leased to Walsingham for a fee. This would benefit Walsingham financially and also might employ Johnson and Lisle Cave, Walsingham's secretary, each at the fee of 200 marks per year. This scheme was overtaken by one promoted by the Company of the Staple itself which was somewhat embarrassed when an official inquiry in early 1577 pointed out that virtually all remaining Staplers were also acting as questionably legal wool brokers. This project suffered the same fate as *Antwerp in England*.[13]

Although the export trade in raw wool was manifestly in decline from the beginning of the sixteenth century, a decline which accelerated dramatically after the loss of Calais in 1558, what discussion there was of the problem was focused on the size of sheep flocks, little more than a convenient symbol for the far-reaching changes in land-holding and land-use in the countryside and their social effects. When the export trade in woollen cloth, especially the expensive traditional heavy broadcloths, also began to decline again discussion focused on the market in raw wool and the activities of the hated (but probably essential) broggers. There was little attempt to widen the discussion or try to understand the way trading in cloth and other staples had changed fundamentally since the early decades of the sixteenth century. One belief remained fixed firmly in the minds of many at the time; English wool was of a quality which could not be matched by any other supplier and was the envy of the world.

---

11 B. Winchester *op. cit.* I, 513.

12 SP 12/109/39.

13 B. Winchester (1953), *op. cit.* 1, 514–16.

In the mid-sixteenth century, when the decline of the wool trade was still not fully appreciated, John Coke, the clerk of the Statutes of the Staple at Westminster re-wrote a pamphlet originally produced in the early fifteenth century, the Debate of the Heralds of England and France. He wrote in praise of England's 'ryches in bestiall':

> Also we have shepe beryng the finest woll of the worlde whose value in the olde tyme was esteemed to the weight of golde wherof we make fine scarlettes clothes carseis stocke bredes fryses cottons worsteds says and coverlettes beyng as wel covetd by you and other nacions christened as also by the Jues Turks sarasynes and all other infydeles.

In the early seventeenth century, at the time when the export of raw wool was banned by Parliament[14], and the export of cloth was in difficulties, Michael Drayton wrote a poetical description of England, the *Polyolbion*. This contains an almost ecstatic description of the Cotswolds, its sheep and their wool.

> But, noble Muse, proceed immediatly to tell
> How Eushams fertile Vale at first in liking fell
> With Cotswold, that great King of Shepheards ...
> Yet hardly doth she tythe our Cotswolds wealthy locks.
> Though Lemster him exceed for finenesse of her ore,
> Yet quite he puts her downe for his aboundant store.
> A match so fit as hee, contenting to her mind,
> Few Vales (as I suppose) like Eusham hapt to find:
> Nor any other Wold, like Cotswold euer sped,
> So faire and rich a Vale by fortuning to wed.
> Hee hath the goodly Wooll, and shee the wealthy Graine:
> Through which they wisely seeme their houshold to maintaine.
> He hath pure wholesome Ayre, and daintie crystall Springs.
> To those delights of his, shee daily profit brings:
> As to his large expense, she multiplies her heapes:
> Nor can his Flocks deuour th'aboundance that shee reaps;
> As th'one with what it hath, the other stroue to *grace*.[15]

Drayton's conceit of a marriage between the Vale of Evesham and the Cotswolds serves to emphasise the riches of both with the value of Cotswold wool only exceeded by the famed 'Lemster ore' from the Marches. The common belief, accepted almost without question, in this whole period was that English wool was the finest in the world.

---

14 The export of wool was banned in 1614.

15 M. Drayton (1624), *Polyolbion*, song 14, p. 233. Consulted online via EEBO TCP 23/1/17.

Chapter 13

Did the Wool Trade Make England Rich?

We have already seen that, in the opinions of many contemporaries, especially those writing before the end of the fifteenth century, the answer to this question is a resounding, 'yes'. It was only in the first decades of the sixteenth century that the wool trade began to be seen in a rather different light. For some, at that time, it was the reason why many humble folk had been reduced to homelessness and abject poverty by the decay of tillage and the ever more extensive spread of pasture lands across the countryside. More long-lasting than this impression was the potent symbol of the Lord Chancellor seated on the woolsack in the House of Lords; in that place wool was seen as the undisputed source of the wealth of medieval England. Was this belief justified?

There is no one answer to this query; we need to consider separately the way the wool trade may have affected the wealth of the crown and the governance of the realm, the lands of the Church, and finally English society. We have already discussed the way in which the revenues from the wool trade accruing to the crown, coming largely from the customs dues and subsidies, were of great value to English kings. This elastic source of revenue allowed them to pursue policies which would otherwise have been impossible for the rulers of the largest part of a relatively small island off the coast of northern Europe. These dues financed wars and policies which gave English rulers the ability to increase greatly their power and influence in neighbouring realms. The fact that this source of income as well as more general taxation had to be discussed in Parliament from the late thirteenth century has been credited in creating the particular form of late medieval English government. The degree of consultation of and assent by parliament to taxation required by the conventions of the late medieval governance of England was a potent lever in the development of the nature of the realm of England. For the crown there is ample justification for the Lord Chancellor's comfortable seat.

The question of whether the wool trade enriched the church is more complex. It depended whether the wool came from flocks owned by a bishop or by a monastic house, the location of the lands and the precise period under discussion. All these factors could greatly influence whether the wool trade was in truth a source of wealth. It can be argued that involvement in the export trade in wool was not in the end to the benefit of many of the monastic houses which were renowned for the size of the flock of sheep grazing on their lands in the late thirteenth century. Many of these were members of the Cistercian order, some with spectacular sites and buildings which are often popularly supposed to have been built from the profits of the wool trade. The careful and detailed analysis of the surviving financial sources relating to prominent houses like Rievaulx, Croyland and Pipewell, however, has shown that it was all too easy for houses like this to become greatly indebted to the Italian and other merchants and their factors that had contracted with them to buy their wool clip. The system of advance payment for wool provided monasteries with the ready cash needed to support ambitious building plans but could easily lead to disaster if bad weather or attacks of disease badly affected the productivity of the flocks. The sad words of the Abbot of Pipewell, as he summed up his time in office in 1323, echo down the years. *Leger est aprendre mais fort est a rendre.* It is easier to borrow than to pay back debts. This was a hard lesson to learn for some.

The picture for monastic and ecclesiastical wool producers was not, however, uniformly black. Many bishops traded successfully and profitably in wool for much of our period with this trade providing a steady income. Successive Bishops of Winchester with extensive and well-run estates are one example. As late as the early decades of the fifteenth century, when many landowners had leased their pastures to tenants and no longer maintained their own flocks, Henry Beaufort, the Bishop of Winchester was described as 'the chief merchant of wolles in your lande' by Humphrey, Duke of Gloucester. Beaufort ran flocks of several thousand sheep on the Winchester manors on the Hampshire and Wiltshire downs. A good proportion of his vast wealth probably came from the sale of their wool.[1] Other bishops and monastic houses with estates in the best wool-producing areas in the Cotswolds and the Midlands also continued to run their own sheep walks and sell wool for most of our period. This applied to the Bishops of Worcester and the Abbeys of Cirencester and Winchcombe, all of which produced the best quality Cotswold wool. Winchcombe maintained its own flocks at least until 1485, when more than 2900 sheep were shorn at the centre of its operations at Sherborne. 14 woolsacks were filled with the clip which if sold at the usual price of good Cots at the time (£12) would have produced £168.[2] Ecclesiastical lands in places suited to sheep-walks which were kept as demesne as well as those which were leased to tenants were capable of producing a good income for their owners. A lot depended on good management but there is little doubt that these estates were valuable and exploited to the manifest benefit of their owners.

Much of what has been said about ecclesiastical estates also applies to large lay estates. The Duchy of Lancaster for example persisted with demesne sheep farming on its manors in southern England until the early 1440s, when the pastures were leased to two local men. They clearly expected to be able to make good profits from their new business venture even though the duchy wool was not of the best quality selling for around £5 per sack. The tenants on Duchy lands could also profit from their

---

1 G. L. Harriss (1988), *Cardinal Beaufort: a Study of Lancastrian Ascendancy and Decline,* Oxford: Clarendon Press, 412.

2 E. B. Fryde (1996), *Peasant and Landlords in Later Medieval England,* Stroud: Sutton, 91–5; D. Hurst (2005), *Sheep in the Cotswolds,* Stroud: Tempus, 120–6.

involvement in the wool trade. It is notable that one of the men who took some of the Lancaster land on lease in the villages of Aldbourne and Ogbourne in Wiltshire may have come from villein stock, but was on his way to becoming a man of substance.[3] Other noble or gentry estates like those of the Counts of Aumale also did well from the trade. The church in this period was always wealthy compared to society as a whole while the same applied to the nobility and holders of extensive lands. Particularly from the end of the fourteenth century there is also reliable evidence of how the wool trade affected the wealth of the growing middle ranks of society.

This level of society made up initially of wool merchants, graziers and leaseholders, many of them also acting as the much maligned broggers, perhaps provides the best evidence of the effect of the wool trade on the wealth of individual Englishmen. It was possible (if rare) for a successful merchant's family to climb the social ladder to the very top. The best example of this is provided by the de la Poles in the fourteenth century. It was no mean feat for the family of William de la Pole to rise from the status of a merchant of Hull (coming perhaps from Ravenser) to that of Earl of Suffolk in one generation. Michael de la Pole, William's eldest son was not only an earl but a close associate and adviser of Richard II. Moreover the family was sufficiently secure in their exalted social position to recover from the disgrace and confiscations resulting from Michael's impeachment in the political turmoil of the end of Richard's reign. One testimonial to the family's power is the magnificent church of St Agnes in Cawston in Suffolk probably originally built by Michael de la Pole and later embellished by other members of the family in the fifteenth century. The dedication to St Agnes may have been thought particularly appropriate by the family since this saint is usually represented accompanied by a lamb.

Many other successful traders in wool, particularly those based outside London, were also responsible for commissioning buildings of great quality. One of the most notable is one of the earliest, Stokesay Castle, built between *c*.1280 and 1290 in Shropshire in the Welsh Marches by Laurence of Ludlow. A casual visitor would be more likely to identify it as the castle of a Marcher lord than the home of a merchant. It was also not unusual in the fifteenth century for members of the Company of the Staple based in London to own rural estates. The Cely family had an estate in Essex, Bretts Place at Aveley, but it was not on the scale of Stokesay Castle for which Laurence received a licence to crenellate in 1291.

Few surviving domestic rural buildings can be linked with any certainty to wool merchants; most of those surviving are substantial houses often with attached outbuildings for wool storage in market towns. Wool traders of less exalted social status in the late fourteenth and fifteenth centuries often made their mark on their home towns by extending or embellishing the parish church. This was a powerful way of acquiring merit in the eyes of the Church and also in those of their fellow townsmen. The quality of the so-called 'wool' churches still to be found in several centres of the wool trade in the Cotswolds testifies to the success of their aims. The largest parish

---

3 E. B. Fryde (1996), *op. cit.*, 110–2.

Figure 34. Cawston Church exterior (photo: author)

church in Gloucestershire, St John the Baptist in Cirencester, was originally founded for the Abbey, a religious house with extensive flocks on its lands in the Cotswolds. Particularly in the fourteenth century, the Abbots and other churchmen contributed to the magnificent building. Later local wool merchants were also involved. Around 1430–1460, a merchant family called Garstang created a chantry chapel in the east bay of the south aisle placing both their arms and their merchant mark on the oak screen. In the early sixteenth century before the dissolution of the monasteries was even contemplated, many of the wealthiest burgesses paid for the almost complete rebuilding of the nave of the church in the latest fashionable Perpendicular style, including a great window over the chancel arch, something which has been seen as a characteristic of the Cotswold 'wool' churches. The piers in the aisle carry shields bearing the arms or merchant marks of the contributors to this enormous enterprise. One known donor was Henry Tapper who left £20 for work on the rood screen in 1532. There are also memorial brasses to wool merchants from the fifteenth century in the Trinity Chapel.[4] We cannot quantify the amount of money that funded these benefactions nor do any domestic buildings from our period survive in the town which was almost entirely rebuilt from

---

4 D. Verey (1970), *Gloucestershire, 1 The Cotswolds,* Harmondsworth: Penguin, 161–6, 170–1.

Figure 35. Cawston Church interior; painting of St Agnes (photo: author)

Figure 36. Stokesay Castle (Creative Commons CC 1.0 universal public domain dedication)

Figure 37. Cirencester church and South Porch (photo: author)

Figure 38. Garstang Chantry in Cirencester Church (photo: author)

the seventeenth century on. Nevertheless it is clear that a large and relatively wealthy merchant community made its home here with the greater part of their wealth coming from the trade in wool and later also the manufacture of woollen cloth.

The lack of identification of named donors also applies to the Church of St James in Chipping Campden, another centre of the wool trade and the location of one of the most active markets. Here the church was again rebuilt from around 1450 in the Perpendicular style. The nave is very similar to that at Northleach leading to the belief that they were probably built under the supervision of the same master mason. The building of St James' has been associated with William Grevel described on his memorial brass in the church as 'the flower of the wool merchants of all England'. He left a substantial legacy of 100 marks to the 'building of the nave and body of the church' but, since he died in 1401 this was not used for the later Perpendicular work but probably for the earlier north aisle. The extraordinary disposable wealth of the Cotswold wool merchants is also demonstrated by the very rare survival of vestments in this Church including the remarkable embroidered altar frontal done in the richest style with much gold thread.[5]

---

5 G. Powell and J. Wilson (1997), 'The Chipping Campden altar hangings', *Transactions of the Bristol and Gloucestershire Archaeological Society* 125, 233–45. While they may not be part of the bequest of William Brodway, their date is not in question.

Figure 39. Merchant's mark of a donor on a nave pillar, Cirencester Church (photo: author)

Grevel's name is also associated with a house in the High Street which is said to have been his home and place of business. It may, however, be a barn dating from the fourteenth century which was converted into a dwelling in the late sixteenth century.[6] The popular belief in a connection with Grevel reveals the way in which the memory of the success of the wool trade is still central to the identity of the town. A connection with another wool merchant family, the Calfs, in more certain since their rebus is built into a Tudor fireplace in another nearby house. This, now known as the Wool Staplers' hall, was extensively restored in the early twentieth century but seems to have fourteenth century origins.[7] Both buildings clearly show the degree of domestic comfort which burgesses in this period were beginning to expect and also that wool storage and other 'business' requirements would usually be closely associated with a merchant's home, usually in buildings at the rear.

Much more is known about the donors who contributed to the rebuilding of the church of St Peter and St Paul at Northleach in the same style as that at Chipping

---

6 Listing text English Heritage Id no. 126139 Chipping Campden High Street Grevel's House.

7 Listing text English Heritage, Id no. 1172611 High Street Chipping Campden Woolstaplers' Hall.

Figure 40. Chipping Campden; brass of William Grevel in the church (photo: author)

Figure 41. The transfiguration of the Virgin from the altar frontal (c. 1400), Chipping Campden (photo: author)

Campden. This is largely because the church contains a remarkable collection of the memorial brasses of wool traders and their wives. John Fortey (d. 1458), whose brass shows him with one foot on a sheep and the other on a woolpack, is credited with helping to finance the new nave with its spectacular clerestory and great chancel arch window. This is because the damaged inscription on his brass includes the words, 'and after his diseese the rofe made'. His will included bequests to 24 churches in nearby villages and a bequest of £300 to 'finish and complete the work he had started in the new middle aisle'. All told his will included over £600 in charitable bequests, a very considerable sum to be able to bequeath in ready cash. John Fortey's standard of living is also revealed in the clauses in his will leaving no fewer than four furred robes to close friends or relations and the bequest which provides funds, for four years after his death, for the support of a student at Oxford.[8]

Another wealthy man commemorated by a brass in the same church is Thomas Busshe who died in 1525. He was member of the Company of the Staple at Calais, (their coat of

---

8 TNA, PROB 11/4/248. Will of John Fortey woolman. Dated 15 July 1458. His other charitable bequests included 4d for every prisoner in Gloucester Castle at the time of his death and £200 worth of woollen and linen cloth to make raiment for the poor.

Figure 42. Grevel's House (photo: author)

Figure 43. The Wool Staplers' Hall in Chipping Campden (photo: author)

Figure 44. Exterior of Northleach Church (photo: author)

Figure 45. Northleach; brass of John Fortey (photo: author)

arms is on the brass) and left a large and valuable estate. His widow received £400, his daughters £266 and his sons £500 in cash; there were also lands in Oxfordshire, Wiltshire, Gloucestershire and Berkshire, all in good wool-producing areas.[9] He is described as the lessee of lands belonging to the Bishop of Worcester and had clearly made the transition from merchant to grazier and landowner. He was assessed for the 1522 subsidy as having goods worth £800, making him the richest man in the county outside Gloucester itself. In 1575 a large property in the main street of Northleach was known as *Bush's Great House*. It had a considerable range of buildings behind the main house which could presumably have been connected with his extensive wool business. The building was mainly demolished in 1936 but some of the range of outbuildings survives. The wealthy wool merchants of Northleach had strong family ties as well as many business links. Another brass is that of William Midwinter, the local woolman who traded extensively with the Cely family in the 1470s–1480s and was married to Alice, the widow of John Busshe, Thomas' father. Alice died in 1503. A property near the *Great House* known as *Walton House* is associated, again in popular belief, with the Midwinter family.[10]

The most munificent of all the bequests left by prominent wool men in the Cotswolds to a parish church is probably that of John Tame who died in 1497. He had already spent what must have been a large sum of money virtually rebuilding the church of St Mary at Fairford in the latest Perpendicular style with his merchant mark on the tower. He had moved to this village from Cirencester around the 1480s as his pasture lands were largely in this area. His will makes no mention of the building work, which gives rise to the speculation that the church was largely finished by late January 1496 when the will was written. The will, however, does include money to further embellish the church and its services. These gifts include two sets of vestments valued at £80 and £50, many items of ritual silver for the celebration of the mass worth £70 10s in all, a mass book valued at £8 and £35 for a fourth great bell. He also wished to set up a foundation for a chantry within the church endowed with the sum of £240. The chantry chapel was to include an elaborate tomb for himself and his wife.[11] His son Edmund saw that this work was completed as the will directed. Edmund was also responsible for the final element in the decoration of the church as a whole, the elaborate scheme for the stained glass windows.

The church must have presented an appearance of astonishing colour and richness when first completed. The walls were painted with traces of the pictures still visible within the tower and on the north wall of the aisle. The windows are filled with a magnificent series of stained glass images which endeavour, 'to present the entire

---

9 TNA will of Thomas Busshe; PROB 11/21/625; dated 20 November 1525.

10 C. Davidson Cragoe, A. R. J. Jurica and E. Williamson (2001), 'Parishes: Northleach with St Mary at Fairford Eastington', in N. M. Herber ed., *A History of the County of Gloucester: Vol. 9, Bradley Hundred. The Northleach Area of the Cotswolds,* London, Victoria History of the Counties of England. 106–45. *British History Online* http://www.british-history.ac.uk/vch/glos/vol9/pp106–45 [accessed 31 January 2017].

11 TNA will of John Tame PROB 11/12/22.

Figure 46. Brass of Thomas Busshe (photo: author)

catholic faith'[12]. There are scenes from the most familiar stories in both the old and new testaments. The great west window is now a copy after damage by a storm in 1703 but the image of the Last Judgment is still powerful and dramatic. There is good evidence that the scheme was devised and probably carried out by the workshop of Barnard Flowers, Henry VII's Master Glass Painter, who also worked on the Henry VII chapel at Westminster Abbey and the chapel of King's College Cambridge.

John Tame was both rich and pious; the total value of his estate is hard to quantify since none of his lands in Kent, Oxfordshire, Wiltshire, and Gloucestershire are valued in the will. He left small sums to a large number of people, many clearly his servants or friends including his shepherds, one called Ingram, William Palmer of 'Esthech' and Richard of Bardon. Other small sums went to mend local roads, and 40s went to his brother's old servant. Edmund, his favoured son and successor in the wool business, continued to rise up the social ladder. He adapted and lived in the old manor house in the village, acquired manorial rights over much of the land and served both as a JP and as High Sheriff of Gloucestershire. He finally acquired a coat of arms which was carved on the

---

12 D. Verey (1970), *Gloucestershire*, I, 246.

Figure 47. Brass of John Midwinter (photo: author)

Figure 48. Fairford Church exterior (photo: author)

church tower and also on his father's tomb in the church when it was completed c.1520.[13] This family, once merchants and graziers had achieved undoubted gentry status.

A similar group of wealthy pious and community minded merchants and clothiers contributed much to the building and embellishment of very similar churches in the prosperous cloth making districts of East Anglia. The links between the two branches of what may loosely be called the business of wool, the one dealing predominantly in the raw material and the other in the manufacture and sale of woollen cloth were strong, even if at times each thought that the other was attempting to profit at their expense. The building of the church of St Peter and St Paul at Lavenham was largely funded by generous donations from three generations of the Spring family which, in the course of the fifteenth and early sixteenth centuries, built up a very successful cloth making business in the town. Thomas Spring II, who died in 1486, built the vestry in which he was buried with his wife Alice. A brass covers his resting place showing Spring II himself, his wife and their ten children. He also left a legacy of £200 towards the building of the church tower.

---

13 H. F. Holt (1871), 'The Tames of Fairford', *Journal of the British Archaeological Association* 27, 110–48.

Figure 49. Head of John Tame of Fairford from his brass (photo: author)

Figure 50. Lavenham Church; much of the building work in the 1490s and early 1500s was funded by the Spring family of wealthy clothiers (photo: author)

This was a major community project involving many of the clothiers who lived in or near Lavenham; at least 18 legacies from this group of people were left to the church either for unspecified building work or particularly for the work on the tower between 1486 and 1523; the last being from Thomas Spring III specifically said to be for 'ad edificationem campanilam in stepyl ecclesiae ...300 marks'.[14] The steeple, not surprisingly, dominates the countryside round about and made plain the wealth and piety of the most important burgesses. The lords of the manor, the de Vere family also contributed to the work but the main benefactor was Thomas Spring III. His will directed that a chapel should be created with an elaborate parclose which would contain his tomb. His merchant mark and his coat of arms also appear frequently carved on bosses throughout the church. On his death in 1525 he held 25 manors scattered throughout East Anglia; without doubt he would have been accounted a gentleman by this time.[15] To his contemporaries he was perhaps the epitome of the

14 P. C. C. Logge 25; Barbara McClenaghan (1924), *The Springs of Lavenham and the Suffolk Cloth Trade in the Fifteenth and Sixteenth Centuries,* Ipswich: W. E. Harrison. Appendix B, 60.

15 His landholdings at death are listed in B. McClenaghan (1924), *The Springs of Lavenham and the Suffolk Cloth Trade in the XV and XVI centuries*, Ipswich, Harrison, appendix D, 86–8.

Figure 51. Lavenham Guildhall (photo: author)

'new rich' of the time. John Skelton was happy to mock him and his wealth in his poem
Why come ye nat to court?

> Good Springe of Lanam
> Must count what became
> Of his clothe makyng
> Though his purse wax dull
> He must tax for his wul
> By nature of a new writ
> My Lordes grace nameth it
> Aquis non satisfacit
> In spight of his tethe
> He must pay agayne
> A thousand or twayn
> Of his gold in store
> And yet he payd before
> An hundred or more
> Which pincheth hym sore
> My Lordes grace will bryng
> Down thys hye sprynge
> And brynge it so lowe
> It shal not ever *flow*.[16]

---

16 J. Scattergood, ed. (1983), John Skelton, *The Complete English Poems*, 'Why come ye nat to court', ll. New Haven and London: Yale University Press, 933–52.

Figure 52. Lavenham, merchant's house and market square (photo: author)

The town of Lavenham, perhaps because its decline in the later sixteenth century from being the centre of the manufacture of broadcloth in Suffolk to relative rural obscurity was relatively swift, also contains several secular buildings which owe their existence to the success of the trade in woollen cloth. The most spectacular is probably the guildhall in the Market Place, built for the Guild of Corpus Christi in 1529 just after Spring III's death when the boom in cloth exports was well under way. A nearby building, part of the *Swan Inn*, was originally the hall of a rival guild that of the Blessed Virgin. Both guilds would have had many members involved in the wool and cloth trades who would have conducted some of their business on these premises.

Other churches in the villages in this part of Suffolk were well supported by the wealth of the clothiers and woolmen. Towns and villages also found the money to build large and magnificent churches either because there was a religious house in the parish as at Blythburgh as well as the wealthy gentry family of Hopton or because of the support of the lord of the manor and the gentry as happened at Long Melford. All perhaps testify to the prosperity of this region during the 'good times' of the trade in woollen cloth. The same can be said of Paycocke's at Coggeshall a house built *c*.1500 for Thomas Paycocke and his bride. The house contains a mass of wood carving which is both well designed and a testament to the owner's pride in his calling and his success. In the hall his initials T. P. and those of his first wife M. P. appear along with his merchant's mark. This also appears on the band of carving on the exterior of the house and also a magnificently set of carved gates lead under an archway to the rear of the building where business was contracted

Figure 53. Long Melford Church (photo: author)

and wool and cloth were probably stored. This is not the house of a gentleman, but it is a house which speaks of economic success and personal self-confidence.

Clearly looking at the achievements of a small group of individuals mainly from the fifteenth and early sixteenth centuries cannot provide any but the most superficial answer to the question of whether the wool trade increased the wealth of the people of England. There are, however, some conclusions that can be drawn. Even in the late thirteenth century most of the most successful religious houses actively engaged in the wool trade selling to the agents of Italian and Flemish merchants would pack *collecta* along with the produce of their own flocks. This wool was gathered up from the flocks of tenants on their lands and other neighbouring villages. In a small way this opened up to those engaged largely in subsistence agriculture the possibility of a cash crop and trade. This early acquaintance with 'commercial' agriculture probably also helped create the mind-set which allowed the more entrepreneurial villagers to take the steps including taking on leased lands and investing in sheep which fuelled the rise of some families up the social and economic scale. It is also the case that gentry families became equally keen to exploit the economic potential of their lands in the same way.

Figure 54. Paycocke's House, Coggeshall, the rear showing possible wool store (photo: author)

The way in which the Commons in the 1340s and 1350s devoted a considerable amount of time to the affairs of the wool trade seems to signify that this was of concern not only to merchants but also to landowners. The hostility to the extension of pastoral agriculture prominent in the sixteenth century was generated by the perception that this was so popular and so profitable that it threatened the stability of society. There was no hint in any of the outpourings of the critics that engaging in trade was socially demeaning as was the belief commonly held in France. The close links between the wool trade and the cloth trade helped to create an appreciation of entrepreneurship in the wider English community. John of Newbury and Dick Whittington could both be folk heroes. In much the same spirit families which entered the highest ranks of the nobility like the Spencers, and the Townshends were proud that they originally owed their wealth to the wool trade.

Perhaps one of the best examples of how people of all ranks were eager to take advantage of the opportunities offered to those who participated in the wool trade are the Heydons of Norfolk. Sir John Heydon, who died in 1550, inherited a large estate in Norfolk from his father which supported large flocks of sheep. His father, Sir Henry, had been a prominent lawyer with connections to the court while his mother was a member of the extended Boleyn family. The family seat was Baconsthorpe Castle,

Figure 55. Baconsthorpe Castle: gatehouse and cloth making range (photo: author)

a large and magnificent fortified manor house near Holt. Sir John used part of the eastern service range of the inner court of the castle as the base for a successful cloth making business adapting this building to what was in many respects an early form of factory. The adapted building had large windows for the benefit of the workers and a tank under one tower may have been used for fulling cloth. The business failed in the seventeenth century under the burden of debts run up by Sir John's successors. It was, however, an example of the willingness to exploit business opportunities to be found in all levels of society at the time.

The wool trade in its heyday from the mid-thirteenth to the mid-sixteenth centuries did rather more than make England richer than it might have been without this lever to prosperity. It provided the wherewithal for the expansive policies of the English Crown both within the British Isles and across the Channel. It framed the arguments and conflicts between assemblies and the Crown which drove the development of the governance of medieval England. It allowed individuals to commission beautiful buildings to delight future generations. Finally it allowed commercial and enterprising attitudes to develop and flourish in all ranks of society. By the time of its decline these things were too deeply embedded in English life to disappear.

Bibliography

Abbreviations

BL	British Library
CCR	Calendar of the Close Rolls
CPR	Calendar of the Patent Rolls
EcHR	*Economic History Review*
EEBO	Early English Books Online
EHR	*English Historical Review*
Letters and Papers	Gairdner, J., ed. (1882), *Letters and Papers, Foreign and Domestic Henry VIII preserved in the Public Record Office, the British Library and elsewhere.* London: Longman, Green
ODNB	*Oxford Dictionary of National Biography*
Parliament Rolls	*Parliament Rolls of Medieval England,* ed. C. Given-Wilson, P. Brand, S. Phillips, M. Ormrod, G. Martin, A. Curry and R. Horrox (Woodbridge, 2005), *British History Online* http://www.british-history.ac.uk/no-series/parliament-rolls-medieval.
PCC	Prerogative Court of Canterbury
SP	State Papers
TNA	The National Archives at Kew

MSS Sources

Archivo di Stato di Prato; Fondaco di Firenze, Carteggio da Londra. Prato.
Archives of the Fondaco Datini, Fondaco di Firenza, Carteggio da Londra. Florence

The National Archives, Kew

Enrolled Customs Accounts
Enrolled Customs Accounts E356
PCC Register of wills proved in the Prerogative Court of Canterbury
Pipe Rolls E372
Probate Canterbury Wills
State Papers Domestic Edward VI and Elizabeth I

British Library

Cotton Vespasian E IX *The Noumbre of Weyghtes*
Westminster Abbey Muniments Room. WAM 12258 John Heritage's Account Book

Primary Sources consulted online

Via British History online

Calendar of State Papers Domestic: Edward VI, Mary and Elizabeth, 1547-80, ed. R. Lemon (London, 1856), *British History Online* http://www.british-history.ac.uk/cal-state-papers/domestic/edw-eliz/1547-80.

Calendar of State Papers Domestic: Elizabeth, 1581-90, ed. R. Lemon (London, 1865), *British History Online* http://www.british-history.ac.uk/cal-state-papers/domestic/edw-eliz/1581-90.

Calendar of State Papers Domestic: Elizabeth, 1591-94, ed. M.A. Everett Green (London, 1867).

Parliament Rolls of Medieval England, ed. C. Given-Wilson, P. Brand, S. Phillips, M. Ormrod, G. Martin, A. Curry and R. Horrox (Woodbridge, 2005), *British History Online* http://www.british-history.ac.uk/no-series/parliament-rolls-medieval.

Mystery Plays

The Chester Plays; the Paynters Playe Http://ummutility.umm.maine.edu/necastro/drama/chester/play_o7.txt

Towneley plays: the Second Shepherds' Play (1966). London: EETS http://quod.lib.umich.edu/c/cme/Towneley/1:13?rgn=div1;view==fulltext

Via Early English Books on line (EEBO)

Deloney, T., (1626), *The Pleasant Historie of John Winchcomb in his Younger Yeares called Jack of Newbery*, London.

Drayton, M., (1624), *Polyolbion*.

Instructions geuen by the kynges maiestie to his commissioners temp. Edward VI Proclamation 1602.

Printed Primary Sources

Alcock, N., (1981), *Warwickshire Grazier and London Skinner 1532-55*, Oxford: Oxford University Press.

Bailey, M., (2007), 'The sheep accounts of Norwich Cathedral Priory 1484–1534'. In M. Bailey (ed.) *Poverty and Wealth; Sheep Taxation and Charity*, Norwich, Norwich Record Society.

Barstow, H. G., trans. (1998), *1208-9, Pipe Roll of the Bishopric of Winchester*, Chandlersford: H. G. Barstow.

Blanchard, I. S. W. (1971), *The Duchy of Lancaster's Estates in Derbyshire 1485-1540*, Derby: Derbyshire Archaeological Society Record Series 3.

Bond, E. A. ed., (1866-68), Chronica Monasterii de Melsa, a Fundatione Usque ad Annum 1396, Auctore Thoma de Burton, Abbate. Accedit Continuatio ad Annum 1406, Rerum Britannicarum medii aevi scriptores (Chronicles and Memorials of Great Britain and Ireland during the Middle Ages, London, Longmans, Green and Co.

Camden, W. *Britannia*, facsimile edition 1970, Hildesheim and New York: Georg Olms.

Carpenter, C., (1996), Kingsford's *Stonor Letters and Papers 1290-1483*, Cambridge: Cambridge University Press.

Carroll, C. W. and Wilson, L. H., (2012), *The Medieval Shepherd: Jean de Brie's le Bon Berger (1379)*, Tempe: Arizona Center for Medieval and Renaissance Studies.

Childs, W., (1978), *Anglo-Castilian Trade in the later Middle Ages*, Manchester: Manchester University Press.

Childs, W. R., (1986), *The Customs Accounts of Hull 1453-1490*. York: Yorkshire Archaeological Society.

Cobb, H. S., (1961), *The Local Port Book of Southampton 1439-1440*, Southampton, Southampton Record Series V.

Fryde, E. B., (1964), *The Wool Accounts of William de la Pole, a Study of Some Aspects of the English Wool Trade at the Start of the Hundred Years' War*, York: St Antony's Press.

Fryde, E. B., (1966), *Some Business Transactions of York Merchants; John Goldbeter, William Avastre and Partners 1336-1359*, York: St Antony's Press.

Fussell, G. E., ed. (1936), *Robert Loder's Farm Accounts 1610-1620*, London: Camden 3rd series 53.

Gairdner, J., ed. (1882), *Letters and Papers, Foreign and Domestic Henry VIII: preserved in the Public Record Office, the British Library and elsewhere,* London: Longman, Green.

Hanham, A., ed. (1975), *The Cely Letters 1472-1488,* Oxford; Oxford University Press for the Early English Text Society.

Haydon, F. S., ed. (1863), *Eulogium Historiarum Sive Temporis Chronicon,* London: Rolls Series III.

Hicks, M., ed. (2015), *English Inland Trade 1430-1540,* Oxford: Oxbow Books.

Hingeston, F. C., ed. (1860–1865), *Royal and Historical Letters During the Reign of Henry IV King of England and of France,* London: Rolls Series II.

Hockey, S. F., (1975), *Accounts of Beaulieu Abbey,* London: Camden 4th Series for the Royal Historical Society 16.

Jenks, S., (2006), *Robert Sturmy's Commercial Expedition to the Mediterranean 1457-8,* Bristol: Bristol Record Society.

Kowaleski, M., (1993), Local Customs Accounts of the Port of Exeter 1266–1321, Devon and Cornwall Record Society New Series 36.

Lamond, E. (1890), *Walter of Henley's Husbandry,* London: Longman, Green & Co.

Lockwood, S., ed. (1997), *Sir John Fortescue: on the Laws and Governance of England,* Cambridge: Cambridge University Press.

Lydgate, J., (1906) *The Lytell treatyse of the horse the sheep and the goos printed at Westminster by Wynkyn de Worde 1499,* Cambridge: Cambridge University Press.

Malden, H. E., (1900), *The Cely Papers; Selections from the Correspondence and Memoranda of the Cely Family, Merchants of the Staple 1475-1488,* London: Camden 3rd series I.

Melis, F., (1972), *Documenti per la storia economica secoli xiii-xvi,* Florence: Leo S. Olschki.

More, T., (1972), trans. Paul Turner, *Utopia,* London: Folio Society.

Nicolas, N. H., ed. (1834–37), *Proceedings and Ordinances of the Privy Council 2,* London: Eyre and Spottiswode.

Oschinsky, D. (1971), *Walter of Henley and Other Treatises on Estate Management and Accounting,* Oxford: Oxford University Press.

Owen, D. M., (1984), *The Making of King's Lynn: a Documentary Survey,* Oxford: Oxford University Press for the British Academy.

Page, M., ed. (1996), *The Pipe Roll of the Bishopric of Winchester, 1301-2,* Winchester; Hampshire County Council for the Hampshire Record Society.

Page, M., ed. (1999), *The Pipe Roll of the Bishopric of Winchester, 1409-10,* Winchester: Hampshire County Council for the Hampshire Record Society.

Pagnini, G. F., Pegolotti, F.B. and Uzzano, G., (n.d.), *Della Decima e di varie alter graveze imposte dal commune di Firenze 2.* Florence: Nabu Public Domain Reprints.

Pegolotti, F. B., (1936), *La Pratica della Mercatura,* ed. A. Evans, Harvard: Medieval Academy of America.

Rich, E. E., (1937), *The Ordinance Book of the Merchants of the Staple,* Cambridge; Cambridge University Press.

Schanz, G., (1881), *Englische handelspolitik gegen Ende des Mittelayer mit besouderen Beruckstigung des Zetalter der beiden ersten Tudors Heinrich VII und Heinrich VIII,* Leipzig; Daucher and Humbolt.

The Statutes at Large; Great Britain, London: Eyre and Strahan 1769–1800.

Tawney, R. H. and Power, E., (1924), *Tudor Economic Documents: Being Select Documents Illustrating the Economic and Social History of Tudor England.* London: University of London Historical Series.

Tusser, T. (1878), *Five Hundred Pointes of Good Husbandrie,* ed. W. Payne and J. Herrage, London: Trubner.

Warner, Sir G., ed. (1926), *The Libelle of Englyshe Polycye: a Poem on the use of English Sea-Power,* Oxford: Clarendon Press.

Secondary sources

Allison, K. J., (1957), 'The sheep-corn husbandry of Norfolk in the sixteenth and seventeenth centuries', *Agricultural History Review* 5, 12–30.

Allison, K. J., (1958), 'Flock management in the sixteenth and seventeenth centuries', *EHR* 11, 98–112.

Allmand, C., (1992), *Henry V,* London: Methuen

Amor, N.K., (2004), 'Merchant Adventurer or jack of all trades? The Suffolk clothier in the 1460s', *Proceedings of the Suffolk Institute of Archaeology and History* 40, 414–34.

Armitage, P. L., (1983), 'The early history of English longwool sheep', in *The Ark, The Monthly Journal of the Rare Breeds Survival Trust* 10, 90–7.

Arnoux, M., (2013), 'Border trade route or market? The Channel and the medieval economy from the twelfth to the fifteenth century,' in D. Bates ed. *Anglo-Norman Studies* XXXVI, 39–52.

Badham, S., (2006), 'Thomas Adynet and his brass at Northleach, Gloucestershire,' *Transactions of the Monumental Brass Society* 17, 347–53.

Bailey, M., (2007), *Medieval Suffolk: an Economic and Social History 1200-1500,* Woodbridge: Boydell.

Baker, R. L., (1956), 'The establishment of the English Wool Staple in 1313,' *Speculum* 31, 444–53.

Baker, R. L., (1976), 'The government of Calais in 1363', in W. C. Jordan, *Order and Innovation in the Middle Ages: Essays in Honor of Joseph R. Strayer,* Princeton: Princeton University Press, 207–14.

Barron, C. M. and Sutton, A. F., (2014), *The Medieval Merchant,* Harlaxton Medieval Studies XXIV, Donington: Shaun Tyas.

Batemen, N., (2004), 'From rags to riches: Blackwell Hall and the wool cloth trade c. 1450–1790,' *Post-medieval Archaeology* 38, 1–15.

Bell, A.R., Brooks, C. and Dryburgh, P. R., (2006), *Advance Contracts for the sale of Wool, 1200–1327,* Kew, List and Index Society

Bell, A.R., Brooks, C. and Dryburgh, P. R., (2007), *The English Wool Market c.1230-1327,* Cambridge: Cambridge University Press.

Bell, A. R., Brooks, C. and Moore, T. K., (2009), 'Interest in medieval accounts: examples from England, 1272–1340,' *History* 94, 411–33.

Bell, A. R., Brooks, C. and Moore, T. K., (2011), 'Credit finance in thirteenth century England: the Riccardi of Lucca and Edward I 1272–94,' in J. Burton *et al.* eds *Thirteenth Century England XIII,* Woodbridge; Boydell, 101–16.

Bell, A. R., Brooks, C. and Moore, T. K., (2014), 'The credit relationship between Henry III and merchants of Douai and Ypres 1247–70,' *Economic History Review 67,* 123–45.

Beresford, M. W. (1955), 'The poll tax and census of sheep,' *Agricultural History Review* 12, 15–29.

Biddick, K. and Bijleveld, C. C. J. H., (1991), 'Agrarian productivity on the estates of the Bishopric of Winchester in the early thirteenth century: a managerial perspective,' in B.M.S. Campbell and M. Overton *Land Labour and Livestock: Historical Studies in Agricultural Productivity,* Manchester; Manchester University Press, 95–123.

Bigwood, G., (1980), 'Un marché des matières premières: laines d'Angleterre et marchands Italiens vers la fin du XIIIe siècle,' *Annales d'Histoire économique et sociale* 6, 193–211.

Bindoff, S.T., (1944), 'Clement Armstrong and the treatises of government,' *Economic History Review (EcHR)* 14, 64–73.

Bischoff, J.P., (1983), '"I cannot do't without counters": Fleece weights and sheep breeds in late thirteenth and early fourteenth century England,' *Agricultural History Review* 57, 143–60.

Bivens, D. R., (1974), 'The wool trade and the finances of English monasteries c. 1300,' *Studies in Medieval Culture* 4, 330–7.

Blanchard, I., (1996), 'Northern wools and Netherlands markets at the close of the Middle Ages,' in G.G. Simpson *Scotland and the Low Countries,* East Linton: Tuckwell, 76–88.

Bowden, P. J., (1956), 'Wool supply and the woollen industry,' *EcHR* 9, 44–58.

Bowden, P. J., (1962), *The Wool Trade in Tudor and Stuart England,* London: Macmillan.

Braddick, M. J. (1996), *The Nerves of State: Taxation and the Financing of the English State 1558-1714,* Manchester: Manchester University Press.

Bridbury, A. R., (1982), *Medieval Clothmaking: an Economic Survey,* London: Heinemann.

Britnell, R., (2003), 'The woollen industry of Suffolk', *Ricardian* XIII, 86–90.

Brown, A. T., Burn, A. and Doherty, R., (2015), *Crises in Economic and Social History: a Comparative Perspective,* Woodbridge: Boydell.

Carlin, M. (2011) 'Cheating the boss: Robert Carpenter's embezzlement instructions (1261–1268) and employee fraud in medieval England,' in B. Dodds and C.D. Liddy eds *Commercial Activity: Markets and Entrepreneurs in the Middle Ages,* Woodbridge: Boydell, 183–97.

Carus-Wilson, E. M. (1967), *Medieval Merchant Venturers,* London: Methuen.

Carus-Wilson, E. M. and Coleman, O., (1963), *England's Export Trade 1275-1547,* Oxford: Clarendon Press

Childs, W. R., (1978), *Anglo-Castilian Trade in the Later Middle Ages,* Manchester: Manchester University Press.

Childs, W. R, (2001), 'Yorkshire in Europe: foreign markets for wools and cloth c. 1350–1500', in S. D. Hogarth and V. Wallace eds *Yorkshire People and Places: a Millennium Celebration,* York: Yorkshire Philosophical Society, 57–71.

Chorley, P., (1987), 'The cloth exports of Flanders and northern France during the thirteenth century: a luxury trade? *EcHR* 40, 349–79.

Chrimes, S. B., (1977), *Henry VII,* London: Eyre, Methuen

Davidson, C., Jurica, A. R. J. and Williamson, E., (2001), 'Parishes: Northleach with St Mary at Fairford Eastington', in N.M. Herber ed. *A History of the County of Gloucester: Volume 9, Bradley Hundred. The Northleach Area of the Cotswolds,* London: Victoria History of the Counties of England, 106–45.

Desan, C., (2014), *Making Money: Coin, Currency and the Coming of Capitalism,* Oxford: Oxford University Press.

Donkin, R.A., (1958), 'Cistercian sheep-farming and wool sales in the thirteenth century', *Agricultural History Review* 6, 2–8.

Donkin, R.A., (1969), 'The Cistercian Order and the settlement of northern England,' *Geographical Review* 59, 403–16.

Donkin, R.A., (1978), *The Cistercians: Studies in the Geography of Medieval England and Wales,* Toronto: n.p.

Dyer, C., (1972), 'A small landowner in the fifteenth century,' *Midland History* 1, 1–14.

Dyer, C., (1995), 'Sheepcotes: evidence for medieval sheep-farming', *Medieval Archaeology* 34, 136–64.

Dyer, C., (2012), *A Country Merchant 1495-1520, Trading and Farming in the End of the Middle Ages,* Oxford: Oxford University Press.

Eckenrode, T.R., (1973), 'The English Cistercians and their sheep during the Middle Ages,' *Citeaux Commentarii Cistercienses* 24, 250–66.

Faith, R., (2012), 'The structure of the market for wool in early medieval Lincolnshire,' *EcHR* 65, 674–706.

Farr, M.W., ed. (1959), *Accounts and Surveys of the Wiltshire Lands of Adam of Stratton,* Devizes, Wiltshire Archaeological Society.

Fraser, C.M., (1959), 'The life and death of John of Denton,' *Archaeologia Aeliana* 37, 303–325.

Fryde, E.B., (1983), 'The English cloth industry and the trade with the Mediterranean, c. 1370 c. 1480,' *Studies in Medieval Trade and Finance,* London: Hambledon Press.

Fryde, E. B., (1988), *William de la Pole: Merchant and King's Banker (†1366)* London: Hambledon.

Fryde, E. B., (1996), *Peasants and Landlords in Later Medieval England,* Stroud; Sutton.

Gras, N. S. B., (1918), *The Early English Customs System,* Cambridge MA: Harvard University Press.

Gray, H. I., (1924), 'The production and exportation of English woollens in the fourteenth century,' *EHR* 39, 13 35.

Griffiths, R. A. (1998), *The Reign of King Henry VI,* Stroud: Sutton.

Grummitt, D., (2008), *The Calais Garrison: War and Military Service in England, 1436-1558,* Woodbridge: Boydell.

Hanham, A., (1973), 'Foreign exchange and the English wool merchant in the late fifteenth century,' *Bulletin of the Institute of Historical Research* 46, 160–75.

Hanham, A., (1985), *The Celys and their World: an English Merchant Family of the Fifteenth Century,* Cambridge: Cambridge University Press.

Hanham, A., (2005), 'The Stonors and Thomas Betson; some neglected evidence,' *The Ricardian* 15, 33–52.

Hare, J., (2006), 'The Bishop and the Prior: demesne agriculture in medieval Hampshire,' *Agricultural History Review* 54, 187–212.

Harriss, G. L., (1960), 'The struggle for Calais; an aspect of the rivalry between Lancaster and York'. *EHR* 75, 30–53.

Harriss, G. L., (1963), 'Aids, loans and benevolences,' *Historical Journal* 6, 1–19.

Harriss, G. L., (1975), *King, Parliament and Public Finance in Medieval England to 1360,* Oxford: Oxford University Press.

Harriss, G. L., (1982), 'Theory and practice in Royal taxation: some observations,' *EHR* 97, 811–19.

Harriss, G. L., (1988), *Cardinal Beaufort: a Study of Lancastrian Ascendancy and Decline,* Oxford: Clarendon Press.

Harriss, G. L., (1993), 'Financial policy', in G.L. Harriss, ed. *Henry V: the Practice of Kingship,* Stroud, Sutton, 159–79.

Haward, W. I. (1933), 'The Financial transactions between the Lancastrian government and the merchants of the Staple from 1449–1461.' In E. Power and M M. Postan eds *Studies in English Trade in the Fifteenth Century,* London, Routledge, 293–320.

Holmes, G., (1993), 'Anglo-Florentine trade in 1451,' *EHR* 108, 371–86.

Holt, H. F., (1871), 'The Tames of Fairford', *Journal of the Archaeological Association* 27, 110–48.

Hunt, E. S., (1990), 'A new look at the dealings of the Bardi and Peruzzi with Edward III.' *Journal of Economic History* 50, 149–62.

Hurst, D., (2005), *Sheep in the Cotswolds; the Medieval Wool Trade,* Stroud: Tempus.

Jamroziak, E., (2003), 'Rievaulx Abbey as a wool producer in the late thirteenth century: Cistercians, sheep and debts,' *Northern History* 40, 197–218.

Jenkins, D., ed. (2003), *Cambridge History of Western Textiles* I, Cambridge, Cambridge University Press.

Jenkinson, H., (1913), 'William Cade, a financier of the twelfth century,' *EHR* 28, 209–27.

Johnson, N.D. and Koyama, M., (2014), 'Tax farming and the origins of state capacity in England and France, *Explorations in Economic History* 51, 1–20.

Kiser, L. J., (2009), 'Mak's heirs: sheep and humans in the pastoral ecology of the Towneley First and Second Shepherds' Plays,' *Journal of English and German Philology* 108, 336–59.

Lee, J. S., (2015), 'Crises in the late medieval English cloth trade,' in A.T. Brown, A. Burn and R. Doherty, *Crises in Economic and Social History: a Comparative Perspective,* Woodbridge; Boydell, 325–49.

Lennard, R., (1929), 'What is a manorial extent?' *EHR* 44, 256–63.

Lennard, R., (1959), 'Statistics of sheep in medieval England: a question of interpretation,' *Agricultural History Review* 7, 75–81.

Li Ling-Fan, (2015), 'Information asymmetry and the speed of adjustment: debasements in the mid-sixteenth century,' *EcHR* 68, 1203–1225.

Lloyd, T. H. (1972), 'The medieval wool-sack: a study in economic history,' *Textile History* 3, 92–99.

Lloyd, T. H., (1973), *The Movement of Wool Prices in Medieval England,* Cambridge: Cambridge University Press for the Economic History Society.

Lloyd, T. H. (1977), *The English Wool Trade in the Middle Ages,* Cambridge: Cambridge University Press.

Lockwood, S., ed. (1997), *Sir John Fortescue, On the Laws and Governance of England,* Cambridge: Cambridge University Press

Madden, J.E., (1963), 'Business monks, banker monks, bankrupt monks: the English Cistercians in the thirteenth century,' *Catholic Historical Review* 3, 341–64.

Martin, G. H., (1955), 'Shipments of wool from Ipswich to Calais, 1399–1402,' *Journal of Transport History* 2, 177–81.

Mcclenaghan, B., (1924), *The Springs of Lavenham and the Suffolk Cloth Trade in the 15th and 16th Centuries,* Ipswich: n,p.

Melis, F., (1959), 'Una sguarda al mercato dei panni di lane a Pisa nella seconda metá del trecento,' *Economica e Storia* 6, 321–98.

Miller, E., (1965), 'The fortunes of the English textile industry during the thirteenth century,' *EHR* 18, 64–82.

Moreton, C. E. and Richmond, C., (2000), 'Beware of grazing on foul mornings; a gentleman's husbandry notes,' *Norfolk Archaeology,* 43, 500–503.

Munro, J. H., (1970), 'An Economic aspect of the collapse of the Anglo-Burgundian Alliance, 1428–1442,' *EHR* 85, 225–244.

Munro, J. H., (1994), '1357 Wool Price Schedule and the Decline of Yorkshire Wool values' *Textiles Towns and Trade,* Aldershot: Variorum, 119–69

Munro, J. H., (2003a), 'Medieval. Woollens: textile technology and industrial organisation c 800–1500', in D. Jenkins ed. *The Cambridge History of Western Textiles,* Cambridge: Cambridge University Press, 181–227.

Munro, J. H. (2003b), 'Medieval woollens: the Western European woollen industries and their struggle for international markets' *c.* 1000–1500, in D. Jenkins ed. *The Cambridge History of Western Textiles,* Cambridge: Cambridge University Press, 228–324.

Munro, J. (2005), 'Spanish *Merino* wools and the *Nouvelles draperies*: an industrial transformation in the late medieval Low Countries,' *EcHR,* 58, 431–84.

Myers, A. R., ed. (1969), *English Historical Documents IV 1327-1485,* London: Eyre and Spottiswode.

Nightingale, P., (2000), 'Knights and merchants, trade politics and the gentry in late medieval England,' *Past and Present* 169, 36–62.

Noble, E., (2009), *The World of the Stonors: a Gentry Society,* Woodbridge: Boydell.

O'Connor, S., (2008), 'A nest of smugglers? Customs evasion in London at the outbreak of the Hundred Years War,' in M. Davies and A. Prescott *London and the Kingdom,* Donnington: Paul Tyas, 293–304.

Oldland, J., (2010) 'The variety and quality of English woollen cloth exported in the late Middle Ages,' *Journal of European Economic History* 39, 211–51.

Oldland, J., (2011), 'Making and marketing woollen cloth in late-medieval London,' *London Journal* 36, 89–108.

Oldland, J., (2014), 'Wool and cloth production in late medieval and early Tudor England,' *EcHR* 67, 25–47.

Oldland, J., (2008), 'The London fullers and shearmen and their merger to become the Clothworkers' Company', *Textile History* 39, 172–92.

Ormrod, W. M. (1999), 'England in the Middle Ages,' in R. Bonney ed. *Rise of the Fiscal State in Europe c.1200-1815,* Oxford: Oxford University Press, 19–52.

Ormrod, W. M., (2000), *The Reign of Edward III,* Stroud: Tempus.

Ormrod, W. M. (2008), 'Poverty and privilege: the fiscal burden in England XIIc–XVc.' In S. Caraciocchi *La Fiscalitá nell economica Euopeo sec. xiii-xviii,* Firenze: Firenze University Press, 637–56.

Ormrod, W. M. (2009), 'The origins of tunnage and poundage; Parliament and the estate of merchants in the fourteenth century,' *Parliamentary History* 28.2, 209–27.

Ormrod, W. M., (2013), 'Henry V and the English taxpayer,' in G. Dodd ed. *Henry V: New interpretations,* Woodbridge: York Medieval Press with Boydell, 187–216.

Page, F. M., (1929), '"Bidentes Hoylandiae": a medieval sheep farm' *Economic Journal* 1, 602–13.

Page, M., (2002), *The Medieval Bishops of Winchester. Estate, Archive and Administration,* Winchester: Hampshire County Council, Hampshire Papers 24.

Page, M., (2003), 'The Technology of medieval sheep farming: some evidence from Crawley, Hampshire, 1208-1349,' *Agricultural History Review* 51, 137–54.

Pedersen, K. V. and Nosch, M.-L.B., (2009), *The Medieval Broadcloth: Changing Trends in Fashions, Manufacturing and Consumption,* Oxford: Oxbow Books.

Postles, D., (1980), 'Fleece weights and the wool supply, *c.* 1250-*c.*1350', *Textile History* 12, 96–103

Powell, G. and Wilson, J., (1997), 'The Chipping Campden altar hangings', *Transactions of the Bristol and Gloucestershire Archaeological Society* 125, 233–45.

Power, E., (1920), *The Paycockes of Coggeshall,* London: Methuen.

Power, E., (1924/1937) 'Thomas Betson: a merchant of the Staple in the Fifteenth century,' in *Medieval People,* London: Methuen, 123–57.

Power, E., (1926), 'The wool trade in the reign of Edward IV', *Cambridge Historical Journal* 2, 17–35.

Power, E., (1933), 'The wool trade in the fifteenth century,' in E. Power and M.M. Postan, eds *Studies in English Trade in the Fifteenth Century,* London: Routledge, 39–90.

Power, E., (1941), *The Wool Trade in English Medieval History,* Oxford: Oxford University Press.

Power, E. and Postan, M.M., (1933), *Studies in English Trade in the Fifteenth Century,* London: Routledge.

Rahn Phillips, C., (1982), 'The Spanish wool trade, 1500-1780,' *Journal of Economic History* 42, 775–95.

Rahn Phillips, C. and Phillips, W.D., (1997), *Spain's Golden Fleece: Wool Production and the Wool Trade from the Middle Ages to the Nineteenth Century,* Baltimore: Johns Hopkins University Press.

Ramsey, P., (1953), 'Overseas trade in the reign of Henry VII: the evidence of customs accounts,' *EcHR* 6, 173–82.

Ramsey, P. H., (1976), 'Two early Tudor cloth merchant's Sir Thomas Kitson and Sir Thomas Gresham,' in Spallanzani, M. *Produzione Commercio e Consume dei Panni di lana (nei secoli xii e xviii)*, Firenze: L. S. Olschki, 385–89.

Richmond, C., (1981), *John Hopton, a Fifteenth Century Suffolk Gentleman,* Cambridge: Cambridge University Press.

Rorke, M., (2006), 'English and Scottish overseas trade 1300–1600,' *EcHR* 59, 265–88.

Rose, S., (2008), *Calais, an English Town in France,1347-1558,* Woodbridge: Boydell.

Ruddock, A. A., (1951), *Italian Merchants and Shipping in Southampton 1270-1600,* Southampton: Southampton Record Series I.

Rushen, P. C., (1911), *History and Antiquities of Chipping Campden,* London: privately published.

Ryder, M. L. (1966), 'The history of sheep breeds in England,' *Agricultural History Review* 12, 1–12, 65–82.

Ryder, M. L. (1984) 'Medieval sheep and wool types,' *Agricultural History Review* 32, 14–28.

Saul, N., (2006), 'The wool merchants and their brasses,' *Transactions of the Monumental Brass Society* 17, 315–34.

Scattergood, J., ed. (1983), John Skelton, *The Complete English Poems*, New Haven, Conn. and London: Yale University Press.

Schofield, R., (2004), *Taxation under the Early Tudors 1485-1547,* Oxford: Blackwell.

Slavin, P., (2015), 'Flogging a dead cow: coping with animal panzootic on the eve of the Black Death', in A.J. Brown, A. Burn and R. Doherty eds *Crises in Economic and Social History; a Comparative Perspective,* Woodbridge: Boydell, 111–35.

Soas, P. E., (2006), 'Direct taxation in England: the experimental subsidies of the fifteenth century,' *Bulletin for International Taxation* 60.4, 157–76.

Spufford, P. (1979), 'Calais and its mint. Part 1' in N.J. Mayhew ed. *Coinage in the Low Countries (880-1500),* Third Oxford Symposium 0n Coinage and Monetary History, Oxford: British Archaeological International Report Series, S54, 171–83.

Spufford, P. (2002), *Power and Profit: the Merchant in Medieval Europe,* London: Thames and Hudson.

Spufford, P. (2012), 'Debasements of the coinage and its effects on exchange rates and the economy: England in the 1540s and in the Burgundian-Hapsburg Netherlands in the 1480s,' in J.H. Munro ed. *Money in the Pre-industrial World: Bullion, Debasements and Coin Substitutes,* London: Pickering and Chatto.

Stanford Reid, W., (1959), 'The Scots and the staple ordinance of 1313,' *Speculum* 34, 598–610.

Stephenson, M. J., (1988), 'Wool yields in the medieval economy', *EcHR* 41, 368–91.

Stone, D., (2003), 'The productivity and management of sheep in late medieval England,' *Agricultural History Review* 51, 1–22.

Stow, J. (1908), 'Limestreete warde', in C.L. Kingsford ed. *A Survey of London. Reprinted From the Text of 1603,* Oxford: Clarendon Press, 150-63

Summerson, H., (2005), 'Most renowned of merchants: the life and occupations of Laurence of Ludlow (d.1294),' *Midland History,* 30, 20–35.

Sutton, A. F., (1998), *A Merchant Family of Coventry, London and Calais c. 1450-1515,* London: Worshipful Company of Mercers.

Sutton, A. F., (2012), 'Agnes Don-Breton, Merchant Stapler, widow and matriarch of Southampton and London c. 1450-1516,' *The Ricardian* 22, 59–94.

Thirsk, J., ed. (1988), *The Agrarian History of England,* Cambridge; Cambridge University Press.

Thornton, C., (1991), 'Efficiency in medieval livestock farming: the fertility and mortality of herds and flocks at Rimpton, Somerset, 1208–1349,' in P.R. Coss and S.D. Lloyd, *Thirteenth Century England* IV, Woodbridge; Boydell, 25–46.

Thrupp, S. L., (1962), *The Merchant Class of Medieval London,* Ann Arbor: University of Michigan Press.

Unwin, G., (1918 reprinted 1962), *Finance and Trade under Edward III,* London: Frank Cass.

Verey, D., (1970), *Gloucestershire, the Cotswolds,* in N. Pevsner ed. *The Buildings of England,* Harmondsworth: Penguin.

Waites, B., (1977), 'Pastoral farming on the Duchy of Lancaster's estate in the fourteenth and fifteenth centuries,' *Yorkshire Archaeological Journal* 49, 77–86.

Waites, B., (1980), 'Monasteries and the wool trade in North and East Yorkshire during the thirteenth and fourteenth centuries,' *Yorkshire Archaeological Journal* 52, 111–33.

Ward, O. R., (2009), *The World of the Medieval Shipmaster: Law, Business and the Sea c. 1350–c.1450,* Woodbridge: Boydell

Williams, D. H., (1965),' The Cistercians in Wales,' *Archaeologia Cambrensis* 114, 2–47.

Winchester, B., (1955), *Tudor Family Portrait,* London; Jonathan Cape.

Zell, M., (1996), 'Crediit in the pre-industrial woollen industry,' *EcHR* 49, 667–91.

Unpublished Theses

Oakley, A. M., (1959), 'The establishment of the Calais Staple', M.A., University of Leeds.

Stephenson, M. J., (1987), 'The productivity of medieval sheep on the great estates,' Ph.D., University of Cambridge.

Winchester, B., (1953), 'The Johnson Letters 1542–1552,' Ph.D., University of London.

Index